next now

Also by The Authors

The Future of Men (2005)
Buzz: Harness the Power of Influence and Create Demand (2003)
Next: Trends for the Near Future (1999)

next now
trends for the future

Marian Salzman

Ira Matathia

palgrave
macmillan

NEXT NOW
Copyright © Marian Salzman and Ira Matathia, 2006.

First published in 2006 by
PALGRAVE MACMILLAN™
175 Fifth Avenue, New York, N.Y. 10010 and
Houndmills, Basingstoke, Hampshire, England RG21 6XS.
Companies and representatives throughout the world.

PALGRAVE MACMILLAN is the global academic imprint of the Palgrave Macmillan division of St. Martin's Press, LLC and of Palgrave Macmillan Ltd. Macmillan® is a registered trademark in the United States, United Kingdom and other countries. Palgrave is a registered trademark in the European Union and other countries.

ISBN-13: 978-1-4039-7564-5
ISBN-10: 1-4039-7564-7

Library of Congress Cataloging-in-Publication Data is available from the Library of Congress.

A catalogue record for this book is available from the British Library.

Design by Newgen Imaging Systems (P) Ltd., Chennai, India.

First edition: December 2006

10 9 8 7 6 5 4 3 2 1

Printed in the United States of America.

contents

acknowledgments

Thanks to Airie Stuart, vice president and editorial director of Palgrave, for commissioning *Next Now*, for she forced both of us to focus on the near future with a rigor we haven't had since we last tackled a *Next* update, six years ago (that edition for Planeta, published in February 2001). This is our third book with Airie, and each one is a pleasure, thanks to her and her teams in New York and London.

Since this book has roots in the first *Next*, initially published by Anthos in the Netherlands in 1997, we'd be remiss not to honor the memory of Jay Chiat, founder of Chiat\Day: Jay and Ira started Marian's production of Fame+Flame, our intimate agency trend letter that was the basis of the original *Next* (even if the co-authors did ultimately rewrite most of it, because we couldn't help ourselves).

Thanks, too, to the people of Young & Rubicam, where we worked when *Next* was published and who supported each of its subsequent editions, including the HarperCollins version for the U.K. and Europe, the Pan Macmillan version for Australia and New Zealand, and ultimately the American version, published in September 1999.

We also owe our deepest gratitude and respect to Ann S. O'Reilly, our former colleague and dear friend who rewrote us through each of those editorial adventures and whose thoughtful rigor is still imprinted on our brands—every now and then we remark, "What would Ann do?" as we try to resolve a thought or worry about how a prediction will play in the heartland. Ann has been a collaborator for most of Marian's books, going back to *War and Peace in the Persian Gulf: What Teenagers Want to Know*, an instant book that won a Best Book prize from the New York Public Library in the days when the first President Bush was in office.

There is no organization or group of people to whom we owe a bigger thank you than the management team of JWT, the ad agency formerly known as J. Walter Thompson: Bob Jeffrey, Lew Trencher, and Rob Quish. Also, Marian's team in New York, led by Ann Mack and including Eric Robertson, Julie Sonkin, James Cullinane, Elissa Aguirre, Matthew Haggerty, Joyce Melito, and Randi Fishbein, have all made this book possible in big and little ways. Many of the ideas contained here were developed, tested, tweaked, revised, rewritten, and even reconsidered as Marian bounced them off Ann and the crew. Julie and James undertook the arduous task of fact-checking this manuscript, finding all the right answers, even when that meant hunting for three dozen needles in a half-mile of haystacks. Warm thanks also to Sheridan Winn, Eileen Dolbeare, Helen Jones, and Christine Onorati for their editorial inputs, which are much appreciated—and to Erin Johnson of JWT for her help lining up terrific contributors from among those who live in her seemingly endless Rolodex. Eileen, in particular, was instrumental in creating our visions of "America Inside and Out" and "It's All a Blur," and she found examples and sources to illustrate our hypothesis beyond our expectations. We must thank, too, Stuart Harris, our friend and collaborator for more than a decade; he kicked in more than his two cents, and we are especially grateful for his thoughts on the topics of Chindia, Europe's near future, and our branded universe, which he helped us develop in terms we hope are user-friendly.

It's nearly impossible to get two marketing communications professionals to stop speaking, and writing, jargon, but we really intend for this book to be accessible to all readers, even where we touch on business matters. We can thank Marian Berelowitz and JC Choi for their assistance revising and refining our English (and our thinking); Marian B., in particular, deserves a standing ovation for her tireless rewrites as we bombarded her with yet another suggestion/comment/late-breaking point of view. While we don't hold her at all responsible for any of our oversights, we do give her credit for ensuring we have created a book that we can read with pride.

We also would like to thank Jessica Kirsch and Bella Jowett of CK Publicity in London, both of whom have managed our profiles brilliantly over the last several years and whose fine work results in calls from journalists for comments weekly. In many ways, trend-spotting is as much about the dialogue as it is about the insights, and Jess and Bella have put us and kept us in the game.

This book became our obsession around New Year's 2005, and as we finalize it in spring 2006, we are both working like maniacs, Marian at JWT and Ira launching the U.S. office of No Formula, a U.K. strategic consultancy founded by Glen Flaherty and Nick Fletcher, former colleagues of ours from Euro RSCG Worldwide. The book has both benefited from and been distracted by our day jobs, and we trust that when the fog clears, we'll forget the manic nights and weekends spent agreeing on the Big Nexts, the Nexts, and the small sightings that, in aggregate, paint a picture of the near future. Any errors or omissions are ours and ours alone. The future is yours, and ours, and everyone's. And while we're not sure it's going to be rosy, we are sure it's coming. Fast. Furious. Finally.

next now

introduction

Our Worldview

For all of us, globalization means experiencing time and space faster. It's a high-speed, fast-download global village where connecting—physically and virtually—blends and sometimes blurs the lines of what's local, national, and international. Far is near, near is far.

Ring customer service for questions about your new laptop, and find that you're on the line with India. Take advantage of a last-minute online deal and jet off to Europe for the weekend on a whim. Earn your college degree virtually from the private, cozy comfort of home. And indulge in a game of Massively Multiplayer Online Role-Playing with newfound friends from across the globe.

Technology is faster, better, smarter, and, in this accelerated, borderless, wireless world, we're making instant choices about who we are, what we do, and what we want.

The benefits of global capitalism have spread across borders, and many Americans, Europeans, and East Asians have enjoyed once-unimaginable material and technological gains. With success come even more choices. Amazon.com gives us a universe of books to buy; Netflix offers tens of thousands of DVDs to rent. And there are a dozen ways to order a coffee at Starbucks. But, as Virginia Postrel writes in *Reason* magazine, "the proliferation of choices goes well beyond groceries to our most significant personal decisions."[1]

At the 2006 World Economic Forum in Davos, Switzerland, international thought leaders not only discussed topics like the emerging role of China and India, jobs, oil prices, and democracy, they also attended a seminar titled, "All You Ever Wanted to Know About Relationships—But Were Afraid to Ask." In the ultimate personal conversation gone global, the sexologist who led the session defined relationships and sexuality as among the only truly universal facets of human life.[2] Our desires are going global too—consider English footballer David Beckham, whose metrosexual allure has won over legions of Japanese fans. For more than a decade, we've made our mark watching how trends travel. In this big global society, it's not just an outward flow of ideas and products, it's a two-way exchange. We've kept our eyes wide open to the cultural icons and influences from around the world. We've seen countries from Canada to Chile, from Spain to South Africa swap products and fads in a cross-cultural frenzy. (Indeed, we've also seen violent demonstrations in the Muslim world over culturally insensitive cartoons published in Denmark—the world is that interconnected.) We've watched ethnic flavors infiltrate the U.S. mainstream; in fact, "Mexican sauces"—salsa, picante sauce, and taco sauce—hold a larger market share than ketchup.

We've seen companies turn their international operations into incubators for the next big domestic hit—the perfect case in point: Pillsbury's successful import of Häagen-Dazs' dulce de leche flavor from Argentina in 1998, now its second-best-selling flavor after vanilla. Or consider Muesli, the German/Swiss breakfast cereal introduced commercially in North America by Kellogg's in the late 1980s. Its name was successfully challenged on a trademark basis, because Muesli had existed in Europe for more than 80 years; today it's branded Mueslix—and sits right next to Corn Flakes as an American breakfast staple. We've also tracked which cities are influencers locally and regionally, on a given continent, and beyond. Mumbai matters for India, Jakarta for Indonesia, and Dublin for Ireland. There are also global style capitals—the All-Blacks ensure that New Zealand is a rugby-style capital, Detroit is the center of the universe for the mass-market auto industry, and it's a duke-out between London, New York, and Paris on restaurant cuisine, while Barcelona owns the tapas trend and Argentina is the authentic source for the global tango craze.

As our collective worldview widens, we're seeing forces in the East—China, India, and the Middle East—make huge impacts on our lives. We all know that much of what we buy in the West is made in China, and many of the call centers and back-office facilities of our businesses are in India. But it's not just their products, nor their sheer weight of numbers, that make these countries loom increasingly large in our world. It's the fact that their cultures—ancient and modern—are somehow filling in gaps in our own. Think about the rising role of Buddha: Many people who rate themselves as spiritual rather than religious feel closer to Buddhism than to Christianity, Islam, or Judaism. Part of that may be because Buddhism has a cool quotient that's far more attractive to the young and hip. And for those who want some connection to the Eastern mind-set, there's "spirituality lite," with imports like tantra, yoga, feng shui, t'ai chi, ayurvedic or Chinese medicine, and the martial arts. These offer the authenticity of ancient wisdom without requiring adherence to a religious belief system.

The West, meanwhile, exports its own concepts. In Dubai, Majid Al Futtaim's Mall of the Emirates—all 2.4 million square feet of it—gives America's megamalls a run for their money. In the spirit of American decadence, it houses the world's third largest indoor ski slope, with top-quality snow and even a mid-mountain hot chocolate hut. It's a global sweep of Western values into Middle Eastern infrastructure. It's the Middle East as architect of new innovations in personal Western luxury and indulgence.

With this fast-growing connection of people, nations, and choices, there's a real collision of cultures, too. Integration is by no means seamless. Mahatma Gandhi said people should be the change they want to see in the world, an idea that places the individual in balance with the globe. That's at odds with a consumerism-driven American culture, in which people expect Mother Nature, society, and government to satisfy their growing desires and needs while feeling little responsibility toward them.

As our cultural landscape widens and globalization opens borders, we see tensions rise. With continuing instability and some mishandling in Afghanistan and Iraq (and throughout the Middle East), America is truly at the fore of cross-cultural challenges and emerging trends in how we deal with our fellow global citizens. Our global lens is also focusing on turmoil across vast borders. After the global outburst of altruism aimed at tsunami-ravaged Asia, everyday consumers are beginning to recognize the even greater devastation—in terms of human life and economics—of the HIV/AIDS epidemic in Africa.

The African continent is looming larger in our consciousness, thanks in part to the efforts of activists like Bono, who refuse to let Africa remain forgotten. For conscious consumers who want to buy with an eye to the global trend, there's now Bono's Red brand label, which graces select Armani sunglasses, Gap T-shirts, Converse sneakers, and an American Express card. One percent of profits support the Global Fund to Fight AIDS, Tuberculosis, and Malaria. It's a global philanthropic gesture threaded with commerce. It's T-shirts and sunglasses as fashion and justice, and as Bono reminds us, "It is sexy to want to change the world."[3]

The Irish rocker also proclaimed: "Red is a 21st-century idea. I think doing the Red thing, doing good, will turn out to be good business for [the companies involved]."[4] No wonder Bono graced the cover of *Time* as one of its Persons of the Year in 2005, alongside none other than Bill and Melinda Gates, whose foundation has a similar (developing) worldview.[5] For Bono it's not just money, it's influence—both George Bush and Tony Blair are ready audiences for Bono's appeal.

Like it or not, we are living in a globalized world, one that challenges the haves to stand up and take responsibility for the have-nots—perhaps because it's right, but also because it may be the only means of self-preservation in an increasingly dangerous world.

Observing the Now Then

In the September 17, 2001, issue of *Advertising Age*, we wrote, "America, long the prom queen, had been largely oblivious to—or at least willing to ignore—indications that members of her court were speaking cattily behind her back. Now she must face the reality that not everyone likes her. . . . We're all vulnerable—and not just to terrorism and the plots of extremists, but to the sentiments of the people in the markets in which we trade. As Europe unifies and as Asia wields greater strength, it may behoove us to realize that we are now part of a pack—still the strongest member, but increasingly beholden to the others."[6]

The New Normal became a catch-all phrase to sum up the forces that realigned in the United States after September 11, 2001, a date that seems to stand for the beginning of what's now. America suffered an overwhelming and pervasive grief that bright morning, and since then we have all pondered what constitutes the New Normal. The first, simple answers: an emphasis on loved ones, in-home entertaining, more religious and spiritual moments, and even a renewed debate about family values and what we value. But even outside the United States, where the symbolism isn't as personal, the fall of 2001 was a key social marker—once America's vulnerability was highlighted, a New Normal was born.

Other negative moments have certainly added to the pervading sense of either pragmatic optimism or genuine pessimism. Think of the collapse of Enron and what it meant to the world's accountants and businesspeople (before the Enron and WorldCom scandals, Sarbanes-Oxley wasn't a concept, let alone a hated term in the business world). The timing syncs up first with confirmation of pedophilia in the Catholic Church and then, three-plus years later, the death of a much-loved Pope. Around the world, people are less trusting, more manic, and more at odds with one another than ever before. They're happiest when bound in safe spots, hopefully well wired, where they can manage the outside from the inside.

We want to create our own worlds, and we value "quality space" as much as "quality time." "Increasingly, we are all in our own virtual bubbles when we are out in public, whether we are texting, listening to iPods, reading, or just staring dangerously at other people," observes Lynne Trusse in her book *Talk to the*

Hand: The Utter Bloody Rudeness of the World Today, Or, Six Good Reasons to Stay Home and Bolt the Door. "It used to be just CIA agents with earpieces . . . who regarded all the little people as irrelevant scum. Now it's nearly everybody."[7] For Trusse, a mass rudeness has resulted from our efforts to make private spaces, away from it all even while we're in it all. We're too in the zone to bother with simple courtesies.

Technology is our new appendage, and as we struggle to manage it, we'll have to redefine the terms of undivided attention. This may be a snapshot of the New Normal: anti-social behavior, even rudeness; personalized environments where we control everything we possibly can; an overarching desire to keep "them" (the irrelevants) away from us; and an awareness of the importance of living life in and of the moment.

Noted author and entrepreneur Jesse Kornbluth, whom we both consider a dear friend, reviewed a version of this book and cautioned us against being too Pollyanna-ish, underestimating people's feelings of "pessimism and fear." He quotes singer Matthew Ryan's line "It's not your job you're fighting for/You're fighting for your life," and explains: "You make life sound like a knowledge worker's paradise: the independent operator with lots of autonomy, etc. May Mr. Autonomous (me) point out I spend $17,700 a year (for a small family) for a health plan that sucks? I see a country in debt beyond reason, terrified of the 2007 balloon-mortgage bubble." He continued, "I could very easily make the case that the middle class will become the rentier class; that we're seeing the rise of corporate feudalism; that the only real freedom to be found is in cyberspace. (Do you know they're arresting people for drunkenness in Texas bars?) On the other hand, this may be a learned 'liberal' response."

On his site HeadButler.com, Kornbluth examines the current mind and mood as described by Martin Seligman of the University of Pennsylvania, former head of the American Psychological Association and author of *The Optimistic Child*. Seligman argues that a quintessentially American optimism started fading in the 1950s and has now turned into outright negativity. As Kornbluth explains it, "Starting in the 1950s, Seligman suggests, real optimism was eroded by the fake happiness of television sitcoms and books like *The Power of Positive Thinking*. Smart Americans refused this blinkered boosterism. And life proved them right: assassinations, Vietnam and Watergate more or less confirmed it was folly to believe that all was well in the best of all possible countries." In the 1970s, he explains, "a booming business sprang up to make the bad feelings go away. Self-help books and programs promoted 'self-esteem,' and a worldview built on a comforting idea: 'I'm okay, you're okay.' Except that we're not okay, says Seligman. We anticipate one negative event after another. And our typical response to our unhappiness is to find some fast-acting external 'cure'—shopping, sex, thrill-ride media, food—that wears off fast and leaves us looking for our next quick fix."[8]

We've tried hard to write an optimistic book, with an eye on the more positive scenarios for the future, but we're living in a time of great pessimism and we'd be remiss not to caution readers that everything is not going to be okay, despite all our best wishes to the contrary.

What to Expect from *Next Now*

This book and the worldview it encompasses is intended not to pick up where we left off when we completed our 1999 publication, *Next: Trends for the Near Future* (Overlook Press), originally published in Holland in 1997, and not as an aggregation of our public and private forecasts over the last several years. Rather, we take a look the social forces that are pushing and pulling against each other to shape the tense and dynamic period 2007–2010, since 2010 once stood for the end point of the near future.

By design, *Next Now* has a narrow time window, and doesn't offer big-picture trend analysis so much as it tells you what to expect in the next four to five years. Unlike other books we've written, we're not primarily focused on the trends affecting big business, or even the business world—it's about how you live now, and how you might come to live. A travelogue into the near future.

To highlight the key themes, we are utilizing the same devices as we did in our previous *Next:*

- "Big Nexts" are the megatrends that transcend place and point of view, and touch almost everyone.
- "Nexts" are the key trends that will shape life and work as we count down to 2010.
- "What's Nexts?" are sprinkled throughout the book. Here, we speculate on probable scenarios, a technique we have incorporated into our trend-tracking style for more than a decade.

We kick off *Next Now* with a survey of our current anxieties and collective cynicism, a Now Audit of today's realities, then move right into our Globalization Next—it's globalization that's now the overarching force behind most of the major cultural shifts in everyday public life and in our institutions.

Marian Salzman
Ira Matathia

Section I

The Whole Next World

chapter one

big next: the age of anxiety

There's a Swedish proverb that says worry gives a small thing a big shadow. If that's the case, we're experiencing a real cultural eclipse. There's a pall on our collective consciousness as we negotiate the troubles of daily life with even bigger things on our minds like cataclysmic natural disasters, terrorism, disease pandemics, and war.

When we wrote *Next*, fear was already one of the overarching trends that we thought would change everything, a "Big Next," right in Chapter 1. We were feeling beset by scandal, not just in the arena of big business, but among "government leaders, celebrities, and just about everyone else in the media spotlight." We wrote about the consequences:

> One result of having weathered scandal after scandal is that we've grown more cynical. We're wiser to the ploys of politicos, preachers and priests, teachers, and, yes, advertisers and marketers. We're bombarded with infinitely more messages than we were a dozen years ago. We're worried about our futures, our countries, our jobs, our cities and villages, our schools, violence down the street and overseas. And we're anxious about what the millennium holds.[1]

We had good reason to be anxious about the turn of the century. A quick glance at the news reveals myriad worrisome issues: A single summary in the

New York Times touches on "carnage" in Sudan, Iran's nuclear program, the rise of HIV/AIDS among minorities, church-burnings in Alabama, and Internet piracy.[2] We're overwhelmed by things to worry about, from bird flu to terrorist strikes, and it's a real assault on our comfort zones.

It's interesting to note how many of these anxieties we would have been thinking about ten years ago. Of the lot, beyond avian flu, the closest one to being new is Internet piracy (though we did talk about the impact of online-payment fears in the nascent days of e-commerce). The new fears, the new threats are really the old ones—of course, the most profound difference is that we view everything through the prism of 9/11.

Before 9/11, there was talk of people drowning in information, too many inputs; Marian's reaction was that many people, especially the upper-middle class, were actually feeling emotionally overloaded: too many choices, too many paths not taken. Today, we have anxiety overload, and we respond by bouncing from strong and fierce—"It won't get me"—to cautious and fearful—"Can I beat the odds?"

It's not just that our fears are amplified—we're continuing to lose faith in institutions (government, corporations, media, church, even the United Nations) that once helped us navigate the world's woes. We're at the cynical tail end of just over 200 years of ideologies spawned by the enlightenment and the American and French Revolutions. The notion that fairness and good sense could prevail in society all but dissipated in the twentieth century, in the wake of the ideological horrors of Nazism and fascism. Then the end of colonialism, the spread of 1960s liberalism, the end of Soviet communism, and the triumph of market-based capitalism raised some hopes.

But little can be achieved if our institutions are revealed to be inadequate and even corrupt. Skepticism and cynicism are born. International polls show that trust in these institutions is at an all-time low. It feels like nothing is sacred anymore.

Next: Our Institutions Fail Us

The attacks of September 11, 2001, assaulted all of our presumptions about the reality of terrorism and the ability of our government to protect us. "Terrorists are working to obtain biological, chemical, nuclear and radiological weapons, and the threat of an attack is very real," reads the U.S. Department of Homeland Security's Web site.[3] An official advisory system may measure the risk of a terrorist attack on a daily basis, but people are skeptical about how the much the government can really do if an attack hits. And it doesn't help matters that in the spirit of the Cold War backyard bunker, Americans are encouraged to take personal responsibility, with survival kits and emergency plans.

Ultimately, we must fend for ourselves, a notion vividly reinforced by images of stranded survivors on rooftops begging for help and the horrific conditions in the New Orleans Superdome after Hurricane Katrina hit. That was followed by a 505-page report called "A Failure of Initiative" that detailed the inaction of government agencies and leaders in their response to the disaster. It's not hard to see how the government has made the American public uneasy. All one has to do to up the ante of anxiety is ponder the allegations against government leaders, from wiretapping to prisoner abuse to inept disaster preparedness. Gallup polls showed President Bush's job approval rating was at an unimpressive 42 percent (about half of what it was in the months after 9/11) by February 2006.[4]

In many—perhaps most—countries, politicians and public officials are now assumed to be basically untrustworthy. Chronic mistrust of politicians and officials might be regarded as part of the culture in such developing countries as Nigeria, the Philippines, and Bangladesh, but it's also endemic in developed countries like Italy (not coincidentally run by that country's biggest media mogul) and Greece, which rank 40th and 47th, respectively, in Transparency International's Corruption Perception Index.[5] And two of the administrations that have trumpeted their principles most loudly—the Bush and the Blair governments—appear to have misrepresented the case for war in Iraq. Trust in them has fallen accordingly.

At the same time, our trust in corporations has eroded as misdeeds by names ranging from Enron, Tyco, and WorldCom in the United States to Ahold and Parmalat in Europe, pile up. It paints an impression of big business as a world of self-serving greed and duplicity. A survey by the World Economic Forum found that trust in both large national companies and global companies recovered to pre-Enron levels in 2004, but again declined; trust in global companies specifically is now at its lowest level since tracking began five years ago.[6]

Next: Fearing Mother Nature

The cover of the November 2005 issue of *Wired* raises the red flag on "Earthquakes, Tsunamis, Meltdowns: America's Next 10 disasters." Between them, the Asian tsunami, the earthquake in Pakistan, and Hurricane Katrina gave the media ample material to dramatize the ramifications of natural disaster.

And while the tsunami of late 2004 killed a vast number of people—well over 100,000—we are told that that number could be dwarfed if a major earthquake were to hit a densely populated area. Many people know they're at risk: Many Japanese live in a major earthquake zone; the big cities in California are built on the San Andreas fault, a geological time bomb. (A major quake in

California "would be much worse than Katrina," says David McLean, a structural engineering expert with the Pacific Earthquake Engineering Research Center.)[7] Densely populated Italy is home to three active volcanoes, and Mexico City, with a population of 18 million, is just 40 miles from an active volcano.

> The odds are long, but under one scenario, the Eastern seaboard of the United States could be destroyed by a tsunami set off by the Cumbre Vieja volcano on the Atlantic island of La Palma. Seismologists fear its next eruption could dislodge an unstable 12-mile-long slab of rock, which would crash to the sea bed and cause a tsunami that would hit the Americas nine to 12 hours later. Cities including Boston, New York, and Miami would see 80-foot waves; South America would be equally overwhelmed.[8]

Mother Nature has become a force we can't trust. *The 700 Club*'s Pat Robertson and Christian radio commentator Charles Colson have gone so far as to suggest that natural disasters are payback and punishment for America's sins. (Robertson would later see divine retribution for Israel's withdrawal from the occupied territories in Ariel Sharon's stroke.) Colson, former special counsel to President Nixon, even suggested that God allowed Katrina to happen as a reminder to the United States of the importance of winning the "war on terror."

> New Zealand has been voted the world's safest destination by readers of the U.K. travel magazine *Wanderlust* several times. But it too has its share of dangers: Auckland sprawls across a field of at least 50 volcanoes. And scientists say the Alpine fault has a 70 percent chance of causing a major earthquake in the next 20 years; such an event could cost the small country up to $11 billion.[9]

Our fears of nature are now amplified by the specter of global warming. Many scientists believe global climate change has reached a pace at which surprising and sudden effects are possible. In 2005, for example, scientists discovered that the Gulf Stream, which raises the temperature in Europe by an average of 5 degrees, had already weakened by about 30 percent. There was widespread belief that the severity of Katrina was due to global warming. As Bill Clinton put it at the 2006 World Economic Forum, climate change is the only problem "that has the power to end the march of civilization as we know it."[10]

Attempts to stabilize greenhouse-gas emissions, linked to climate change, have stalled. In December 2005, at the UN Conference on Climate Change in Montreal, the United States refused to ratify the Kyoto Protocol; neither China nor India attended, although China opens a new coal-burning power station every two weeks and will soon overtake the United States to become the world's largest emitter of carbon dioxide. One recent response—motivated as much by business self-interest as concern for the planet—is the $3 billion dollar pledge to invest in renewable energy by Virgin's Sir Richard Branson at the second Clinton Global Initiative.

Climate change is just one of the dire environmental crises we're warned about. There are many, including the fact that by 2050, four more planet Earths would be required to sustain the projected population of nine billion people, according to British scientist John Guillebaud.[11] New maps show that the Earth is rapidly running out of fertile land and that food production will soon be unable to keep up with the world's population. The UN reports that during the next 20 years, the average supply of water per person is expected to drop by a third. As early as 2000, 30 countries containing 20 percent of the world's population were short of water, and the UN warns that figure will rise to 50 countries by 2025. An environmental assessment by the World Wildlife Fund and the Worldwatch Institute in Washington found that humans are exploiting about 20 percent more renewable resources than can be replaced each year.[12]

Next: Rising Global Health Fears

A few years ago, the phrase "the next pandemic" would have been meaningless to most. Globalization and global mobility provide outstanding opportunities for pathogenic bugs of all sorts. This was already the case when journeys overseas took weeks, not hours. The SARS outbreak in China caused a major panic before it was contained. And now the U.S. Centers for Disease Control writes in "Preparing for the Next Pandemic" that "Many scientists believe it is only a matter of time until the next influenza pandemic occurs. The severity of the next pandemic cannot be predicted, but modeling studies suggest that the impact of a pandemic on the United States could be substantial."[13] The top candidate for pandemic is Avian Influenza A (H5N1), one of the few "bird flu" viruses that also affects humans. Around half of those who become infected from birds will die, but the big danger is that the strain could mutate into a form that's highly infectious and transferable among humans. Such a change could mark the start of a global outbreak.

And just as the Asian tsunami and Hurricane Katrina quickly and massively turned life upside down for huge numbers of people, so would a pandemic. It would disrupt everything from air travel to tourism and the international food trade; mass transportation and public places would be shunned; and Westerners may well have to rethink social habits such as kissing, hugging, and even shaking hands.

While the dangers of an influenza pandemic are only hypothetical, the dangers of another pandemic, the global spread of obesity, are clear: increased incidence of type 2 diabetes and its associated complications, increased risks of cardiovascular disease and cancer. This phenomenon has been dubbed "globesity" by the World Health Organization. One way or another, the coming years are virtually certain to see a rise in global levels of anxiety about health.

> A few years ago, we completed a study on globesity that found its way onto the cover of the *Economist* and page 1 of the *New York Times*. One of our key findings was that XXL-sized people were changing businesses, since current dimensions of everything from coffins to toilet seats in hospitals do not accommodate the truly obese.

What's Next? Hajj Scares

The annual pilgrimage to Mecca presents a perfect storm of elements that could set off an epidemic: A mass of people, many from countries that are still batting infectious diseases like polio and cholera, congregate in close quarters. In January 2006, as many as 2.5 million Muslims participated in the Hajj. Disease outbreaks have occurred before, with documented cases of cholera epidemics reported in the 19th century. Meningitis became an issue in 1987, after an international outbreak following the Hajj that year. Saudi Arabia now makes meningitis vaccinations mandatory. While the government has taken various other precautions, even equipping the airports in three cities with thermal cameras to pinpoint travelers with dangerously high fevers, the pilgrimage could well serve as an "epidemiological amplifying chamber" for the avian flu, says Ziad Memish, co-author of a study on the topic in *The Lancet*.[14] If one person in the throng carries the virus, reports *Seed* magazine, the odds that it would mutate into a human-to-human strain "would increase by orders of magnitude."[15]

Next: Master of My Destiny

As a response to fears and anxieties related to health concerns, corporate scandals, government ineptitude, terrorism, and all the other complexities of modern life, people are seeking more personal control. We're taking matters into our own hands, whether it's home-schooling and eating homegrown organic foods or screening potential mates online for the perfect match. Our desire to be autonomous isn't new—even in small children, the human desire for self-determination is clearly present. What's new is the extent to which personal control has become a social phenomenon. We find custom-designed dates online. Peer-based ratings systems for eBay transactions help guard against people who don't play by the rules. Local grass-roots groups intend to take matters into their own hands and become the real "first responders" in the event of a terrorist attack. We self-diagnose our ailments online, disillusioned with the medical establishment. We swoon for celebrities like Angelina Jolie who go head to head with world leaders in the name of social justice.

Next: Consumers Take Charge

Since the 1980s, the thrust of free-market economics has been to facilitate more individual control, get people to accept more responsibility for their lives, and give them more power to do so. The result has been that in every walk of life, consumers now expect to call the shots. Their demands increase every year, encouraged by technological breakthroughs and a stated "customer is king" attitude.

Consumers now have the means for greater autonomy. After the introduction of ATMs, having to coordinate with banking hours and stand in line for a teller was replaced by the freedom to get ahold of cash whenever and wherever one needs it. The TV remote control brought freedom from unwanted shows and commercials, the ability to seek out pleasurable content quickly and easily. WiFi gives us freedom from wires and lets us access the Internet at will. Interactive technology is all about giving the user control: The Internet, TiVo, PVRs, and self-service touch screens have all gotten consumers used to being in charge of their experiences. And the Internet lets the most proactive consumers seek detailed comparisons and reviews before making a purchase, blog about their experiences with products, then hound brands that have let them down. And now connectivity is also available via the cell phone so that location has been taken out of the equation entirely.

In today's highly competitive markets, there's huge scope for consumers to exercise control by playing brands off one another. And as consumers' expectations for fulfillment increase, the result is fidgety, volatile behavior. The process tends to be one of diminishing returns—as personal control grows, so do people's demands, expectations, and complaints. For personal-control freaks, enduring satisfaction is a rarely achieved ideal. Dissatisfaction is always waiting in the wings—so they move on to the next thing.

Next: Back to School at Home

Home-schooling allows parents to determine exactly how and what their kids learn. Both the number and the proportion of U.S. students who were home-schooled increased between 1999 and 2003, and it's an increasingly popular option among the educated elite.[16] As Michelle Conlin writes in *Business Week,*

it's "no longer the bailiwick of religious fundamentalists or neo-hippies looking
to go off the cultural grid."[17]

In spring 2003, approximately 1.1 million students were being taught at home, up
from 850,000 in spring 1999, according to the U.S. Department of Education.[18]

What's the reason for the shift? Fear and safety concerns, for one. In the 2003
National Household Education Surveys Program, the most frequently cited reason for home-schooling was concern about the environment of schools, with
issues including safety, drugs, and negative peer pressure.[19] We note with dismay
that by October 2006, there has been story after story reported on violence in
schools, including a deadly shooting in Montreal and another in Colorado, and
a principal killed by a disgruntled student in Wisconsin. Some parents are also
concerned that outdated educational standards are keeping their kids behind in
a competitive international landscape. Conlin writes that, "More parents believe
that even the best-endowed schools are in an Old Economy death grip in which
kids are learning passively when they should be learning actively, especially if
they want an edge in the global knowledge economy."[20]

With vast resources and curricula available on the Internet and home-school
networking groups providing a social outlet, learning at home will become more
attractive to parents and increasingly accepted in the culture. It's the ideal way to
take control of education.

Next: The Rise of Mavericks and Whistleblowers

As frustration with government and corporate misdeeds grows, more and more
people are becoming whistleblowers, revealing perceived misconduct and speaking
out in the name of truth despite the risks. As controversy builds around prison-
abuse cases and other national-security issues, even military officials are becoming
more vocal against the government. In a February 2006 hearing held by a subcom-
mittee on national security, military officers revealed their roles as whistleblowers in
various government scandals. One, Specialist Samuel Provance, said he was
demoted and humiliated after revealing that senior officers had covered up abuse of
detainees at the Abu Ghraib prison in Iraq. He said, "Young soldiers were scape-
goated while superiors misrepresented what had happened and misdirected attention away from what was really going on. I considered all of this conduct to be
dishonorable and inconsistent with the traditions of the Army. I was ashamed and
embarrassed to be associated with it."[21] Champions of government accountability
and honesty who brave the risks and social stigma will be the next American idols.

What's Next? More Independent Activists

Public mavericks like Cindy Sheehan are demanding that the government provide cogent explanations and take responsibility for its actions. The anti-Iraq war activist, sometimes referred to as the "Peace Mom," waged extended demonstrations and set up camp outside President Bush's Texas ranch to protest what she believes is an unjust war. Sheehan, whose son died in Iraq, hopes to pressure the government to bring troops home from Iraq and to hold politicians accountable for their actions. While the public has responded with a mix of support and criticism, there's no doubt that she stands as an icon of independent action against the establishment.

Next: Relying on Who and What We Know

Because we mistrust our politicians, we'll turn to alternative leaders to tackle our problems—think Bono or Bill and Melinda Gates as the key to ending HIV/AIDS. We mistrust the media, so we seek more independent outlets, like Thesmokinggun.com. And grounded in our own sense of truth, we'll stick with who and what we know.

Futurist Faith Popcorn puts it straight—we'll pick our friends and friends of our friends over the traditional institutions: "Disillusioned by the old authorities, and unable to know everything themselves, people turn to their friends to tell them what, and who, to trust. They inform each other on everything from how to invest and what to buy to whom to have sex with. Expect everyone to have their own panel of 'curators,' experts and opinionated pundits to cut through the clutter."[22] We can see another of Faith's observations as a very likely reaction to all this stress and strain—"cocooning," the idea of reverting into a small circle of people and a tightly confined, managed home space.

It's why we love Facebook, Friendster, MySpace, Ecademy.com, Classmates.com, LinkedIn, and other online social networking sites so much. We can stay connected to each other in a seemingly safe network or "place for friends." The question remains whether these sites will offer the same communal benefits once they are acquired, one after another, by big business. No doubt, this is why we heard such an outcry when it became clear just how much our personal information has become fodder for online predators. We've made friendship a commodity to ensure our security and control as much as our social fulfillment.

Next: Wiki Gives Everybody a Shot

Beyond our own personal networks, we're getting the lowdown from our peers rather than from established authorities by virtue of the wiki (which means

"quick" or "fast" in Hawaiian). It's the next generation of openness and participation over the Internet, a type of Web site that allows users to add and edit content. It's an ideal way for the masses to participate in and control content.

Most famous among wiki sites is Wikipedia, the self-described "communal
encyclopedia that anyone can edit."[23] It began in 2001 and has become the largest
reference site on the Internet, with 13,000-plus active contributors working on
somewhere around three million articles in more than 100 languages.[24] The site,
produced by a nonprofit company headquartered in St. Petersburg, Florida, promotes open collaboration and encourages anyone to contribute knowledge—
central to Wikipedia's philosophy is collective participation and a sense of trust. At
the same time, Wikipedia is the first Web site to point out that not everything you
read will be accurate and unbiased. "Trolls" who post deliberately misleading
entries, however, aren't tolerated, and content is usually corrected quickly.

Debate rages on about whether Wikipedia is the ultimate example of open,
honest collaboration or simply a portal of misinformation crafted by people who
are not experts. But what's really significant is that it finds a perfect balance: control without being overly controlling. It's fluid, ever-changing, and open to all,
but it's also, for the most part, an accurate and tightly run site managed by a
global editorial staff.

Wikipedia is the 17th most-visited site globally.[25] (In comparison, the 69th-
place site is About.com, the citizen-expert site acquired by the New York Times
Company in 2005 for $410 million.) Wikipedia's founder, Jimmy Donal "Jimbo"
Wales, a minor Internet rock star already, is only just beginning. He has Wikia up
and running, a for-profit wiki company that manages Wikicities, a collection of
more than 250 wiki communities, and Wikiasari, a search-engine project.

It's also just the beginning for a concept called Web 2.0 that, like Wikipedia,
is about "harnessing the collective wisdom of users," explains *Investor's Business
Daily*. Web 2.0 services use a development technique called Ajax that mimics
desktop software and makes Web sites "faster and easier to use," says the newspaper. "If you've used Google's Gmail service, Yahoo's Flickr photo-sharing site,
or Microsoft's Windows Live, you've seen Web 2.0 in action."[26] The common
link for the buzzword is that Web 2.0 is the social Web, because it helps users
contribute and reuse information.

The social Web demands genuine collaboration between user and content
provider, and typically includes other users, too. User-contributed content will
forever modernize the media world, with online media leading the charge.

"We have become so imbued by the conventional wisdom of managerial capitalism
that we think the only way to do things is via hierarchical, top-down, tightly

controlled organizations that are highly tuned and incredibly fragile. Wikipedia is none of these things, yet it works brilliantly. There's a lesson there for control freaks."
—John Naughton, *The Observer*[27]

Next: Fear and Mistrust as an Engine for Entertainment

Poking fun at calamities and mistrustful behavior effectively desensitizes us, helping us cope. Like a good nervous laugh after a moment of discomfort, it's a defense mechanism of sorts to help us minimize magnitude. Late-night talk shows and comedy writers give us jokes and tales of conspiracies so far flung that we essentially forget the facts and, consequently, the worry.

We make fun of everything. We're a "joke-drunk America," noted Peter Mehlman, a senior writer for *Seinfeld* and television producer, after a shooting accident in the Texas woods put Vice President Dick Cheney at the center of a political and media storm. The jokes spread across e-mail and proliferated on TV faster than details of his victim's condition. Said Mehlman: "It's a testament to our universal cynicism that comedy writers are now virtually impotent when it comes to shocking or offending people anymore."[28] If the truth hurts, we want to see it and make fun of it.

That's especially true in a time when the truth feels so elusive. At the core of the Cheney incident was a nagging concern that the 24-hour gap between the event and its report indicated some manner of cover-up; then four days passed before Cheney publicly commented on the incident. We're living in an era where the American Dialect Society's 2005 word of the year was "truthiness," defined as "the quality of stating concepts or facts one wishes to be true, rather than concepts or facts known to be true."[29] The word itself is a joke, part of the tongue-in-cheek lingo of Stephen Colbert, faux news-show host on Comedy Central's *The Colbert Report*.

The Colbert Report spun off from *The Daily Show*, the self-proclaimed "nightly half-hour series unburdened by objectivity, journalistic integrity or even accuracy."[30] Nonetheless, young viewers are turning to such shows for real information: In a poll by the Pew Research Center for the People and the Press, 21 percent of Americans aged 18 to 29 cited *The Daily Show* and *Saturday Night Live* as places where they regularly learned presidential campaign news.[31] It's an ironic twist that a disillusioned younger generation would spurn the mainstream media for its lack of objectivity and truth in favor of a fake news show that prides itself on mockery and subjectivity. What's the appeal? It's wildly open, uncensored, and unrestrained.

It's why the satirical newspaper *The Onion* enjoys such widespread popularity, with more than 3 million monthly visits to its Web site and a total print circulation of nearly half a million.[32] The cynic has become both satirist and symbol of free expression. Comedy has always served as a thin veil for truth-telling—there's truth in jest, as they say—but watch as even more critiques and indictments of people and institutions get delivered with a punch line.

Next: Truthiness is the Modern Way

We're awash in uncertainty. Lying in all its forms—from little white ones to grand-scale deception—has become part of our cultural mainstream. It's a time of quasi-truth that makes discerning real from fake or true from false an almost impossible task. Think of Clinton's tortured phrasing to explain misdeeds so that the whole truth became "truth lite." Or the political "blame game" that ensued after Hurricane Katrina, with people pointing fingers at New Orleans itself, the state government, and various components of the federal government. Essentially, it's a shoulder-shrugging way to shirk accountability, a way to cloud the truth and dance around the facts.

Living in a culture of rampant lies is unsustainable, unstable, and essentially anxiety producing. So more people are demanding the truth. There's a real rise of interest in "owning up." There's now such a widespread fascination with uncovering the truth that we've actually co-opted it as our own brand of entertainment. Think DNA tests to prove paternity as featured on daytime talk shows, which are now broadcast globally. And consider the Style Network show *Diary of an Affair*, which titillates viewers with this promise: "Imagine hearing true confessions of real women and men who strayed from their partner to pursue perilous and provocative acts with another. *Diary of an Affair* allows you to live vicariously through the intimate details of an infidel's torrid tale." We want all the details of the lie, the acts that led up to the deceit, and the story of what happened when the truth was revealed.

Nothing exemplifies the movement to bridge the truth gap as a form of popular entertainment than the outing of memoirist James Frey, who in early 2006 was found to have faked substantial portions of his life story in *A Million Little Pieces*. The book had been catapulted into the spotlight—to the tune of 3.5 million copies sold—after Oprah selected it for her book club. First, Frey had the audacity to weave fiction and fact in a move of sheer, subjective truthiness. Second, his falsehoods were outed not by the media establishment but by a Web site with a small staff called Thesmokinggun.com, which hunted down primary sources and documents through simple Freedom of Information requests to reveal the life Frey truly lived. (Remember, also, the indiscretions of Bill Clinton were first reported online by Matt Drudge.) At first, Oprah supported Frey in a semi-endorsement of truthiness: "Although some of the facts have been questioned—and people have a right to question, because we live in a country that lets you do that—the underlying message of redemption in James Frey's memoir still resonates with me."[33]

The masses, however, had no tolerance for wavering on the truth, even if it was done by the doyenne of daytime. After she was barraged by criticism, Oprah rescinded her support. "I made a mistake," she said, "and I left the impression that the truth does not matter. And I am deeply sorry about that, because that is not what I believe." Oprah promptly had Frey on her show and gave him a verbal flogging—exactly the kind of truth and TV the public wants. Watch as even more independent outlets use exposés as leverage for appealing to the populace.

Next: Corporate Scandal Breeds
Corporate Conscience

Corporations now face levels of scrutiny that were unimaginable even a generation ago. Media outlets compete to dig up sensational stories about corporate malfeasance—after all, the media-consuming public loves to see high fliers brought down and mighty corporations humbled. And with the Internet available to all, interest groups can easily spread damaging information that undermines trust. Plus, the Sarbanes-Oxley Act, passed by the U.S. Congress in 2002, includes provisions that protect whistleblowers who reveal securities fraud and other violations from retaliation by public companies. Even the business buzz word "transparency" has crept into everyday parlance. Business is under the gun to start playing by the rules. In this environment, corporations have to be beyond reproach and do all they can to assuage consumer fears and doubts. That means embracing and enforcing whole rafts of politically correct initiatives, such as equal-employment policies and strict rules against discrimination and harassment, and doing their best to act as "good guys." In the complex business environment of the early 21st century, corporate social responsibility looks more like a wise obligation than a smart option. And while some argue that the "business of business is business"—that market forces will ultimately exert the necessary pressures to make corporations behave in socially responsible ways—corporations that embrace social responsibility before they are forced to are much more likely to benefit from enhanced reputation and trust.

A proactive stance on social responsibility doesn't just enhance a corporation's trustworthiness, it can also signal strategic opportunities. Consider the growing market for generic (i.e., non-patent-protected) drugs, the push for healthier meals at fast-food chains, and the growing demand (as well as the regulatory pressures) for cleaner fuels such as natural gas. Social pressures often indicate unmet social needs or consumer preferences. Businesses can gain both a market and a trust advantage by spotting and supplying these needs before their competitors.

When General Electric launched its Ecoimagination initiative in mid-2005 to develop environmentally friendly products in energy, water, and other product lines, CEO Jeff Immelt told *The New York Times*, "We wanted a marketing campaign that could span lots of our divisions, and hooking it to the environment seems logical."[34] In other words, GE (which happens to be one of the most notorious and long-standing polluters of New York's Hudson River) has come up with an initiative that's about saving the environment, while differentiating the company and providing products customers want. Some advocates believe this is the new direction of business, because linking corporate citizenship with the bottom line is a connection that executives are more likely to embrace.

And Therefore Next

In the space of a decade, it seems there is even more to be afraid of than we had imagined. In some ways, we are poised at a crossroad as we look ahead: Do we succumb to our fears and anxieties, become a society of fatalists, and throw care to the wind as we "carpe diem," or do we continue to accept the sacrifice of small (for now) individual liberties in the name of "security"?

chapter two

big next: the shrinking globe

Perceptions of Globalization

The process of globalization goes back at least 500 years to the Age of Discovery, when advances in ship-building technology made longer voyages possible for Columbus and others. Ever since those early days spent traversing the spice routes, technologists and traders have tried to find ways of shrinking time and space to bring the world closer. Now, we live in a world of 6.5 billion people in which cheap, instant, and continuous global communication is taken for granted. It would amaze the pioneers, but they likely would have no trouble understanding the dynamics of today's globalization—it's a logical extension of a centuries-long process.

In trying to find a defining characteristic for the modern era, Richard N. Haass, president of the Council on Foreign Relations, suggests that globalization perhaps comes closest. The term encompasses "the increasing volume, speed and importance of flows across borders: people, ideas, greenhouse gases, manufactured goods, dollars, euros, television and radio signals, drugs, germs, e-mails, weapons, and a good deal else," Haass wrote as 2006 began.[1] There can be little doubt that whatever happens in the world today happens in a globalized context, so that events have increasing potential to be felt continents away.

Next: Clashing Values, Disconnected Continents

Coming into closer proximity with each other—physically and virtually—involves significant change, and many people fear change. Often these rising tides of change breed violent tension.

The 2004 murder in Amsterdam of Theo van Gogh, a liberal and a film-maker, vividly illustrated the trend. Riding his bicycle to work, Van Gogh was shot several times by Mohammed Bouyeri, 26, an articulate, educated, second-generation Moroccan immigrant. As Van Gogh begged for mercy, Bouyeri slit his throat, then pinned a five-page note to his stomach with the knife; the note threatened Western governments and Jews, and made reference to an Egyptian extremist group. Bouyeri's statement was "a glimpse into the chasm that is opening up between the graying, secular, permissive societies of Europe and the predominantly young, unassimilated children and grandchildren of Muslim immigrants," as *The Boston Globe* put it.[2]

The fall 2005 riots in Paris and throughout France also clearly attested to the wave of cultural conflict. A group of immigrant teenagers were playing soccer in a suburb street. The police arrived and the teens fled, fearing ID checks. Two of them, one of Malian and the other of Tunisian descent, were accidentally electrocuted in a power substation as they ran away; a third teen, whose parents are Turkish Kurds, was injured and hospitalized. Spurred by the deaths, thousands of rioters, most of immigrant North African backgrounds, participated in violent protests.

The gap between native European people and the immigrants living there is becoming a defining challenge for the continent's future. And it's hardly the only place where values, belief systems, and agendas are clashing. The technologies driving globalization, such as satellite broadcasts and the Internet, are bringing conflicting values and agendas into homes around the world.

Next: Continued Rise of Islamic Fundamentalism

In his *Globalised Islam*, originally published in France in 2002, Islam scholar Olivier Roy "takes a broad look at the way in which militant Islam is expressed and organised in a world where people, ideas and electronic messages move swiftly across borders that used to be sealed."[3] According to *The Economist*, "Precisely because traditional cultures, societies and extended families are breaking down, both among immigrants and in their home countries, a younger generation of Muslims in the West is attracted by the idea of a simple, stentorian version of their faith . . . compatible with modern patterns of consumption." It's their way of rebelling, both against elders and against their host cultures."

Other young Muslims are embracing different fundamentalist creeds such as Wahhabism, which purports to be a more pure version of Islam. The son of a Moroccan immigrant in Holland, or of a Bangladeshi in Britain might find the village traditions of his parents oppressive; by embracing fundamentalism, he can sweep away those old cobwebs and adopt a new identity, unencumbered by family customs. In a way, Muslim fundamentalism, promoted by freelance clerics in radical mosques, is comparable to the strict Protestantism preached by evangelicals in the United States. These young Muslims, confused about their place in the world, just want to be born again, too.

In the late 1970s, a highly Westernized Iran installed a government that embodies fundamentalist Islam's response to modernism. This backlash has spread to become a trend even in the heart of non-Islamic countries.

The Middle East itself is a hot spot that emotionally involves people—and polarizes opinions—thousands of miles away. From Connecticut to Kansas, the war in Iraq, oil prices driven by the Middle East, and (lack of) accord between Israel and Palestine now infuse our consciousness.

Next: Two Lost Continents?

In the very early days of globalization, Europe regarded South America and Africa as ripe for ruthless exploitation. Five centuries later, and partly as a consequence of that exploitation, the two continents are struggling to develop. And in today's globalized world, their plight is both morally unacceptable and strategically dangerous.

Capital now flows primarily from poor to rich countries. In 2004, emerging economies, including the newly industrialized economies of East Asia, sent almost $350 billion to wealthy nations.[4] Yet according to the economic textbooks, capital seeking the highest returns should move from capital-intensive countries to poorer ones.

Next: Latin America, A World Apart

In the case of Latin America, countries in the region have not learned how to compete, says *Miami Herald* columnist Andrés Oppenheimer.[5] His book *Cuentos Chino* outlines his belief that Latin America is in danger of falling behind much of the developing world and could become irrelevant if it continues on its current path. He draws on studies by the CIA's long-term think tank and the European

Parliament's Rolf Linkohr, both of which contradict the prevailing view that Latin America is enjoying a healthy recovery.

The crux of the problem, Oppenheimer believes, is that Latin America lacks the income to invest in the research and development projects needed to produce sophisticated goods—only 1 percent of the world's research investment goes to Latin America, versus the 27 percent that goes to Asia.[6] The region's growing number of populist regimes is unlikely to attract foreign investment for R&D. Likewise, those regimes will hinder efforts to reform outdated educational systems and to create highly skilled work forces that could compete with China, India, and Central and Eastern European countries.

This is happening in a globalized economy where an increasing proportion of trade is made up of knowledge-based products in the form of software or intellectual property. Information and knowledge are key aspects of today's economies, essentially weightless commodities (bits and bytes rather than atoms) ideal for trading. And participation in the information/knowledge economy requires increasingly higher levels of specialized education. Oppenheimer says the most startling difference between China, India, and Central and Eastern European countries, and countries like Venezuela, Argentina, Brazil, and Mexico is the approach to education, science, and technology.

> While Chinese and Eastern European universities are graduating engineers, scientists, and technicians, Mexico, an oil-producing country, turns out 15 times more psychologists than engineers.
>
> —Andrés Oppenheimer, *Cuentos Chinos*

Issues of economic viability are deeply rooted in Latin America's history under the yoke of colonial powers. And while the region has long since readjusted its relationship with the old colonists, Spain and Portugal, for the last century it's had every reason to be suspicious of domination from the north. It was Theodore Roosevelt who said the United States would consider Latin America in its sphere of interest, making the United States the dominant power in the Western Hemisphere—one that would speak softly but carry a big stick.

Resulting attitudes toward the *yanquis* have been a major factor in Latin American regionalism. Latin politics oscillates between courting the economic and military benefits of friendship with the United States, and stoking national pride and regional solidarity by defying an Uncle Sam who is often considered evil and sometimes written off as loco or at least senile.

Hugo Chávez, Venezuela's president, has made his disdain for the Bush administration amply clear and places himself at the fore of populist movements in the region. "We need to save life on the planet, we need to save the human race by changing the course of history," he proclaimed at the 2006 World Social Forum in Caracas. And more recently, at the September 2006 U.N. General Assembly, President Chavez publicly referred to President Bush as el Diablo, "the Devil," further exacerbating the divide between Venezuela and his followers, and the U.S. and its allies.

> About 220 million of Latin America's half-billion residents live in poverty. Close to 100 million people in the region are "indigents," according to United Nations figures.[7]

In Bolivia, president Evo Morales is the first member of the indigenous majority to lead the country since the Spanish arrived 500 years ago. He brashly called himself the Bush administration's "nightmare" during his campaign, speaking out against almost every item on Washington's Latin America agenda, notably its attempts to fight coca-leaf production, as well as efforts to privatize natural resources and liberalize trade.[8] The popularity of these anti-Washington positions is a growing trend in South America, where left-wing leaders now govern 300 million of the continent's 365 million people. (Some of which, like Brazil and Chile, have worked hard to cooperate with the United States.)[9]

Next: Africa Struggles for Survival

Unlike Latin America, Africa was not decolonized until well after World War II, and the post-colonial era is still fresh in many minds. One result is an atmosphere of regionalism in which leaders, in trying to present a united front to the world, are unwilling to speak out against others. This has made it difficult for opposition parties to gain traction.

Robert Mugabe of Zimbabwe is the last leader of that era still in power and the only leader still trying to stir the embers of liberation grievances against the European powers. One disastrous effect: His government has seized thousands of white-owned commercial farms since 2000 under a land-reform program that critics say has crippled the agriculture-based economy and contributed to widespread hunger. Zimbabwe's economy has contracted by as much as 35 percent; unemployment is at 80 percent, and agricultural output has plummeted by 90 percent.[10] In the face of wide-scale political repression by Mugabe's government, the opposition party, the Movement for Democratic Change, has had fierce internal debates on the most appropriate election strategy.

At a recent signing of an agreement, South African Intelligence Minister Ronnie Kasrils praised Zimbabwe's "advances and successes" in the 25 years since its independence from Britain and said the two countries share a "common worldview." South African President Thabo Mbeki argues that his policy of quiet diplomacy is the only way to bring about economic and political reform. At the same event, Zimbabwe's Minister for National Security, Dydimus Matasa, said that the greatest threat to Southern Africa's security comes from outside, from "influences whose aim is to effect regime change, especially with regard to countries led by former liberation movements."[11]

Africa is the only continent that became poorer in the past 25 years, according to the BBC.[12]

The drive toward reform and development is made even more complex and harrowing by the continent-wide struggle with HIV/AIDS. More than three-quarters of the 3.1 million global AIDS deaths in 2005 were in sub-Saharan Africa,[13] and the region accounted for two-thirds of the approximately 4.9 million people newly infected with HIV/AIDS in 2005.[14] An extra 1 million health workers are needed in sub-Sahara Africa to fight conditions such as HIV, AIDS, malaria, and tuberculosis, if health is to improve over the next decade, according to a Joint Learning Initiative report sponsored by the Global Health Trust. One reason for the shortage is that rich nations poach medical personnel, a practice that hits poor and politically struggling countries the hardest.[15]

It's believed that in the course of three years, approximately 2,000 doctors and nurses left Ghana in search of greener pastures, and there are more Malawian doctors in the British city of Manchester than in Malawi.
—Joint Learning Initiative report

Social forces exacerbate the HIV/AIDS crisis. Many young girls are forced into sex or pushed into marriage as early as 13 or 14. Getting their partners to use condoms is culturally unacceptable. Says Babatunde Osotimehin, chairman of Nigeria's National Action Committee on AIDS, "Abstinence is not an option for these girls, nor is getting their partners to use condoms. . . . In Nigeria, only 23 percent of men and 8 percent of women use condoms regularly, and, as elsewhere, almost none of them use condoms with a spouse or primary partner."[16] Hope for turning the tide against HIV/AIDS is pinned on microbicides, which are undergoing large-scale efficacy trials. These are products such as topical creams, gels, and vaginal rings that would reduce the transmission of HIV/AIDS during intercourse.

South African professor Sipho Seepe argues that the continent's recovery must start with humble, but pragmatic, aspirations. In an article in *All Africa* titled, "Getting Small Things Right First," he suggests that running through the subtext of the world's "aid brigade" is the notion that Africa is a lost continent, unable to help itself—the quintessential misstep if ethical globalization is going to have a chance.[17]

Next: More Coordination and Cooperation

Latin America and Africa are big geographic expanses with even bigger problems. Some people may dismiss the areas as lost causes, but others are focused on achieving change. Bishop Desmund Tutu of South Africa insists, "Today we face a new, global apartheid where the rich become richer and the poor become even poorer. Such a system cannot be sustained. Our task is to correct the legacy of this injustice and shape a new economic system which can ensure sustainable development for all."[18]

There's an emerging movement across nations to emphasize just and equitable trade as a vehicle for sustainable development, an idea sometimes referred to as "ethical globalization." In 2002, Mary Robinson, former president of Ireland and former United Nations High Commissioner for Human Rights, founded Realizing Rights: The Ethical Globalization Initiative, in collaboration with The Aspen Institute, Columbia University, and the International Council on Human Rights Policy. The initiative is aimed at getting key international stakeholders to adopt concepts of human rights, gender sensitivity, and accountability in government and policy.

Next: New Economic Underpinnings Needed

Trade has always driven globalization. And since rules governing trade were largely based on the concept of "might makes right," trading relationships were generally biased against the weak. The proponents of globalization are advocating for more fair rules. It's clear that aspiring to anything less than a win-win situation for both weak and strong risks ending up as lose-lose.

At a contentious World Trade Organization meeting in Hong Kong in December 2005, a consensus emerged among the developing nations of the world. It was agreed that poor countries need stronger economic foundations before their markets can be thrown open to international competition. Free trade can kill economies if introduced too quickly; neo-liberal economic policies are little help to the world's poorest nations.

An increasing number of voices are arguing that trade is not enough to end poverty and reduce the massive income disparities that bedevil countries from China to Chile. Columbia University economist Joseph Stiglitz, a Nobel laureate, argues that poverty reduction requires not just market liberalization but also massive investments in aid. Other economists advocate aggressive programs to boost literacy, improve healthcare, and build infrastructure.

One new proposal would grant the world's poorest countries "duty free" and "tariff free" access to American, European, and Japanese markets in exchange for anything they can export except weapons, writes *Newsweek International* Hong

Kong bureau chief George Wehrfritz. This would allow those countries to shield their in-bound trade. However, the United States will balk at textiles; Japan will rule out rice. "Still, the scheme could encompass up to 95 percent of what the poorest nations export and grant them exclusive incentives to ramp up not just commodity production but manufacturing as well," according to Wehrfritz. Key to this, he claims, is the idea of sequencing as practiced by China's opening of its markets: "Phased openings rather than shock therapy or big bangs."[19]

There is rising interest in promoting this win-win notion of fair trade. A private meeting held by the Swiss government for 30 trade ministers during the 2006 World Economic Forum in Davos highlighted the need for sweeping industrial and agricultural reform and a model that would give developing countries a shot at new markets. Peter Mandelson, European Union Trade Commissioner, encouraged the economic community to capture the spirit and to maximize the "mood music."[20]

But following the failed attempt by the 149 member states of the World Trade Organization to achieve wide-ranging reform at the Hong Kong meeting in 2005, the fate of world trade is uncertain. And there's a lot at stake, especially considering that despite growing global prosperity, the gap between rich and poor continues to widen.

> The 50 least developed countries, most of which are in sub-Saharan Africa, represent 11 percent of the global population but less than 1 percent of the world's gross domestic product, according to UN figures.[21]

Next: Scientific Research for the Common Good

Science can be a unifying force, and it's always been international, with researchers from around the world migrating between laboratories to pioneer new fields. That's because science operates with its own precise language—data and facts are hard and fast, often indisputable, the perfect nexus for people from Chicago to Beijing to agree on. Perhaps the first and most tangible expression of the true end of the Cold War was the U.S.-Soviet Union collaboration in space (which, a generation before, had been the clearest and most emotional measure of America's competition with the Soviet bloc).

As communications technologies become more sophisticated and countries become more collaborative, research is now multi-locational and synchronous. At the start of the third millennium, the human genome was decoded by two rival groups of researchers. The honors were shared between a private company, Celera Genomics, and the Human Genome Project, a joint venture among four taxpayer-funded American laboratories, a charitably funded British lab, and a scattering of other contributors from around the world.

Increasingly, too, international teams of scientists are forming, with the backing of their governments, to tackle real-world problems like ecology and climate control. Often, threat of disaster is a motivating force for teamwork. Under the sponsorship of UNESCO, coastal countries have concluded their consultation on setting up a tsunami-warning system in the Indian Ocean. At a meeting in Geneva in November 2005, an international gathering of disease specialists and government officials agreed on a £1 billion global action plan to combat bird flu.

As cooperation increases, more new players are emerging in the R&D community. The UNESCO Science Report 2005 notes that while North America still accounts for more than a third of the world's scientific activity, its share is diminishing. Make room for the little guy—a small number of emerging scientists from countries like Turkey, from newly industrialized areas of Asia, and from a number of countries in Central and Eastern Europe, are making their mark. With new players come new opportunities and advances to benefit the greater good.

At the 2006 World Economic Forum, there was talk of "science in the wild," the notion that for the last 100 years, scientific exploration has been done behind closed doors but today the "doors of the laboratory are being torn down." Many areas of research— including climate change and human behavior—are being explored with more engagement with the outside world. The trend will be for scientists to seek more connection with the international public.

These trends in the scientific community will spark new scientific agendas and innovations. And this is critical, with issues like climate change becoming increasingly urgent. Glaciers are melting as the atmosphere warms up, and last year scientists discovered that the Gulf Stream, which keeps Europe's average temperature some five degrees warmer than it would otherwise be, has already weakened by about 30 percent.[22] There will be a collective drive for science to find ways to address the problem.

Next: Globalized Awareness

Technology and the media have allowed people to gain access to images, events, and discussions that are happening beyond their local and national borders. This is fostering more globalized perspectives and shifting what people perceive as the big issues. For those whom the mainstream media reaches, the class-based, ideologically driven, and nationally specific politics of previous generations are being displaced by more global concerns: international politics, international trade, technology, the environment, poverty, disease, security, and terrorism.

Such global issues may be far removed but feel increasingly personal. For some, strong feelings about issues affecting other parts of the world may lead to the opinion that one's own national government is largely irrelevant. Instead, these people may put their faith in transnational organizations and join pressure groups as agents of change.

The modern globalized mind-set was invoked and leveraged by the Live Aid event of July 1985, which staged rock concerts in London and Philadelphia to raise money for famine relief in Ethiopia. Thanks to satellite link-ups, the live broadcast of the concerts drew an estimated 1.5 billion viewers in 100 countries. The 20th-anniversary event, Live 8, was held in July 2005 in 11 spots around the world from London to Toronto to Johannesburg and is estimated to have reached 3 billion people. (An interesting fact: More people in the United States watched the concert on America Online than on television. Widely criticized for misplaced commercial breaks, the TV broadcasts were a travesty when compared with the concerts themselves.)

The differences between Live Aid and Live 8 reflect the development of a globalized mind-set over the past 20 years. The more global 2005 event reached twice as many people. Its goal was more far-reaching, too: It was part of the Make Poverty History campaign that aims to put pressure on world leaders. People can now be brought together for an essentially "global" cause because most of the barriers that used to separate them have been knocked down.

According to the American Association of Fundraising Counsel Trust for Philanthropy, donations to charities involved in international affairs increased by nearly 15 percent in 2003, while total charitable giving grew by less than 3 percent.[23]

Next: Greater Accountability as a Force for Change

"The Internet is increasing the perfection of information and its increasing transparency," said Amazon.com founder Jeff Bezos at the Aspen Institute's 2005 Aspen Ideas Festival. "If in the old world, it was possible to fool consumers, it's not going to be possible in the new world. What the Internet does is really reveal everything."[24]

It's the notion that nothing happens in isolation anymore. It's chaos theory in fast-forward. In a highly complex system, according to the theory, small variations in one part of the system can have a big impact on the whole—the idea is contained in the popular claim that a butterfly flapping its wings in Tokyo could cause a tornado in Indonesia. (Mathematician and meteorologist Professor

Edward Lorenz, one of the pioneers of the theory, actually summarized it this way in a historic 1963 paper: "One meteorologist remarked that, if the theory were correct, one flap of a seagull's wings could change the course of weather forever.")

These days, local events can have real ripple effects with the force to cause big changes. Actions are more likely to have consequences. At the start of 2006, protests from around the world forced Russian President Vladimir Putin to patch together a face-saving deal after shutting off the flow of natural gas to Ukraine. He had been attempting to force the neighboring country to pay market rates. Russia is a powerful nation that has the ability to destabilize not just Eurasia but, given its nuclear arsenal, the entire world. It could have put the screws on Ukraine for decades.

Sixty countries now have some version of Freedom of Information Acts, and the numbers are growing, according to the Brookings Institution.[25]

Just three days later, Russia restored 100 percent of the piped gas after criticism from around the world. Not so surprising, really, given that the gas that supplies Ukraine also supplies much of Western Europe, and supplies had been reduced by as much as 40 percent.

Next: Blogistan's Loud Voices

In other parts of the world, the blogosphere is giving repressed citizens a way to speak out. Iran's hard-line president, Mahmoud Ahmadinejad, may have banned the music of Eric Clapton and advertisements featuring football player David Beckham (whom we already noted is beloved not just in England and Spain but also in Japan), but he can't stop the blogs.

There are more than 100,000 active blogs in Iran, according to British journalist Ben MacIntyre. "Farsi is the 28th most spoken language in the world. Now it ties with French as the second most-used language in the blogosphere," he wrote, as 2005 drew to a close. "This is the place Iranians call 'Weblogistan': a land of noisy and irreverent free speech."[26]

Iraq too has bloggers, often providing a window into places reporters can't go. "Blogging pseudonymously during the last days of Saddam Hussein's regime, Salam Pax's personal experience of the Iraq war gave us a perspective that no professional journalist could possibly give us," noted Personal Democracy Forum.[27] More recently, Baghdad Burning (riverbendblog.blogspot.com), an anonymous Iraqi woman's journal, has been among the most widely read reportage blogs. In early 2006, it was short-listed for the Samuel Johnson Prize in the U.K., an award for nonfiction. To help bloggers avoid repercussions in repressive or turbulent regions, Reporters Without Borders has even published a "Handbook for Bloggers and Cyber-Dissidents."[28]

The blogosphere is more than 60 times bigger than it was three years ago, and it's doubling in size every six months, according to David Sifry, founder of blog search engine Technorati.[29] Upward of 35 million blogs were being tracked by Technorati as of this writing—that's a lot of eyes and a lot of voices now openly in the mix and connecting with the world. More and more, we're seeing the mainstream press pick up and report on the contents of blogs, thereby giving bloggers a greater level of responsibility (moral, if not necessarily legal).

Next: Tourism as an Engine for Reconstruction and Peace

Tourism makes the obscurities of globalization a little more real for people, and personal experience brings greater cross-cultural awareness and understanding. "Travel is the one social and cultural phenomenon that can overcome the 'fear of the other,'" suggests Louis D'Amore, founder of the International Institution of Peace through Tourism, who describes tourism as the first "peace industry."[30]

And today, cultural exchanges, volunteering vacations, and community tourism (where visitors are taken off the beaten path to meet locals in rural areas) are fast-growing areas of the travel industry. Rick Lathrop, founder and executive director of Global Service Corps, told *Newsweek International* in 2005 that participants for programs like teaching English to monks in Thailand or volunteering in rural health clinics were up 30 percent over the year before.[31]

However, while tourism can help the peace process, peace is essential for tourism—an issue in the Middle East and elsewhere. So there is a genuine interdependence that likely will ensure tourism is encouraged by every moderate government around the world.

> "Tourism and peace are inseparable. The forces unleashed by tourism are so powerful that they can change apparently irreversible situations and bring about reconciliation where none was considered possible."
> —World Tourism Organization Secretary-General Francesco Frangialli[32]

Tourism promotion can be compelling proof of a country persevering after severe terrorism attacks against its infrastructure and, indeed, tourists themselves. Egypt witnessed brutal acts of terrorism in both 2005 and 2006, yet tourism continues to grow. Sri Lanka is another example. Tourism to India still thrives, although interest in visiting the Kashmir region has fallen sharply. Bali,

Indonesia, is finally beginning to reestablish its connection to tourists more than a year after the most recent attacks and three years after deadly attacks killed 202 people—mostly foreigners in Bali on vacation.

Next: Globalization as a Force for Gender Equality

The more people see into each other's countries and lives, the more the differences stand out. And few differences are more striking, and more relevant, than the situation of women around the world. Globalization throws a spotlight on the progress or plight of women, and aspires to minimize and even eliminate the mistreatment of women.

The past three decades have seen a steadily increasing awareness of the need to empower women and give them broader access to basic human rights and health care, but progress has been grindingly slow. Women still comprise more than two-thirds of the world's illiterate adults. The abortion of female fetuses, forced marriages, and bride burning are still prevalent in the Asian subcontinent. Even in developed countries, women hold only 15.6 percent of elected parliamentary seats.[33]

The World Economic Forum 2005 report, "Women's Empowerment: Measuring the Global Gender Gap," concluded that gender equality challenges the most entrenched of human attitudes: It takes far more than changes in the law to change practices in the home. The report found that the Nordic countries stand out as the most advanced in the world in terms of narrowing the gender gap. Seven Eastern European countries, including Latvia, Lithuania, and Estonia, are among the report's top 25.[34]

Still, there is some evidence of growing support for equality: According to the Pew 2002 Global Attitudes Project, large majorities in 41 of 44 countries believe the more satisfying way of life is when both spouses work and share childcare responsibilities. Only in Pakistan, Egypt, and Jordan did majorities believe it's better for women to stay home and take care of the children.[35]

In the World Economic Forum's ranking of countries that are narrowing the gender gap, the U.K. ranked 8th, France 13th, and the United States 17th. At the bottom of the 58-country list were Pakistan, Turkey, and Egypt.[36]

The definition of the term *gender gap* is broadening. From the growing awareness of the need to uplift women worldwide has come the concept of gender as an overarching socioeconomic variable, seen in relation to class, race, age, and ethnicity. Gender equality is no longer regarded as synonymous with requiring some sacrifice or adaptation by men. The new view is of a stage of human social development in which rights, responsibilities, and opportunities are not determined by sex. The emphasis is on what men and women—people—can do to realize their full potential.

Fundamental to the idea of ethical globalization is an affirmation of a common humanity that doesn't stop at national borders. Simply, if globalization is going to work in the interest of everybody, all individuals need to be treated equally and with dignity.

And Therefore Next

All the ideas we cover in this book are, in many ways, a subset of the concept of globalization. Culture and ethnicity underlie the shifting balances that are fundamentally changing the world order. Today, we no longer think about United States–USSR, United States–Europe as the axes that drive change across the world. When we consider the future now, the pundits are as likely as not to look at the BRICs—Brazil, Russia, India, and China—as the axis of primary influence. And technology and connectivity are the mechanisms by which these influences are spreading—the Internet is, in many ways, the clipper ship of these times.

How adept will we become at finding ways to accommodate mores that are far afield from the dominant thinking of the West? How do we manage the assault on ever-shrinking global resources with the inexorable increase in demand from the rapidly emerging world? Will we find better ways to manage the impact of "progress" on our habitat? How will we deal with the distribution of wealth—that growing gap between the haves and the have nots? These are the questions that will determine what kind of collective future is in store for the human race.

chapter three

big next: yin meets yang in chindia

It's said that as he looked at a map of the world, Napoleon Bonaparte pointed to China and proclaimed, "There lies a sleeping giant. Let him sleep! For when he wakes, he will shake the world." China and neighboring India had enjoyed healthy trade before the European powers came to the forefront—in 1500 the two countries accounted for as much as 49.3 percent of the world's gross domestic product, according to economic historian Angus Maddison.[1] As the Western powers grew, Asia faded into the background, and China and India's combined GDP fell to about 29 percent of global output by 1870. A century later, they accounted for less than 8 percent.

Now, in the twenty-first century, China is awake. And as neighboring India comes into its own, an even greater giant looms on an Eastern horizon. The two nations, dubbed Chindia by Indian economist Jairam Ramesh in 2005, are linked by a lot more than geography. With blooming economies and a mutual hunt for new markets, Chindia is poised to shake up international economics, politics, and culture.

We've always talked about the ever-accelerating rate of change, and perhaps it's nowhere more evident than in the case of China and India. Consider that on June 30, 1997, China was making headlines for removing the last vestige of foreign influence, gaining control of Hong Kong from the imperial British. What a difference a decade makes. China is on the offensive and is quaking world markets, certainly in terms of what it buys and, we believe, imminently with what it sells.

When we wrote *Next*, our colleague Stuart Harris began his thoughts on China by noting that "China is big—very big." Now, Chindia is even bigger—a lot bigger.[2]

It's home to a third of the world's population, nearly 6.5 billion people. With a growth rate of about 9 percent a year since the 1970s, China is now among the world's biggest economic superpowers, standing behind only the United States, Japan, and Germany. India's GDP was expected to expand by 8.5 percent in 2006, according to a Credit Suisse First Boston forecast[3]—compared with 4–6 percent growth in smaller Asian economies like Thailand or Singapore.

And while Chindia currently accounts for just 6 percent of global GDP (compared with the U.S. share of 28 percent and the EU's 34 percent), it's poised to account for as much as 45 percent by the middle of this century, reports *Business Week*.[4]

"There are at least 100 million individuals with 'middle class' purchasing power (enough disposable income to indulge in nonessential goods ranging from a can of youth-cool Pepsi to a meticulously appointed living room). And this 'middle class' is unlike any other in history in terms of scale, growth rates and ambition."
—*Billions: Selling to the Chinese Consumer*, Tom Doctoroff[5]

As the economies grow, consumer demand will skyrocket in Chindia. Its burgeoning middle class will demand its own shot at the good life with high-end home appliances and status symbols like nice cars and diamonds that project power and style. The Chinese middle class alone is estimated at 175 to 250 million people. A recent Diamond Trading Company ad for men's diamond wear in China promises that "One sparkle is enough to make a powerful man." And the statistics speak to a desire to project modern images of status and beauty. Engagement-ring penetration in one Chinese market is up to 80 percent, from just 10 percent in 1994, according to Diamond Commitment Jewelry Research. By 2008, China is expected to overtake the United States in homes connected to broadband. Demand for passenger cars is expected to reach 3 million in 2006, putting China third in the world, according to a report in *Business Week*.[6]

China has the largest base of cell phone subscribers in the world: 350 million in 2006. And that's expected to grow to 600 million by 2009. India has 55 million cell phone subscribers—a tenfold increase over the 5.6 million in 2000.[7]

There are bigger choices and more business options than ever before in Chindia, and young Chinese and Indians have the opportunities, ambition, and drive to succeed. They're optimistic about their futures and careers, and all too ready to compete with American students and industry. Watch for a rising prominence of Indian and Chinese schools as the international cream of the crop are enticed to Bangalore and Beijing, and watch for an even smarter class of Chindian youth in American universities—both on campus and enrolled in online courses. Look for more success stories like that of Infosys, the Indian-born global software services company that in 1999 was the first Indian business to do a public offering on the U.S. stock market. It's an example of India as a global competitor, not simply a back-end support for multinationals. There's a boundless determination in India that many compare with the pumped-up optimism of Silicon Valley circa 1999.

> "Speaking for India, 20 percent of the world's population under the age of 24 are Indians and 70 percent of our population is less than 36 years old. Given these statistics, I am confident that our youthful workforce, with its boundless energy and enthusiasm, is raring to compete at the global level."
> —Nandan Nilekani, president and CEO of Infosys[8]

China and India possess the weight and the dynamism to transform the global economy. Chindia will disrupt workforces, industries, companies, and markets in ways we can not quite imagine. How these Asian giants integrate with the rest of the world will largely shape the 21st-century economy. As former Harvard University President Lawrence Summers puts it: "What is happening in India and China . . . has the potential to be one of the three most important economic events in the last millennium, alongside the Renaissance and the industrial revolution."[9]

Next: Buddhism to Billions—the Ties That Bind

"India and China are non-identical conjoined twins, joined at the Himalayas," writes correspondent Randeep Ramesh in the *Guardian*.[10] History between the two countries is measured in centuries and marked by a long-standing shared trade and belief in Buddhism. Buddhism spread from India to China along the Silk Route—or the Tea Horse Route, as the Chinese call it—and with it, a cross-border trade took place in silver, raw wool, silk, cotton, and tea. Years later, it was machine parts that the mules carried across the Himalayas, until the borders were closed and trade came to a bloody end in 1962 during the Sino-Indian War.

Historic differences are being overshadowed by rapidly multiplying economic ties. In 1994, Chindia's bilateral trade was $300 million. In 1997, it jumped to $1 billion, and in 2004 to $10 billion. Analysts then predicted it might double by 2010, but Chindia is now set to reach this target in 2007, according to India's Commerce Minister, Karnal Nath.[11] And, too, there's the rising prominence of the

BRIC countries (Brazil, Russia, India, and China) and their combined potential that could dominate the world economy by 2050. Set forth by Jim O'Neil, chief global economist at Goldman Sachs, the BRIC thesis proposes that the four countries could represent over 40 percent of the world's population and a GDP of $12 trillion by the middle of the century. While the four are not bound by a political alliance or formal trade agreement, they did sign a cooperation agreement in 2002. The alliance only further strengthens the Chindia giant by providing the two manufacturing-and-services countries with exactly what they need: natural resources. Brazil is rich in commodities like soy and iron, while Russia has oil.

China's and India's respective industrial strengths are more complementary than competitive and help contribute to goodwill business dealings. China has the "hard" infrastructure of a global manufacturing center, while India has the "soft" infrastructure of a world leader in information technology services. This balance will help to keep foreign businesses engaged in both countries. And the Internet and plunging telecom costs are making it easy for multinational companies to manufacture in China while designing software and circuitry in India.

Motorola is a perfect example of the rising business advantage that Chindia offers. A 2005 *Business Week* article points out that Motorola's R&D group in Bangalore developed the software and user interfaces for the RAZR cell phone, while most of its hardware was assembled in China.[12] More businesses will take advantage of the cheap cost to develop and produce in both countries.

> "Chinese officials have long insisted that if their country is the workshop of the world, then India is the globe's office. The logic is that both can work together to corner markets. Many IT firms already employ hundreds of programmers in China."
> —Randeep Ramesh in the *Guardian*[13]

There are still big shifts in thinking between the two countries that could impede success. China is the world's largest autocracy, while India is the world's largest democracy. Land reforms took place in China in the late 1970s, but stalled in India. In the decades since the Sino-Indian War, interaction between the two has been slow and cautious. And there's still some baggage involving border disputes, overseas oil competition, and caginess about military power. But by and large, China and India have been all too willing to set aside their differences and put on a good face for the sake of economic evolution.

We already see it in their dialogue and diplomacy. "We don't want to take the lead—we just want to be a partner," said Cheng Siwei, vice chairman of the standing committee of the National People's Congress, about relations with India in early 2006. In an equally good show of cooperation, Indian Finance

Minister Palaniappan Chidambaram has noted that, "India and China are not in a race against each other. We believe that the world has enough room to accommodate both India's needs and China's needs, both for capital, for markets, etc."[14]

If it takes two, China and India will do well to continue to play nicely to grow their billions into more billions of trade dollars. America, meanwhile, will watch along anxiously as it tries to walk the fine line of participation and competition.

Next: A Different Generation Rises

In the summer of 2005, *Business Week* assembled a roundtable of 13 Indian and Chinese thinkers—a sample of everyone from authors and activists to academics and business leaders—to talk about the differences between the younger and older generations in Chindia.[15] The consensus? Seeing vastly more opportunities for itself, the younger generation has a boundless ambition for the future and will push ahead hard in the global marketplace. Wang Yong, a professor at Beijing University, noted that younger Chinese are more individualistic, more consumerist, and more knowledgeable about the world—and in turn, more eager to get ahead and positive about the chances of doing so.

"The biggest difference is Chinese youths today are optimistic and more confident," commented another panelist, Viveca Chan, CEO at Grey Global Group in Hong Kong. "In most urban areas, life has improved significantly, and they no longer need to worry about having enough to eat or to wear. They can afford to go after a higher hierarchy of needs."

But while China is getting older as a nation, India is getting younger. Its average age is only 25, and with a population growth rate nearly twice that of China (1.4 percent), 1-billion-strong India is expected to overtake its neighbor as the world's most populous nation by 2035. And this younger generation has a sense of hopefulness that comes from a history without great hardships.

Known as "liberation children," many are too young to remember the challenges of their parents' generation. Their parents are pushing harder and faster for them to be high-performing overachievers, and they possess a drive and energy that could make India increasingly dominant in everything from economics and education to politics and pop culture. On blogs like Youth Curry: Insights on Indian Youth, they make it clear that their career aspirations go beyond those of their dads, who may have worked at the same company for 30 years—they're going to job-hop and leverage their skills as much as they can.

"When the world was round, say 30 years ago, you would much rather have been born a B+ student in Indianapolis, Indiana, rather than a genius in Bangalore, India. Because the Indian genius, unless he or she could get a visa out of India, really could not plug and play with his or her talent. Today . . . you would much rather be a genius in India, because that genius can now innovate at a global level without ever having to emigrate. That is what the flat world makes possible."

—author and journalist Thomas Friedman[16]

Consider Infosys, whose story may sound familiar—at least, it would if it were a Silicon Valley startup. A group of young programmers left their jobs at an Indian software firm and through what is considered a typically Indian mix of skill and determination, crafted a business model that offered top-quality service on a low-cost, around-the-clock basis. To attract a top-notch workforce, Infosys crafted a culture of empowerment, fulfilling employees' needs with everything from in-house gyms to 24-hour cafeterias and clean, accessible facilities (it's one of the few places in India that offers handicap access). The company is a beacon of hope and profits, representing the electric current of competition and possibility for a new Indian generation with boundless drive and potential.

A Nasscom-McKinsey study forecasts the IT industry in India will employ 4 million people by 2008. By then, according to projections, the sector will contribute 7 percent of the nation's GDP, account for 30 percent of foreign-exchange inflows, and see sales of $70 billion a year.

Perhaps the best representation of Chindia's potential is 10-year-old Ajay Puri, who has Bill Gates "worried," by his own admission. Ajay is the youngest Microsoft Office User Specialist, and at this point he's a tech veteran—he created his own Web site at age three.

On the Youth Curry blog, Indian youth are talking about how to attract top international students to their business schools, known as IIMs (Indian Institutes of Management). And they're frustrated that only one IIM made it into *The Economist*'s top 100 ranking of business schools. They're proud of their institutions and want to be seen as competing at the upper echelons. (But if an American degree still carries more weight, Indian students now have the advantage of distance learning, which makes a foreign degree cheaper and simpler to come by.)

The trend will be to mine the intellectual current running out of Chindia—Americans will at the same time reap the rewards and feel the pressure. As companies like Google, IBM, and Hewlett-Packard set up camp in those countries, capitalizing on the science and engineering whiz kids from Bangalore and Beijing, Americans will feel the flame of competition.

In higher education, China and India graduate more than half a million engineers and scientists a year, compared with 60,000 in the United States, according to a report in *Business Week*. The McKinsey Global Institute projects the number of young researchers in both nations will rise 35 percent to 1.6 million by 2008. The U.S. supply, by contrast, will drop. (Although a Duke University study points out that only about half the engineering graduates have four-year degrees; the rest have "short cycle degrees," meaning three years or less of college training.)[17]

Chindia's intellectual capital is already as much a reason for multinationals to move into China and India as are low labor costs. In a February 2006 survey of more than 200 corporations in 15 industries, more than a third said they would "substantially" change the worldwide distribution of their R&D work over the next three years—with Chindia getting the greatest increase in projects. In the study, presented to the National Academies, the United States's leading advisory groups on science and technology, multinationals said this move was motivated by a search for talent more than lower costs or tax incentives. The tug of war between the United States and Chindia in the IT and engineering industries will only increase in the next years.

What's Next? The Rise of Guanxi

People interested in the value of connections would do well to study the principles of *guanxi*, a core Chinese belief in personal connections between people who can prevail upon each other to perform a favor or service. (In the West, the fancy-term equivalents are social capital or relationship capital.) With *guanxi* the relationship is always personal, even when it involves business. *Guanxi* is about networks of mutual trust and respect.

Next: Resources Chindia Needs to Survive—and Succeed

These big changes also come with some big problems, real causes for concern. While India experiences bursts of economic success, more than 300 million Indians live in extreme poverty. In China, water tables are reaching dangerously low levels, and about 300 million people in China's countryside drink chemically contaminated water. There will be more global action and pressure for both countries to make strides in sustainability—for their people and the environment. At the same time, political, demographic, and other issues may hold Chindia back.

Next: Chindia's Rising Demands

The next thing to watch is the way Chindia comes to terms with the realities of conservation and consumption.

About 90 percent of Chinese cities have polluted groundwater. Chemical spills, including one in the Beijing River in the south and one in the northeast that crossed into Russia, have exacerbated the crisis. About 400 of China's 600 largest cities already suffer from water scarcity, and in the next 25 years, the water situation will face enormous pressure from a new round of economic growth. And when there's no water, there's no food. With a lot of mouths to feed, China will need to balance growth with conservation.

At the same time, China accounts for 4 percent of global GDP but consumes a quarter of the world's steel, a quarter of its coal, half of its cement, and 8 percent of its oil. (In 2003, China raced past Japan to become the world's second biggest consumer of petroleum products after the United States, states a report from the BBC.)[18]

And in India, energy consumption will double in the next seven years as the economy expands by 7–8 percent annually, according to Nikhil Meswani, director of Reliance Industries, India's largest petrochemical and its second largest company.[19] As cities like Bangalore glow with the buzz of computers, phones, and lights in call centers and R&D software labs at all hours, it's clear that India—which is adding more people to the world than any other country—will need more natural resources to keep it powered. China and India's growing middle class means more incremental pressure on oil. With a first generation of cars to fuel, India and China are bidding up this commodity to all-time high prices.

"Regardless of ethical considerations, China has no choice but to secure more energy as the world's most populous nation continues its near double-digit growth."
—Agence France Presse[20]

China is increasingly seeing the need for cross-Himalayan collaboration in such matters. In a tight energy-supply market, bidding wars between Indian and Chinese firms have been pushing up prices. In January 2006, India's petroleum minister, Mani Shankar Aiyar, visited Beijing in the hope of ending one of Asia's most deadly rivalries—the goal now is to pool resources, with joint bidding for assets.

Xia Yishen, director of the China Energy Strategy Center, a government think tank, says China is aware that clashes with other countries over energy supplies will become more common: "We realize that eventually this will be harmful to all concerned and so the necessity of cooperating to share risks and reduce costs in a multilateral way is gaining currency here."[21]

The 2008 Summer Olympics in Beijing helped to spur environmental awareness. The government agreed to spend $12 billion over ten years to clean up air pollution if it was awarded the Games, and Beijing is now undertaking some hefty projects: reducing coal-burning pollution; constructing a natural-gas pipeline; improving electricity distribution; reengineering power supplies; implementing European Standard II auto-emission standards; and increasing the use of clean gas-powered buses and taxis. A massive greenbelt has been built around Beijing's borders—the goal was to cover at least 45 percent of the city in green space.

As just one other preparation for the games, China spent $3.7 billion to ease Beijing's traffic, tripling the length of its highways and quadrupling the capacity of its subway. China walks a fine line between necessary development and meeting its conservation promises.

Next: Thinking Out the Business of Saving or Spending

Overinvestment is the Achilles heel of the Chinese economy; India's flaw is too little investment in regard to rapidly increasing consumption. One rising Asian superpower wants to produce all it can now and consume later; the other wants to spend its future income today.

> "China's investment demand is based on excessive optimism about the future. India depends on capital inflow to fund its consumption-led growth, like a poorer version of the U.S."
>
> —Andy Xie, Morgan Stanley's chief economist for Asia[22]

Tom Doctoroff makes the point that China's excess savings goes right to the heart of the Chinese psyche—even with its newfound success, there is a fundamental trepidation that security is only temporary, that one needs to gird for hard times, and that hard times are a certainty down the road.[23]

China needs to shift as much as $250 billion of its economy from investment to consumption just to prevent new bad loans in the banking system, Morgan Stanley's Andy Xie estimates. China also loses a lot of money. *Business Week* notes that its 9.5 percent growth rate in 2004 is less impressive when you consider that half of GDP went into glutted sectors like crude steel, vehicles, and office buildings. The magazine goes on to warn: "Its factories burn fuel five times less efficiently than in the West, and more than 20 percent of bank loans are bad. Two-thirds of China's 1,300 listed companies don't earn back their true cost of capital, estimates Beijing National Accounting Institute President Chen Xiaoyue."[24]

> "The average Indian company posted a 16.7 percent return on capital in 2004, vs. 12.8 percent in China."
>
> —*Business Week*, based on its study of 346 top-listed companies in both countries[25]

The *Business Week* report points out that India has fewer resources and foreign investments, and as a result is more capital efficient with what it has. But at the same time, merchandise exports are constrained by shortcomings in basic infrastructure, such as power, ports, roads, and airports. And computer software and back-office services, in which the country is the world leader, are still a very small part of the Indian economy.

Next: Reconciling the Chindian Wealth Gap

China and India are both too vast and populous to spread their rapid development evenly. This inevitably has led to huge differences between the minority that is in the right place and has the right resources to make the best of development, and the poor majority that is largely out of the loop.

For the masses of poor in China who resent being left out of the nation's rush to riches, one solution may be revolt—something that is and always has been a concern of the authorities. In India, by contrast, the poor can vote and thereby comment on their situation.

Indeed, the elections of 2004 sent a clear message: Don't let the country's historic shift to a market-driven economy leave behind the more than 30 percent of India's 1 billion people, who still live on less than $2 a day. The few high-tech cities whose residents enjoy the benefits of cell phones, 24/7 electricity, and paved highways are a universe apart from the rural villages with no power or clean water, rutted dirt roads, and few jobs. The next step will be for India's democratic structure to provide a political check on the excessive disparities in wealth and lifestyle, preventing a dangerous boil-over of resentment.

What's Next? India's Worker Shortage

In India, where poverty is pervasive and half the female population cannot read, the economy depends on a thin sliver of the population. The number of people working in IT and business-process exports will jump from about 700,000 in 2006 to 2.3 million by 2010. But only about 1 million people with relevant qualifications are expected to graduate from college by then, leading to a deficit of about half a million people, with business processing the worst hit.[26] The McKinsey Global Institute found that only 25 percent of Indian engineers are capable of competing for outsourced work.[27] The jobs will be there, but the people won't.

This supply of talent may be the biggest constraint on India's growth, says *The Economist*, allowing the United States to entice businesses to stay at home for engineering brain power.[28]

What's Next? China's Aging Problem

Its "one child" policy has had a dramatic effect, and as a result of falling birth rates, China is aging faster than any other country in history. It's unique in growing old before it has grown rich. According to official projections, China's working-age population will start shrinking by 2020. This is going to put some pressure on China in the coming years.

Young Chinese are going to feel that push and pull of family duty as they deal with their aging parents. According to Zhang Wenfan, president of the Chinese Old-Age Association, the elderly will be a big burden for China through 2050, when that population will reach 400 million, accounting for a quarter of the total.

Younger Chinese will struggle to reconcile age-old cultural traditions of respecting and providing for the elderly and newer, more individualistic notions of personal success and independence at home and in the office. As China ages, there's been a real shift in the Chinese family dynamic—gone are the multigenerational families with built-in support for the elderly, replaced by small nuclear families that sometimes live at great distances from the older generations. China must grapple with a version of social welfare, pension, and medical plans.

Next: American Attitudes toward Chindia

"When I was growing up, my parents told me, 'Finish your dinner. People in China and India are starving.' I tell my daughters, 'Finish your homework. People in India and China are starving for your job.' "

—Thomas Friedman[29]

As Chindia wakes, watch as Westerners, America in particular, waver between a certain "Bangalore envy" and "Bangalore rage." A lot of the world's smart money is flowing to where a lot of the world's smart people are—especially as they cost less than smart people in the developed countries. Google and many other future-forward American businesses have set up shop in places like Bangalore. (Google opened its first engineering R&D lab outside the United States there, because it wants to mine the top engineers in the world.)

With envy comes anger. Pay attention to the frustration of Westerners with the Bangalore-based call centers and customer-service hubs: "How come no one in *this* country can help me?" Globalization means never knowing where you're calling—but it's probably India. And though Indians may be smart, they may speak English, they may have access to all the information, they're not living in your world, which can become clear when you struggle to understand each other. As a result, watch as some companies move call centers to Central and Eastern

Europe, places like Hungary, where the distance isn't as hard to decipher over the phone.

Anxiety will be a rising emotion as people get scared—for their jobs and for their future. Laura Tyson, dean of the London Business School, says when she asks people how they feel about China, all she hears is "fear."[30] The projections are big, after all, and their ripple effects unknown.

What's Next? A Taste of Chindia at Home

There will be a rising trend of bringing the East and the Middle Kingdom into middle-class American homes. There's a deepening thirst for interior décor via New Delhi and Beijing. Watch for more retailers giving their bent on the Chindia couch or curtain. Consider Target's 2006 ad campaign to bring the look and feel of the global bazaar to its stores. Sure there's a taste of Latin America, Europe, and Africa, but there's even more of Asia and India—online shoppers can even choose between Asia Traditional and Asia Modern, between India Traditional and India Colonial.

On Overstock.com, you can even buy it for less. There's a subsite at the discount retailer that offers up "unique imported home décor"—here can buy an "Indian Rajastani mirrored window/door toran" to "welcome guests and good fortune into your home." The traditional banner, handmade by "talented artists in India," is embroidered with "lucky elephants and flowers." No matter that few Americans will have any idea of elephants' relevance to Indian myth; more immediately, this could make a unique housewarming gift. Atop a picture of the "Long life wall plaque" from China is a warning to shoppers that it's "Almost Sold Out."

During the holiday 2005 shopping season, saris were a hot ticket at stores like Bloomingdale's. The traditional dresses were fashioned into curtains in the Indian color palette—mostly deep reds, greens, and purples—with the signature elephant imagery woven into the fabric for extra cultural flair. And saris are being transformed into everything from bedding to tablecloths. Demand will only rise for a touch of this vintage exotic.

At the same time, the food and flavors of China and India are taking the supermarket by storm. Americans can pick up India's classic spiced milk chai tea at Starbucks and even Dunkin Donuts, or buy it in boxes from the grocery store. Also at Starbucks: green tea frappuccinos (or order a green tea martini at a swanky bar)—a very Western twist on China's age-old flavor.

Shoppers can find a host of new ready-to-eat Indian dishes from Raja Foods and MTR Foods, which offer masalas, chutneys, and sweets. Choose from a host of classics, including aloo mutter, a mix of green peas and potatoes, and methi mutter malai, peas spiced with chilis, cinnamon, and clove. Our palates are getting more attuned to Indian tastes: *The Philadelphia Inquirer* reports that Americans have doubled their annual spice consumption in the last 20 years, from two to four pounds a person. And what spices are Americans using? More curry, cardamom, and cumin.[31]

We're also crazy about China's green tea, drawn in by the benefits of all those antioxidants. Ferolito, Vultaggio and Sons, the No. 2 ready-to-drink tea company, says its Asian-inspired bottles of Arizona green tea are top sellers. And smaller tea brands are starting to get into the specialty-tea game too, including the Japanese company Ito En, Honest Tea, and Revolution Tea.

Next: Entertainment and Romance, Eastern-style

Next, Americans will be sipping their iced green tea lattes and indulging in chocolate truffles infused with cumin as they enjoy the latest movie from Bollywood. From the rows of titles at Blockbuster to the hundreds of rentals available on Netflix, Indian movies have hit the American mainstream. The Bollywood formula film usually runs about three and a half hours, showcasing hundreds of dancers in routines centered on the story of star-crossed lovers. There's lots of action, complete with car crashes and Hollywood-style explosions, but never any blood—nor any kissing or physical intimacy in the romance scenes. It's ideal camp for clean-cut America.

Sfgate.com reports that students at the University of California at Berkeley compete in the Hindi Film Dance Competition, emulating Bollywood's signature routines set to typical Bollywood soundtracks. It's catching on: Other contests have taken place in cities including Detroit and Los Angeles.[32]

And American entertainment is starting to show an underlying inclination toward a very Indian notion: arranged marriage. Traditional Indian culture sees arranged marriage as the way for boy to meet girl, and while many Westerners respond with resistance and a strong cry against the idea, consider ABC's wildly popular primetime show *The Bachelor* as a case in point. Each season a bachelor or bachelorette is given the opportunity to select a mate from a prescreened group of eager partners—essentially a prearranged relationship. The couple's family and friends, as well as the American public, weigh in on the nuances of the couple's relationship. On Abc.com, there was a message board for viewers to discuss and even vote on their favorite partner. If all goes well, it ends in a marriage proposal with a multicarat diamond ring. *The Bachelor* and others like *Who Wants to Marry a Multi-Millionaire*, *Married by America*, and *Who Wants to Marry My Dad?* are American versions of arranged unions.

And Therefore Next

We concluded our look at China in *Next* with a provocative and, we believe, still largely unanswered question: "Will China be seen as a welcome Asian alternative to Americanization/Westernization? Or will Asians look even more to the West to counterbalance Chinese influence?"[33]

Our response would be "both," as well as "neither." We can't help but wonder whether China's rise and Japan's retreat occurring simultaneously changed the whole idea of the Asian region. Somehow, "Asia" seems much more disparate than other continents. (Even more so than the Americas: North relative to Latin.)

A long time ago, we asked the question to a major consumer electronics brand, "Where is 'wow' now?" "Now," we think, is with the Koreans, and we'll bet our "next" on China. Think of Korea's LG and Samsung—and watch this space for Haier. (Any upmarket parent who has a kid away at college has bought a Haier dorm fridge at Wal-Mart.) The one distinctly Japanese component in this "Asian" brandscape: automobiles, especially the perennial star Toyota (the first foreign firm to make it into the top ten of *Fortune*'s America's Most Admired Companies list).[34]

What of India? The original *Next* had this to say about its potential:

> Perhaps the biggest surprise—and the biggest paradox—in the wired world is India. It has just one ISP, a government-controlled company that provides access at charges, that are far beyond the means of ordinary Indians, and yet it has spawned a thriving IT services sector that is taken very seriously around the world. A selection of Indian software companies looked far from out of place at the 1998 CeBIT, the world's biggest IT trade fair, in Hannover, Germany.[35]

Yup, no doubt the Indians get tech.

As Chindia seduces us with its novel clothes, colors, flavors, and films, its emergence on the global stage serves notice to the developed world. If America does not engage vigorously with China and India, it risks becoming the next Old Europe, hanging on to past glories while trying to slow the march of global progress.

Somebody told us a long time ago: "If everyone in China stood on the shore and stamped their feet in unison, they would create a tidal wave that could flood the rest of the world." And that was just China!

chapter four

big next: europe in a post-european world

For better and for worse, Europe has had a disproportionate influence in shaping the world as we know it. Driven by a dynamic combination of intellectual vigor, technological ingenuity, religious zeal, rivalry, and greed, a handful of European powers dominated the oceans from the time of Columbus until the 20th century, and European colonial masters ruled in much of the Americas, Africa, Australasia, South Asia, and Southeast Asia.

The modern systems of banking, finance, joint-stock companies, and capitalism were invented in Europe and imposed on the rest of the world, as were the opposing ideologies of socialism and communism. Democracy was also invented in Europe, and it remains the de facto benchmark of governance for the international community. Europeans visiting other continents today may find much that's unfamiliar, but in many ways they will feel right at home (and, after all, French, Spanish, or Portuguese are still the first languages of hundreds of millions around the globe). The same is not true in reverse: Chinese visitors, Indians, Africans, and South Americans see little trace of their own cultures in Europe beyond ethnic restaurants.

It has been a European world for about half a millennium. But change is afoot. As other parts of the globe grow both in terms of population and economic power, Europe's influence is waning, in relative and absolute terms. While it's far too soon to write off the continent—there's still plenty of economic clout left in the Old World—it will have to come to terms with the new realities of the 21st-century's post-European world.

In a sense, this takes Europe full circle from our perspective of a decade ago, when we kicked off our "Small World" chapter with what appeared to be the biggest of all the "big nexts"—The United States of Europe:

> For very many of Europe's 350+ million citizens, the next five to 10 years will be the most exciting, promising, and/or disturbing era of their lives. Only those with vivid memories of the 1939–45 war or the radical '60s might find these millennial years less than seminal.
>
> The quarrelsome patchwork of nations, peoples, cultures, economies, climates, and topographies loosely known as Europe is facing the next millennium more united—or at least more closely bound together—than anyone could have dreamed just 50 years ago.
>
> Take a bow, Brussels.
>
> The capital of Belgium has become shorthand for the ambitious project of European integration that started in the early 1950s. The changing names of the project over the decades reflect the broadening ambitions of the "Eurocrats" and the visionary politicians who have driven it—the European Coal and Steel Community (1952), the European Economic Community (1957), the European Community (1967), and now the European Union (1993).
>
> What started out as a forum for collaboration among six countries in a limited area of industry has evolved into nothing less than a drive to create, in effect, a United States of Europe, with its own single currency and supranational legislature currently covering 15 countries, with more in the waiting room.
>
> . . . Slowly but surely, nations across Europe are in the process of uniting their destinies with former foes, of handing over strands of sovereignty previously held dearer than life itself. Long term, for many Europeans it will mean living under rules invented by other Europeans who don't even speak the same language. This sort of prospect used to lead to fighting in Europe, but so far it has only sparked a war of words between the "Europhiles" and the "Euroskeptics" within countries.
>
> With a fair wind, the early years of the next millennium should see the laborious but peaceful emergence of a true European Union, put together by committees rather than by combatants, but nevertheless a heroic achievement. What the late General de Gaulle said of his native France is even more applicable to Europe as a whole: "My friend, you can't expect to unify overnight a country which boasts 257 different types of cheese."[1]

So how did we go from such anticipation to "post-Europe" in just ten years? Read on for some of the developments on the continent itself (and that pesky little island of Great Britain, which continues to hold disproportionate sway as it remains outside monetary union). It's a story that, at least in part, suggests that complete "openness" is not without its very unique challenges. Then go back and review "Chindia"—that just changed the balance entirely.

Now: One Europe

European countries have a long-standing habit of focusing on their differences rather than working with their similarities. At its mildest, this stance generates pride, prejudice, and rivalry on a local level, with acute awareness of distinctive languages, accents, and customs. But it has also produced centuries of wars between nations. Even now, communal violence smolders just below the surface in parts of Northern Ireland, the Basque country of Spain, and, of course, the Balkans.

Long periods of peace have been rare in Europe, which is why after centuries of conflict that culminated in two horrific world wars, the major powers in continental Western Europe decided to pool their interests rather than fight over them. Six countries came together in the European Coal and Steel Community (ECSC), and the seeds of the European Union were sown. Successive waves of expansion over the decades saw the ECSC morph into the Common Market, the European Community, and now the European Union, which has grown from six members to its current 25, with more on the way.

The EU is a large and diverse body stretching from Finland in the north to the Mediterranean islands of Malta and Cyprus in the south. It brings together very diverse economies, political cultures, languages, and religious traditions, as well as different visions of the EU's aims and how it should go about achieving them.

Given Europe's blood-steeped history of continual conflict, the EU in its various stages has been an amazingly ambitious and successful undertaking. For the late French President François Mitterrand, former German Chancellor Helmut Kohl, and other European leaders who lived through World War II, the EU was first and foremost a structure for binding countries together in order to prevent war. And it has succeeded to the point that a European war is now almost unimaginable. As the postwar baby boomers reach their 60s, there are now three substantial generations of Europeans who have never known war or privation; they take peace and prosperity as a given.

Gradually, with peace secured, the EU has given itself a new objective: building a politically and economically united Europe. But with peace now taken for granted and the EU issuing directives that override national law, Europeans are becoming increasingly critical and wary of the EU.

Next: One Union Not Quite United?

As is the case with other large central governments (such as the federal government of the United States), some critics of the EU—also referred to as "Brussels,"
the administrative capital—see it becoming overwhelmingly bureaucratic, with
excessive powers.

Regions and nations that value their differences are suspicious of the desire
for harmonization, coordination, and standardization by means of central control; they fear too great a loss of sovereignty. In January 2002, for instance, historic national currencies such as the Dutch guilder, the German mark, and the
French franc were replaced by a single currency, the euro. Certainly, monetary
union has made trade and travel easier. But it also has been widely perceived as
causing price hikes, and individual countries can no longer use interest rates to
manage their economies. Nor can governments in more inflation-prone
Eurozone countries such as Italy and Greece try to regain competitiveness by
devaluing their currencies.

Then there's the matter of the European Constitution, an attempt to set out
the EU's aspirations in a document that had to be ratified by all member states.
It was an attempt to remedy the fact that the EU and national politicians are
behind much of what has happened in Brussels, rather than citizens of member
countries, who rarely have been directly consulted about what they want from
the EU. For example, the EU's ambition to achieve political and economic solidarity has never been put to a popular vote. Some nations chose to put the constitution to their people in referenda, and against expectations, it suffered defeats
in the Netherlands and France, two core European states. So the EU now faces
the challenge of regaining public support after these rejections.

The interplay of conflicting national aspirations and interests is becoming
more troublesome as the EU grows. How do Europeans reconcile the age-old
instincts of parochialism and regionalism with the drive to join forces in the face
of global competition? In Spain, for example, there were fears of military unrest
in 2005 after a senior general gave a speech to fellow officers opposing an independent Catalonia (he called on the army to take action if parliament approved
the proposed autonomy statutes without amending three aspects: Catalonia's
right to call itself a nation, the establishment of an independent judiciary for the
region of almost 7 million people, and obligatory use of the Catalan language).
In the end, the general was dismissed.

The European experience has shown that national governments tend to
place their own national interests above those of the group—or else to frame the

interests of the group in terms of their own interests. Not surprisingly, progress requires detailed negotiations that are all the more difficult for being conducted in multiple languages. And national politicians then have to sell the results back home, often in the face of skeptical opposition parties and media.

Europeans' deep-rooted differences are typified by language. Despite the spread of English as the de facto lingua franca, language is still a divisive factor, considering that it's not unusual for people to say that inhabitants of a neighboring town have an altogether different accent that nobody can understand. The European Union has 20 official languages, and Irish—a language not even spoken by many in Ireland—has just been added. There are also many nonofficial languages, which in a few cases are spoken by more people than some of the official languages (Catalan, for example).

One of the most divisive issues facing the EU is Turkey's application for membership. Turkey's desire to join the union may very well be the greatest tribute ever paid by an outside power to the EU's brand of liberal democracy. Politically, strategically, and economically, there are good reasons to bring Turkey into the fold and foster progress there. But it's large, poor, and populous, sprawling from Europe into Asia. Culturally, it's a worrying prospect for many Europeans. The Turkish Ottoman Empire was clearly a non-European power, lording over the Balkans and Greece, constantly threatening Austria, and imposing Islam on its subject peoples. Modern Turkey is a secular state, but its population is overwhelmingly Muslim and not European by history or culture. Many Europeans are uneasy at the prospect of assimilating its approximately 70 million people alongside the 12 million Muslims already living in Europe.

As Turkey enters into its EU entry talks, it may decide that Europe looks better from a distance. Accession talks can be humiliating at times, and Turkey may be less adept than the Central Europeans were at quietly putting aside national pride. It is, after all, the rump of an empire with a history as long and lofty as Europe's. That makes its accession to the EU all the more desirable—and all the more difficult.

Next: Employment That Doesn't Last for Life

The economies of continental Europe are widely criticized for their sclerotic labor markets and inability to reduce chronic unemployment. It is certainly true that core countries such as France, Germany, and Italy have a long way to go in reforming their economies. Government initiatives are frequently hampered by street protests and powerful opposition forces. Nevertheless, contrary to the general perception, employment has grown slightly faster in the European Union than in the United States.

> In the United States, the proportion of the population of working-age people with jobs fell from 74.1 percent in 2000 to 71.1 percent in 2003; during that period, it rose from 63.4 percent to 64.3 percent in the land of the euro, according to the European Commission.[2]

But how do European countries stack up against the United States on entrepreneurialism? When it comes to tallying up new patents and small businesses, Europe trails behind America. The continent has a shrinking workforce and an aging population, and as Europe's markets face fiercer global competition, they will have to become more flexible and more productive, with workers putting in longer hours. Harmonization among the 25 EU countries will be key to a competitive edge, as eBay CEO Meg Whitman told *The New York Times*.[3]

If eBay is anything to go by, though, there's plenty of entrepreneurial spirit left in Old Europe. On an average day in France, a comic book is put up for sale on the site every minute (the French consider comic books something of an art form); in Germany, someone buys a bulldozer every three hours; and in Britain, a teddy bear changes hands every two minutes, according to eBay stats cited in *The New York Times*. "Markets evolve at different rates, but there's no difference in people wanting to better their lives," says Whitman. "I see more similarities than differences between European and American entrepreneurs."[4]

> About 170,000 people in the 12 European countries where eBay operates make a living selling on the site, with $947 million in activity recorded in 2004, compared with about 724,000 Americans, notes *The New York Times*. The United States accounts for 55 percent of eBay's $4.5 billion in global sales. Buyers and browsers in the United States total roughly 90 million, versus 50 million in Europe. The eBay market is steadily growing in Europe, with Italy—previously an Internet laggard—topping the list.[5]

Europe may well find that new drive comes from the East—from countries that stagnated and fell behind under the yoke of Soviet communism. Western contracts and investment are flooding into Eastern Europe, which is much cheaper than Western Europe. The lower business costs are helping to drive "near-shoring," outsourcing work within a geographical region rather than offshore. *The Economist* cites estimates by Colling, a Hungarian consultancy, that wage costs in Eastern Europe are 50–60 percent below Western Europe's; while they are 75 percent cheaper in India, Eastern Europe is just a day's drive away for Western Europeans.[6]

About 19 percent of the EU's clothing imports in 2004 came from Eastern Europe, representing a value of €22.3 billion ($25 billion), according to *The Economist*.[7]

For some companies—those that require just a small team of telephone sales people or back-office workers culturally attuned to Europe—the Eastern European countries are a more ideal solution than India. In fact, firms from India and other outsourcing locations such as Turkey and Hong Kong are investing in Eastern Europe, in part to be closer to customers, *The Economist* reports. Besides geographical and time-zone benefits, there's the matter of cultural fit, notes Amitabh Chaudhry, COO of Progeon, a division of India's Infosys IT group that opened a center in the Czech city of Brno with about 100 employees. He also cites the quality of work, a favorable political and regulatory environment, and the availability of multilingual workers. One drawback of the former communist countries is that they lack middle managers and suffer a shortage of hard skills, but companies tend to bring in their own management teams.[8]

Next: What Happens With the U.K.?

In a best-case scenario, the United Kingdom acts as a bridge between the United States and continental Europe, building on what it perceives as a special relationship with the United States and deep ties with the European Union. In the worst-case scenario, Britain is in limbo between the two—humored by the United States but without influence there and scorned by continental Europeans as little more than an American stooge, a U.S. lapdog.

When British Prime Minister Tony Blair (who will be out of office before this book is published) was new to his job in 1997, he wowed France by addressing its National Assembly in French. All over continental Europe, he and his brand of politics were feted as a fresh way forward, combining the European social conscience with sound financial policies and a business-friendly attitude. Six years later, with war in Iraq looming, Blair was doing his level best to play the honest broker between a United States determined to invade and Germany and France, intent on avoiding conflict. When it came to taking sides, Blair threw his lot in with the United States.

Britain's commitment to Europe is always in doubt, both within the country and on the continent. The U.K. remains the odd man out in many ways. When the euro launched across Europe in 2002, Britain was one of three EU economies that chose not to adopt the currency (opting out with Denmark and Sweden), and it's unlikely to do so in the foreseeable future. The British still drive on the left, and while metric weights and measures have been gradually adopted, the old "imperial" weights and measures still persist.

> The U.K. embraces the continent when it comes to football: Any self-respecting English club fields a raft of talent from Europe and beyond. England's hottest club, Chelsea, is owned by a Russian billionaire and managed by Portuguese José Mourinho; its London rival, Arsenal, is managed by Frenchman Arsène Wenger and spearheaded by French star Thierry Henri. Then there's perennial contender Liverpool, managed by Spaniard Rafael Benitez.

Despite Britain's continuing limbo status in Europe, it has three important advantages that ensure it doesn't get wholly detached from the European mainstream. For one, within the EU, Britain stands as a counterweight to the French method of governance and economics that dominated during the European Community's early days. The Nordic countries have an affinity with the U.K.'s more transparent approach to EU affairs, and the new members in Central and Eastern Europe believe they stand a better chance of economic progress with Britain's free-market style.

Also significant is that the U.K.'s economy has been lively, generating jobs at a time when continental European economies are sluggish. The painful reforms of the Thatcher years prepared Britain for the coming changes, and today it's a magnet for young continentals who struggle to find work back home. As Britain's *Sunday Times* reported,[9] the number of French citizens officially registered as living in Britain has doubled since 1993, to more than 90,000—and the real figure is believed to be more than twice that, since most expatriates do not register with the French consulate. "The French never used to feel the need to live abroad, because they had everything they needed at home," said Agnès Catherine Poirier, 32, a French journalist living in London. "That is not the case anymore. London is what Paris was 80 years ago—a cosmopolitan city full of opportunity." While young French people go to Britain for work, older British people go to France for pleasure, buying relatively cheaper properties there. As Jean-Pierre Raffarin, the former French prime minister, commented to Blair, "We send you all our young people, and we are getting all your elderly."

The U.K. also has the advantage of being the only country in Europe where English is the native language. Ambitious young Europeans know that a good command of English is essential in the global 21st century, and the U.K. is the nearest place for them to brush up on the language of Shakespeare. Plus, the freewheeling economy offers plenty of work to fund their stay.

Next: More Extremism

The last half-century in Western and Central Europe has been an uncharacteristically peaceful time, largely marked by social liberalism and political moderation. Certainly, there were the upheavals of the 1960s and the violent antics of small terrorist groups such as Italy's Red Brigades in the '70s and '80s. But extremism has been largely absent from Europe for a long time. That may be changing. There's widespread disenchantment with traditional politics, and some single-issue activists are taking extreme measures.

In the U.K., animal-rights activists have taken an increasingly hard line. For example, in 2004, companies that contracted to build a research laboratory at Oxford University came under heavy fire. A plant owned by RMC Group, the company that supplied cement, was set on fire, and its trucks had their brake pipes and cables cut and their tires slashed; a posting on a Web site for animal-rights extremists claimed that a raid on the company's Bournemouth offices cost RMC £250,000. One supplier stopped delivery of building materials, and then the contractor pulled out of its contract.[10]

In the Netherlands, a bastion of European liberalism, plain-speaking politician Pim Fortuyn was shot to death in 2002 by a lone-wolf left-wing environmentalist. Fortuyn had galvanized widespread support with his robust criticisms of Islam as a backward religion and hard-line views on immigration and crime.

Germany's oldest neo-Nazi party, the NPD, received 1.6 percent of the national vote in the 2005 federal elections with a focus on anti-immigration rhetoric. The NPD also focuses its xenophobic ideology on resistance to global capitalism and opposition to Turkey's entry into the EU—an issue that looks likely to stir passions around Europe.

The challenge for Europe's political establishments is to maintain the culture of moderation that has kept the peace in Europe for so long while addressing the sort of voter concerns that give rise to extremism. It's a tough balancing act, but politicians ignore immoderate passions at their peril. For instance, the French political establishment was shocked in 2002 when far-right maverick Jean-Marie Le Pen trounced the powerful French socialist party in the first round of the presidential elections. He was badly defeated by Jacques Chirac in the second round but intends to run again in 2007.

Next: Marginalizing Nicotine Addicts

There are still parts of Europe where smoking seems almost an obligatory part of the culture. But this culture is slowly fading as the tide of European opinion—and legislation—inexorably turns against smoking. Smoke-friendly places are getting fewer and farther between. Spain (following countries such as Ireland, Norway, and Italy) is one of the latest European countries to clamp down on tobacco, and with good reason. Some 30 percent of Spaniards smoke, and per-capita consumption of tobacco is the second highest in Europe; not surprisingly, smoking is the No. 1 cause of preventable death in Spain, claiming 50,000 lives a year. Smoking is now banned in offices, shops, schools, hospitals, public transport, and theaters. Bars and restaurants over a certain size are required to install separate smoking areas with ventilation systems; smaller places must put up signs stating they are smoke-free.

As growing numbers of Europeans give up smoking and become accustomed to nicotine-free lives, many are becoming more sensitive to, and critical of, smoky atmospheres. But as support for smoking bans grows, vocal opponents are speaking out against what they see as the erosion of personal freedom and the "nanny" state's encroachment into private lives.

The U.K. held out for a long time. All manner of nuanced ideas were put forward with the aim of squaring the circle—somehow limiting smoking without impinging on people's personal freedom. Finally in early 2006 the issue came to a parliamentary vote, which was carried by a substantial majority. Starting in mid-2007, smoking will be banned in almost all enclosed public spaces, including pubs, cinemas, offices, factories, and public transportation. (Scotland had already banned smoking, effective in March 2006.)

Despite all the antismoking action around the fringes of Europe, the European heartland of Germany remains a relatively unrestricted refuge for smokers. Only schools and hospitals have been declared smoke-free zones, leaving other public spaces, including the workplace, open to smoking. Long after the U.K. imposed severe restrictions on cigarette advertising, billboards in Germany were still showing smiling smokers with the line "*Ich rauche gern*" ("I like smoking").

Reducing smoking in Europe has been a long, slow haul. Governments have only gradually recognized their dubious position of conflicting interests. After all, they profit handsomely from the sale of products that their health departments identify as killers. Cigarettes are heavily taxed in Europe, often to the tune of 80 percent of the retail price, which translates into plenty of money for government coffers. In the U.K., tobacco-related excise duties and sales tax contributed nearly £10 billion in fiscal 2003–2004. This is, according to the Treasury, equivalent to almost 3 pence on the basic rate, or 13 pence on the top rate of income tax.[11] And while smokers impose a heavier burden on health-care budgets, they tend to be less of a burden on the pension system, because they don't live as long as nonsmokers. Ultimately, the success of smoking bans in Europe is up to citizens concerned about their health, not the governments.

Next: Goodbye to the Myth of the Slim European

Most Europeans, resigned to the fact that their economies just aren't as dynamic as America's, have been able to console themselves with a sense of superiority in other areas. Europeans opt for quality of life over grueling work hours, after all, and they enjoy weeks more time off than Americans get. Another source of smugness is Americans' physical appearance—in particular, their girth. Sure, all those American TV programs show a nation of lithe, liposuctioned people with perfect smiles, but visitors to the United States and observers of American tourists abroad have a different image: a nation of fat people gorging on fast food.

It's becoming increasingly apparent, however, that when it comes to obesity, Europeans aren't all that different from Americans—they're just a few years behind the curve. Travelers around Europe will have noticed growing numbers of strikingly overweight people in the less gastronomically sophisticated countries, such as the U.K. and the Netherlands. And now the French—always held up as a people who know how to eat well and maintain a chic, svelte look—are going down the greasy path pioneered by Anglo-Saxon countries.

The rate of obesity in the land of fine cuisine and the arts of the table rose from 8 percent of the adult population in 1997 to 11 percent by 2003. Obesity is now climbing at an annual rate of 6 percent—and among children, it's growing by 17 percent. And a 2005 health study by the Organisation for Economic Co-operation and Development notes that while the U.K. and the United States have much higher obesity rates (23 percent and 31 percent), the French figures probably understate the true extent of obesity because they are self-reported.[12] Still, more than 40 percent of the French are considered overweight, and according to a report from the French senate, the proportion of fat people is now the same as it was in the United States in 1991.

Even the home of gastronomic pride is clearly not immune to fast-food habits. France is one of the biggest and most profitable European markets for McDonald's, and KFCs are spreading across the country. The traditional family meal is slowly being edged out by frozen pizzas and fizzy drinks, particularly in poorer households.

There's little doubt that global obesity problems stem from increasingly sedentary lifestyles, combined with a growing consumption of convenience foods. The open question is whether Europeans will bow to the inevitable and sit back and continue to bulge—or whether the prospect of going down the American road will spur them to action.

Next: Melding North and South

In most places around the world, "northern" and "southern" are key factors in culture and identity, be it in the United States, Korea, India, Italy, Sweden, the U.K., France, or Germany. Europe as a whole is no exception.

The origins of European culture undoubtedly lie in the south, in the Mediterranean ("middle of the world") basin, home to the Ancient Greeks and then to the Romans, who effectively unified much of Europe. Roman imperial rule was followed by Roman spiritual rule, as the whole of Christian Europe came under the authority of the pope in Rome. It was probably inevitable that people in the more bracing climates of northern Europe would feel the need to challenge the rules laid down by southerners. So it came to be that Martin Luther sowed the seeds of religious reformation that broke the Catholic Church's hold, setting up a divide in Europe that persists to this day: the Protestant North versus the Catholic South, the Baltic and North Sea nations versus the Mediterranean nations.

Generally, the southern cultures are thought of as more emotionally expressive, more garrulous, more sensual, and more pleasure-oriented. Southern Europeans pay a lot of attention to the quality of their food and drink, for instance, and their cuisine is celebrated by the whole of Europe. The southerners are also devoted to dressing well, which explains the prevalence of big fashion-design houses in France and Italy, with a few in Spain too. While southern Europe values *l'art de vivre, el arte de vivir*—"the art of living"—northern Europe is concerned with order and reliable systems for making life run smoothly.

The northern cultures are considered more emotionally contained, quieter, more stoic, and less pleasure-oriented. In the Protestantism that so influenced northern cultures, each person answers directly to God; wrongdoing cannot be absolved by confession and asking for forgiveness. It is this heritage that may have made northerners more transparent and direct in their business and political dealings, and far more rigorous about accountability.

The north-south divide shows up in Transparency International's Corruption Perceptions Index, which draws on 16 surveys from ten independent institutions that gathered the opinions of businesspeople and nation analysts. The index measures the degree to which corruption—defined as the abuse of public office for private gain—is perceived to exist among a country's officials and politicians. Scores range from 10 (squeaky clean) to 0 (highly corrupt). Iceland (not in the EU) ranks highest with a 9.7, closely followed by the northern countries of Finland (9.6), Denmark (9.5), Sweden (9.2), the U.K. (8.6), and Germany (8.2). France, which straddles north and south, rates 7.5, ahead of

Spain (7.0) and Portugal (6.5). Italy scores a poor 5.0, and Greece gets a lowly 4.3.[13]

The perceptions these figures reflect and the realities they represent are not merely academic. Officials from member states work together to administer the EU, so different attitudes toward transparency and accountability can give rise to a lot of friction. Voters in northern member states get irate at reports of corrupt dealings in the EU, thereby weakening support for the whole enterprise.

With open borders and cheap travel, however, it has never been easier for Europeans to flit between countries and to cherry-pick the most appealing aspects of other cultures. The more they do so, the less stark the divide will become. Northern Europeans might look askance at the political and business cultures of southern countries, for example, but there's no doubt they love the lifestyle. Throughout the summer, northern Europeans head south en masse to soak up the sun, drink the wine, and enjoy la dolce vita.

Next: Russia Nearer but Still over the Horizon

Europe is a relatively small part of the Eurasian land mass. The distance from Helsinki, Finland, in the north to Palermo, Sicily, in the south is about 2,600 kilometers; from Lisbon, Portugal, in the far west to Bucharest, Romania, in the east, it's roughly 3,000 kilometers. By comparison, Russia is a giant: More than 6,400 kilometers separate Moscow in the west from Vladivostok in the east.

Russia is distant from Europe, both geographically and culturally. Its roots are steeped in centuries of Orthodox Christianity—far removed from Western Europe's Catholic and Protestant traditions—overlaid with more than 70 years of totalitarian communist rule. For much of the last hundred years, from the 1917 revolution onward, Western Europe has tended to think of Russia as the great threat in the East. Until the last decade or so, Russia was more or less out of bounds for most Europeans—suspicious, heavily armed, ensconced behind the Iron Curtain, and far, far away from life in the West.

It was Winston Churchill who described Russia as "a riddle wrapped in a mystery inside an enigma."

Since the fall of communism and the Soviet Union, Russia has opened up; it's become more accessible to Europeans, and in turn, Russian tourists are now a familiar sight around Europe. But while tourism and commercial exchanges are certainly helping to improve relations, they don't necessarily amount to bonds of affinity. On that score, Russia and Europe have a long way to go.

The essential question for Europe and Russia is whether Russia is a European country. Russians certainly have a lot in common with Europeans, not least on the tricky issues of race (they're mostly white), religious heritage (Christianity, albeit a distinctive variant), and language (Russian is an Indo-European language). On the surface, that makes Russia more European than Turkey. Yet in spite of these commonalities and the growing links between Russia and the EU, it's unlikely that Russia will find an acceptable fit with the EU anytime soon.

One roadblock is the governance of President Vladimir Putin, which is far from what the EU likes to see in its members. While Russia has transitioned to democracy, Putin's version is inspired more by the authoritarian tradition of the czars and the communist leaders than by Western liberal democracies. Being accepted by Europe is not easy in many respects, as Turkey is finding. To satisfy the EU that it is a suitable candidate for membership, Turkey has had to modify many policies and practices, including its approach to human rights. For the process to continue, Turkey will have to swallow its pride and accept the conditions and, implicitly, the values of Western Europe. Such a process would be extremely distasteful to Russia, which until recently ranked as a mighty superpower whose diktat extended into the heart of Europe.

It's more likely that Russia sees a destiny separate from Europe, as part of the BRIC phenomenon (the countries of Brazil, Russia, India, and China). This doesn't mean that Russia and Europe will turn their backs on each other—they have a lot to offer one another. But their respective interests and outlooks are too different to make common cause in the foreseeable future.

Next: Living with Islam

There are few hotter topics in current affairs than Islam (as attested to by the fact that we tackle the subject in numerous places in this book). In fact, the relationships between the various streams of Islam, and the relationship of Muslims with the non-Islamic world, are crucial issues not just for Europeans but for the whole world.

Islam has been a big issue for Europe for many centuries. Muslim Moors conquered Spain in 711 and ruled there for seven centuries. Throughout the Middle Ages, European nations fought Muslim powers for control of the Holy Land and the Mediterranean Sea. In the 16th and 17th centuries, the Turkish Ottoman Empire pushed into central Europe, laying siege to Vienna, and was thwarted only when European powers banded together. The threat of Islamic "invaders" subsided only with the end of the Ottoman Empire after the First World War.

Europeans didn't have any reason to think about Islam again until the 1960s, when Muslim immigrants began to arrive—Turks in Germany and Holland, North Africans in France, Pakistanis in the U.K. There are now about 12 million Muslims in Europe, and within a generation Muslims will be in the majority in major German, French, and Dutch cities, according to the Foreign Policy Research Institute.[14] But even as the Muslim population expands across the continent, the headline-grabbing activities of militant Islamic fundamentalists have prompted many Europeans to associate Islam with terrorism.

Muslims account for 8.3 percent of the population of France, 5.8 percent in the Netherlands, about 3.5 percent in Germany, 2.7 percent in Britain, 2.3 percent in Spain, and 1.7 percent of Italy.[15]

Global awareness of Islamic extremism has been growing for more than two decades. The Iranian revolution of 1979, the bombing of New York's World Trade Center in 1993, and the Taliban's takeover of Afghanistan in 1996 raised the profile of fundamentalist Islam. The actions of Osama bin Laden and his admirers in 2001, and the subsequent al-Qaeda-inspired bombings in Madrid and London, pushed the issue to the forefront.

Even disregarding al-Qaeda, the rising influence of more traditional, conservative interpretations of Islam has become an issue for Muslims and non-Muslims alike in Europe. Traditional Islam doesn't sit easily with the integration and multiculturalism of non-Muslim countries, nor with such 21st-century principles as female emancipation, the free mingling of men and women, and the separation of religion and state. This leaves millions of Muslims torn between two worlds of conflicting values.

"Despite being born and raised in Europe, many young Muslims adopt anti-Western views. In one large-scale study, almost one-third affirmed that Islam must come to power in every country. Even though they live in Europe, 56 percent declared that they should not adapt too much to Western ways but should live by Islam. Over 33 percent insisted that if it serves the Islamic community, then they are ready to use violence against non-believers. Perhaps most disturbing of all, almost 40 percent stated that Zionism, the European Union, and the United States threaten Islam."
—"Breeding New bin Ladens: America's New Western Front," Foreign Policy Research Institute[16]

Barely more than a generation ago, Islamic attitudes toward religious observance were relatively relaxed. For example, in Pakistan, Malaysia, and Iran, it was mostly older or rural women who wore some form of head covering, while urban women generally chose more Western forms of attire. In Western countries,

Muslim women dressed much the same as everyone else, and men felt few qualms about drinking the occasional beer. It seemed that Islam, like Christianity, was destined to become more tied to cultural identity than to religious observance.

Now, waves of strict religious observance are sweeping through the Islamic world. Muslims are increasingly feeling the need to affirm and proclaim their religious affiliation. Muslim women in both Islamic and non-Islamic countries, for example, are adopting various forms of head covering. Going forward, coming to terms with the problems of cohabitation and finding solutions palatable to both groups will be a matter of urgency in Europe.

Next: Redrawing the Boundaries of Social Liberalism

Since the 1960s, the northern European countries have had a reputation for social liberalism. Well before their southern European neighbors Greece, Spain, and Portugal emerged from rule by right-wing dictators, the Netherlands, Sweden, and Denmark were known for their tolerant attitudes. They attracted many immigrants from southern Europe, as well as from the Balkans and North Africa. But after decades of liberalism and openness, these pioneering countries are facing tough moral and social dilemmas that, ironically, are probably a consequence of their social liberalism. The Dutch and the Danes in particular may be entering an era described by American writer Christopher Caldwell as "post-politically correct."[17] (At the same time, Europe is more than glad to turn over its "menial" jobs to its immigrant population, much the same way that Americans wink at the growing Mexican population, legal and illegal.)

One of the early signals heralding this new era was the runaway popularity of the Netherlands' Pim Fortuyn. His provocative and trenchant criticism of Islam, along with his views on immigrants, resonated deeply among the Dutch. In effect, this flamboyantly gay firebrand highlighted the uncomfortable contradiction at the heart of free-speaking social liberalism. Because Dutch liberalism—or, occasionally, indifference—dictated that immigrant communities be accommodated, rather than assimilated into the mainstream, Muslims felt free to keep to themselves and to express contempt for the liberal society around them.

As Fortuyn's following showed, many people came to resent what they felt was exploitation of their tolerance. Eventually, it became socially acceptable even for "right-thinking people" to express negative views about immigrant groups, especially Muslims. Now the Dutch are prepared to discuss the implications of having fast-growing and unassimilated Muslim communities in their midst.

As liberal European countries go, the Netherlands has been something of a grandstander, with its famed tolerance of soft drugs and its red light districts. Denmark, by comparison, has had a low-key international profile—certainly nothing to offend delicate sensibilities abroad. Yet in the space of a few weeks, this unassuming country became reviled in the Muslim world when a Danish newspaper published satirical cartoons depicting the prophet Mohammed. The cartoons were actually just the latest manifestation of criticism against Islam—criticism that runs all the way to the top. In early 2005, Queen Margrethe spoke out against radical Islam and called on Muslim immigrants to improve their Danish-language skills so they would not feel excluded from society. In an authorized biography, the queen stated that citizens had to take the "challenge" of Islam seriously, saying, "We have let this issue float around for too long, because we are tolerant and rather lazy."[18]

It's not just Islam that's causing a re-evaluation of liberalism. For decades now, officially tolerated drug use and prostitution have been hallmarks of Amsterdam and other Dutch cities. To the extent that criminal gangs were involved, they were at least Dutch gangs familiar to the authorities. But the opening of Europe's eastern borders, as well as the troubles in the Balkans, prompted an influx of ruthless criminal entrepreneurs into the Netherlands.

Some Dutch liberals are now fretting that tolerance of the sex industry is inadvertently helping to fuel sex trafficking. One human rights group estimates that about 3,500 women from Eastern Europe and Asia are trafficked to the Netherlands each year, where they are often held captive and abused in underground brothels or illegal escort agencies.[19] (And this underground is without the same rigid health screening that legal sex workers undergo.) Recent government figures show that Eastern European and African prostitutes (who, respectively, make up 47 percent and 26 percent of sex workers in Amsterdam) are vulnerable to violent abuse, blackmail, and extortion; they fear deportation if they go to the police.[20] Human trafficking is by no means limited to Holland, and Southern Europe especially is seeing an influx from the East—the former Soviet Union—and Africa.

In many more ways than one, soft European liberalism is facing hard challenges in the early 21st century.

Next: The Pain of Aging and Demographic Imbalance

European countries have some of the lowest birthrates in the world—the average woman in the EU bears just 1.48 children. That means Europeans aren't "replacing themselves" with new generations big enough to match the aging and dying population. In 1900, one out of four people on the planet lived in Europe, according to UN estimates; today, the global population has tripled, and Europe represents not much more than one in ten people worldwide. By 2025, projections put the figure at one in fourteen.[21]

The combination of fewer babies and longer life spans will have "major implications for [Europe's] prosperity, living standards, and relations between the generations," according to a European Commission green paper on demographic change.[22] The immediate worry is the fate of generous welfare and social protection systems across the continent, because fewer young workers are supporting larger numbers of elderly pensioners. The only way to keep public pension plans afloat may be the continued employment of older workers—and that will not be at all popular with retirement-age Europeans.

> The gap between working-age people and seniors in Europe is stark. In Italy, the working population will shrink 20 percent by 2035, and an additional 15 percent by 2050; meanwhile, the 65-and-over population will jump 44 percent by 2050. The result will be huge rise in the dependency numbers, doubling from 32 percent in 2005 to 67 percent by 2050. While fertility has been higher in France, the dependency ratio will increase from 28 percent to 51 percent over the same period.[23] The population of Germany will shrink rapidly as well.

The United States owes much of its dynamism to immigration, to the millions of "poor and huddled masses" who continue to swell the ranks of Americans. If Europe wants to maintain its dynamism and its standard of living, it will have little choice but to take a cue from the United States and embrace immigrants. There's certainly no shortage of migrants—huge numbers of young people in developing countries are unable to find jobs at home or are drawn to emigration by the prospect of salaries that can be five times higher in the developed world. A Global Commission on International Migration report puts the global population of migrants at almost 200 million.[24]

Assimilating large-scale immigration is not an easy prospect, especially for the difference-oriented peoples of Europe. Countries that are determined to prevent significant numbers of immigrants from settling will be hard-pressed to find ways of maintaining their economies. And countries that embrace immigration will need to update their economic policies, their social policies, and their mind-sets. When immigrants get a fair chance to work and integrate in a liberal economic environment, they can be enormously beneficial, as shown by Indians in the U.K. But when they are marginalized in more rigid economies, such as France's, they become the focus of social division and resentment.

And Therefore Next

The coming decades will be testing times for Europeans. In ways that appear less than obvious right now, Europe will come to grips with the new questions of assimilation, which will only continue—and continue to generate friction and controversy—given the practical realities of an aging continent that needs young newcomers. What we suspect will happen is that differences, which the EU was intended (at least in part) to minimize, will continue to mark the progress of Europe, versus whatever commonalities might arise from "one Europe." In truth, Europe looks less like "one" than it did pre-Union.

chapter five

big next: america inside, outside, and caught in the (tyranny of the) middle?

When we wrote the concluding chapter to this book's predecessor, *Next*, we discussed our trepidations about predicting where America was heading:

> So why is forecasting what's next for the U.S. a more difficult challenge than forecasting global and regional nexts, as we've done in completing more than a half dozen editions of this book? In some ways, we're disadvantaged when it comes to analyzing life next in the place where it'll impact us most: What we're seeing as next for America isn't all good news, and maybe this somehow causes us to freeze.[1]

A decade later, we think it's fair to say we see America somehow even less advantaged to play on the world stage circa 2007. Other parts of the world have narrowed not only the "wealth gap" but, perhaps more important, the "innovations" and "anything's possible" gaps.

The American Constitution is the ultimate how-to guide, designed to help the people of the United States sustain a "more perfect union" and insure "domestic tranquility." Praised for its optimism and clarity, the document presents a picture of a unified America bound in this almost idyllic marital state. But if the framers were to gaze at today's cultural American landscape, they'd find a radically different state of this union. America is a fractured society, often defined more by turmoil than tranquility. It's a country engaged in wars on terror abroad and on culture at home. We're strongly separated along party lines and splintered around the essence of our values. We're at odds with ourselves.

Our political strategy is defined by many around the world as benevolent hegemony. We celebrate and debate the idea of a secular Christmas. We seek peace through war. We're global but local, and even turned inward. We speak of liberty and freedom as prisoner abuse graphically unfolds in front of us. We separate church and state officially but blur the lines by supporting creationism in school curricula and talking of all things faith-based. We turn out to vote for American idols but not American presidents. We're a land of opportunity mired in credit card debt. We waste and we want. We're a wiretapped democracy— wiretapping ourselves in the name of "homeland security." We're certain we've not yet heard the end of that debate, nor felt the implications.

Almost a third of Americans advocate the teaching of creationism along with evolution in schools, according to a 2005 survey by the Pew Research Center.[2]

These are the dizzying conundrums of this American life. It's no wonder that the 2006 update to Alexis de Tocqueville's 1831 classic about American character called *Democracy in America* is titled *American Vertigo*. More than 170 years later, the *Atlantic Monthly* commissioned French author Bernard-Henri Levy to retrace the steps of his fellow countryman and attempt to capture the new American essence. What does he think? After interviews with everyone from Sharon Stone to a struggling waitress, prisoners to politicians, he terms the United States a "magnificent, mad country, laboratory of the best and the worst, greedy and modest, at home in the world and self-obsessed, puritan and outrageous, facing toward the future and yet obsessed with memories."[3]

America's complex contradictions inspire strong feelings from friends and foes. All over the world, America gets mixed reviews. There's rampant anti-Americanism from Venezuela to Afghanistan, and at the same time, there's overt emulation of America's capitalist, entrepreneurial spirit. A new Silicon Valley is growing in Bangalore. American excess and Western extravagance are laid out on man-made islands in Dubai that hold enormous Vegas-style hotels. American movies dominate the European box office.

America's in and it's out at the same time. It's this push and pull that's redefining our national self-portrait—the ins and outs of a new national identity. How do we negotiate the inconsistencies between how we see ourselves and how the world sees us? We search for stability in everything from religion to real estate, and we respond with even more contradictions. (We go for inconspicuous consumption *and* affordable luxury.)

And we embark on quests for personal meaning in diverse places. Some of us are lured by lotteries and Las Vegas as tickets to the good life. Many people search feverishly for connection with old and new friends in the growing numbers of Web sites centered on everything from romance and religion to business and brands. In our instant-download, fast-paced culture, we're time-crunched by long commutes and constant communication, and we're short on downtime. So we look to leisure activities like yoga and even better sleep to help us decompress (and to that end, we write more prescriptions for sleeping pills than ever before, even as we begin to discover some very unsettling reports about "sleep behaviors" that don't look anything like sleeping—everything from binge eating to driving). But in these pursuits and amid the polarity, what's clear is that Americans are more unclear than ever about what's a good and right way to make good on the national right to pursue happiness wherever we can find it. All the incongruity makes for shaky ground.

Next: In Search of God and Country

When there's uncertainty of any sort, there's a reflex to turn to religion. A 2006 survey by the Barna Group, a consulting and religious research firm, indicates, for example, that 47 percent of Americans say they read the Bible outside of church in a typical week. That's up from 31 percent in 1995, a 20-year low. Similarly, 47 percent say they attend church in a typical week, compared with 37 percent back in 1996.[4]

A turn toward serious religious faith is certainly a byproduct of the mind and mood of America today. The result is another contradiction in today's America (a country led by a president who espouses the core beliefs of evangelical Christianity): the wholesale opening of the political sphere to the influence of religion.

Debate about the interplay between politics and religion will be the next political crescendo as people worry about keeping them separate . . . or not. In the latter category are the evangelical Christians, who now represent three of every ten white, non-Catholic Christian Americans, according to Gallup polling.[5] What do evangelicals believe? Gallup polling finds that most evangelicals (28 percent of Americans) have had a born-again experience and have committed themselves to Jesus Christ, have tried to encourage someone else to believe in Jesus, and believe the Bible is the actual word of God.[6]

This mammoth group takes their faith very seriously, as well as their politics; Gallup finds a strong belief that "the religious calling means that one should take action within the environment in which one lives."[7] That environment includes politics, and evangelicals are mobilized and vocal on debates about prayer and the teaching of evolution in public schools, federal court appointments, and elections, from local races to presidential candidates. *Roe* v. *Wade*, however, is the central flashpoint between believers and others, and the issue of abortion has helped to put religion at the heart of American politics.

Evangelical political power stems in part from the fact that they donate heavily, and they do their research: Barna Group notes that evangelicals "give away almost three times as much money as do other Americans"; they're also "the most well-informed among Christians regarding the interaction between their faith in Christ and current public issues."[8]

Gallup polls show that about eight in ten Americans at least nominally adhere to a Christian faith of one sort or another.[9] And 59 percent say their faith is "very important," according to a survey by the Pew Research Center for the People and the Press.[10] Compare that with a European Values Study, which tracks attitudes in 32 countries, that finds only 21 percent of Europeans consider religion "very important" to them.[11]

Consider the influence of the evangelical activist group the American Family Association (AFA), founded by the Rev. Donald E. Wildmon. With a network of 180 radio stations, a monthly publication with a claimed circulation of 150,000, and a Web site that boasts 5 million monthly page views, the pro-"traditional family values" group casts a wide net. And it's making its voice heard: In 2005 the AFA threw a flare by initiating boycotts against Ford Motor Co. because of the company's support of gay rights. More recently the group took credit for putting enough pressure on NBC and its advertisers to remove from the network's lineup a controversial show called *Book of Daniel*, which depicted a drug-addicted Episcopalian priest who had candid conversations with Christ.

It will be hard to distinguish between soul work and lobbying in the public arena in the coming years, especially with a presidential election on the horizon. It's an ever closer collaboration between church and state that has even President Jimmy Carter, a self-proclaimed devout Christian and Sunday school teacher, concerned. On CNN in November 2005 he told Larry King: "For the first time in the history of our country since Thomas Jefferson said build a wall between church and state, there has been a deliberate and overt, not secret melding of religion and politics or the church and state, which I believe is not only contrary to what our founding fathers intended and what everyone else has agreed to the last 230 years, but also, in my opinion as a Christian, it's different from what I've been taught to believe in my religion."[12]

Just how does religion play within the structure of American society and government? The American Family Association, for example, is out to "promote the Biblical ethic of decency in American society,"[13] and in some ways it's succeeding. This will be the next national conversation as we muddle through the meaning of everything from decency and democracy to prayer and patriotism. And in the next decade, American social order is going to be defined in terms that walk the line between God and country. Those who hold fierce religious beliefs will face off against those who do not, with a silent majority of Americans stuck in the middle, neither evangelical nor agnostic but just plain confused about the rules of the road.

What's Next? Adam and Steve Go to Church

Religious communities are being torn apart by the battle over gay rights and civil unions. A number of the world's 37 Anglican primates are refusing to take communion with the American primate Frank Griswold because he ordained a gay bishop. We're seeing the trend of "Us vs. Them" dividing not just denominations but also congregations and even households.

Next: Religion Is Big American Business

More Americans are turning toward the commercial arena as a place to express personal beliefs and attitudes, even a higher purpose. And with religion on the rise, the market for religious products is booming. *The Economist* reports estimates from market-research firm Packaged Facts that the sector was worth $6.8 billion in 2003 and will expand to $8.6 billion by 2008.[14] And, as the magazine points out, churches serve as built-in distribution channels and congregations as word-of-mouth promoters. Endorsements by churches and religious groups also do wonders for corporations that win their approval. For instance, as *The Economist* notes, evangelicals are big supporters of Chick-fil-A, the popular fast-food chain. The company shows its devotion by closing outlets on Sundays and still boasts $1.74 billion in national sales. What's the corporate philosophy? Chick-fil-A says its "first priority . . . has never been just to serve chicken. It is to serve a higher calling."[15] Perhaps at no time since Hebrew National's breakthrough campaign for its hot dogs, "Higher Authority" (introduced in 1965), has there been such an overt link to religious conviction as a "reason why."

Next: Religion Gets Some Work Done

A sign outside a Protestant church appeals to passersby with an invitation to come in and have their "faith lifted." This is more than a modern play on words

and reflects a rising paradigm shift. Religion as we know it is quite literally getting overhauled, reworked, and redone—it is taking on a new look, a body and
soul makeover. This means that some people are flocking to megachurches and
even living in towns devoted to specific beliefs, and it also means that some
believers are going off the beaten path to pursue a more private, "revolutionary"
form of religion.

Many experts anticipated a waning of the giant congregations known as
megachurches that became a huge phenomenon in the 1990s. But megachurches
are still attracting the flock. A 2005 study by Leadership Network and Hartford
Seminary's Hartford Institute for Religion Research found that more than 1,200
Protestant churches in the United States attract an average weekly attendance of
over 2,000 people; this is double the number of megachurches that existed in
2000.[16] And the trend is projected to increase.

The sheer number of people involved in these churches indicates the extent
of their influence. Dave Travis, executive vice president of Leadership Network,
points out a few ways in which their presence is felt: "Not a week passes without
megachurches figuring prominently in one or more national news stories.
During 2005 alone, four megachurch pastors had books on *The New York Times*
best-seller lists. And megachurch pastors always dominate the lists of the most
influential religious leaders in the country."[17] With savvy marketing and slick
promotions, the churches will become more prominent than ever.

Indeed, they're run by charismatic leaders whom *Florida Trend* magazine
writer Mike Vogel likens to "the pastoral equivalents of visionary, entrepreneurial CEOs." He cites two prominent pastors who have appeared on best-seller
lists: Joel Osteen, author of *Your Best Life Now*, whose Texas church was once the
Houston Rockets' arena, and Rick Warren, who wrote *The Purpose-Driven Life*,
leader of California's Saddleback Church. Vogel notes that such leaders also have
back stories that follow "some familiar Christian and American archetypes: The
saved sinner on a mission, the mainline Protestant turned evangelical, and the
preacher short on university theological education but long on relating to his
flock."[18] Americans identify with a boot-straps tale of redemption. And they're
even more energized by the entrepreneurial excitement of a start-up, whether it's
a business or a church.

Next: Greetings from Ave Maria

If the megachurch isn't big enough, consider an entire town devoted to religious
principles—a modern-day spiritual utopia. Entrepreneur and billionaire Tom
Monaghan, who founded the Domino's pizza chain, has had the idea to blend

civics with religion. He is developing a community of about 11,000 households around a Catholic university, a town that will live together under strict Catholic principles. Ave Maria, as it is called, is 30 miles from Naples, Florida. (Florida, no stranger to novel communities, is already home to Celebration, the pristine planned community developed by the Walt Disney Company.)

The town will adhere to Catholic values, so, for example, contraception and abortion will not be available. But speaking to Katie Couric, Paul Marinelli, the town developer, made clear that, "We will not discriminate against anyone. . . . We're not going to violate the U.S. Constitution or the Florida Constitution." Asked what would happen if a pharmacy chooses to sell contraception, Marinelli said it wouldn't be illegal but would be discouraged. The aim is a community with "a traditional family-value perspective," explained Marinelli.[19] Governor Jeb Bush, for one, is a fan, attending the groundbreaking ceremony and praising Ave Maria as a place where "faith and freedom will merge."[20] America is living out a values-based culture war, and people will continue to use religion to define how and where they live.

If some people choose to live within the geographical boundaries drawn by religion, others are going in the opposite direction, eschewing formal Christian communities or institutions. The Barna Group identifies this trend and explains: "These are people who are more interested in being the Church than in going to church. They are more eager to produce fruit for the kingdom of God than to become comfortable in the Christian subculture."[21] Barna says more than 20 million adults fall in this category.[22] These people are creating new spiritual environments that they believe bring them closer to God and other believers than the structure of a church. Barna says, "They are meeting in homes, at work, in public places—wherever they can connect and share their mutual love for Christ."[23]

What this trend points to is not only a counter response to the megachurch and the formalized routines of faith, but also the growing subcultures within religious culture. Faith in America in the next decade will become even more nuanced in terms of how people self-define and the religious image they project. Where do you turn? Do you believe in separation of church and state? Are you immersed in a religious community? Do you attend a megachurch? Are you evangelical or revolutionary or both? What lights your "bonfire?"

What's Next? Sponsored Houses of Worship

Watch as more churches and religious events secure grand-scale sponsorship deals from big business to secure their brand identities in the hearts and minds of the country's congregations.

What's Next? Spirituality Lite

Not looking for an actual religion, but want a connection to something? That's where such Eastern imports as tantra, yoga, feng shui, t'ai chi, ayurvedic or Chinese medicine, and the martial arts come in. All the ancient authenticity without having to adhere to a religion-based belief system.

Next: Polarity Prevails and Purple Becomes Obsolete

Another form of polarization in the United States is the quick labeling of red and blue, and the mounting sense that moderates have no power. Despite pressures on President Bush to appoint a moderate Supreme Court justice, there were none to speak of on his shortlist. In today's world, Sandra Day O'Connor wouldn't be nominated. While politics is a place where the middle can be healing, the coalition mentality is nonexistent and has no juice—there's no purple thinking.

Red and blue have been extended to the labeling of brands and cultural mind-sets. Red and blue products and experiences have become variables for how people consume in the marketplace, participate in politics, and choose their media outlets. Who's red and who's blue isn't easy to quantify, but the colors clearly demarcate opposing American ideologies.

Ann Kornblut, then a political reporter at *The New York Times*, believes the cultural divide is not as simple as liberal versus conservative, urban versus rural, or elite versus populist. "I think it's a combination of all of those things together, plus what music you listen to, what you like to eat," she told National Public Radio. "It's a divide that's been splitting the country since the 1960s. The words 'red' and 'blue' have taken off, but they really don't describe anything."[24]

To discern the "states of minds" of red and blue states and go beyond the obvious voting tendencies, Kornblut put together a multiple-choice quiz on Slate.com, asking readers, among other things, to identify what the Eighth Commandment prohibits and what Whole Foods refers to, and to choose the correct occupations of Lee Greenwood and Jon Stewart. Presumably, these represent two blue and two red touchstones (discern those for yourself). The quiz is obviously not definitive, Kornblut cautioned on Slate.com, because red and blue are amorphous conditions, highly influenced by "background noise": "the local news, what your neighbors talk about, how you get from one place to another, the kinds of culinary and artistic options available, what I like to think of as the 'cultural soundtrack' that you can hum automatically because it's always on."[25]

We're polarized because we've become so much more fixed on our preferred background noise, leaving little room for discussions of a more purple nature.

"People tend to watch one kind of cable station or another, listen to one kind of radio program or another, and there's no real reason to have to interact with people from the other side if you don't want to," Kornblut notes. "The Internet also makes it a lot easier. You don't have to read the entire newspaper; you can go read the articles that interest you, which I think becomes sort of a reinforcing echo chamber."[26]

Indeed, the rise of cable news is linked to the growing politicization of American culture, says Carroll Doherty of the Pew Research Center,[27] with CNN to blue as Fox is to red. Our traditionally middle-of-the-road media is fading at the expense of information customized with a red or blue bent. As Nicholas Lemann writes in *The New Yorker*, "Newspapers and the network evening-news shows are losing their audiences at an alarming rate, while openly ideological, anti-mainstream-media, quasi-news programs like Rush Limbaugh's radio show have huge followings."[28]

With rising fervor in both camps, there's also a growing trend toward more local, participatory journalism by ordinary citizens trying to counter these media leanings. It's driven by a sense that much of mainstream media has become myopically focused in both directions, so disempowered minorities and the everyman must search for the "real story." Born are blogs as a medium for this growing appetite for circumventing the big media outlets.

Perhaps in the coming years, especially as America heads toward the 2008 presidential election, more people will trend toward purple as an anti-mainstream movement. It will be a counter faction for those who are tired of polarized politics and open to partisans playing together productively. Purple will be the new black when it comes to voting.

Next: From Civic to Carnal, Connections Are King

Strong divides may define America's national character, but so too does a mounting connection imperative. We're a country driven to stay connected. Connections help us construct a sense of identity and derive a sense of belonging.

The Internet alone has given us countless new ways to form connections. According to The Pew Internet and American Life Project, which studies the social impact of the Internet, the Web has become the "new normal" in American life.[29] So many aspects of our lives have moved out of the 3D world and into the digital one: We go to Google instead of the Yellow Pages, eBay or Craigslist rather than garage sales, Froogle rather than shopping malls, Match.com instead of singles bars. But we're not going online just to meet dates: About 100 million

Internet users say they belong to online communities.[30] And true to our diverse and democratic history, Pew notes that "members of online groups . . . say the Internet increases the chances that they will interact with people outside their social class, racial group, or generational cohort."[31]

The Internet is also socially appealing because it allows us to control our levels of intimacy, to be surrounded but not touched. We can belong but stay firmly in control, and this is especially true in the sensitive spheres of politics and sex. This was certainly played out in the 2004 presidential election, when Web sites like Meetup.com and Moveon.org brought likeminded Americans together and gave them the tools to get involved in e-mail advocacy, fundraising, and campaigning. MoveOn, still actively promoting Democratic causes, describes itself as bringing "real Americans back into the political process. With over 3.3 million members across America—from carpenters to stay-at-home moms to business leaders—we work together to realize the progressive vision of our country's founders."[32]

This and other sites like it appeal to time-crunched "real" Americans of all sorts who want to take action but feel overwhelmed by the demands on their time. The sites engender a sense of belonging based on a common cause, and they make it really easy to join in grassroots-style action. As Pew says, "The Internet creates new online town squares and civic storms."[33]

Next: Status Anxiety May Mean More Simplicity

Keeping up with the Joneses has gotten harder and more confusing. In our final chapter, on the future of shopping, we talk about the rising trends of inconspicuous consumption and competitive consumption: the practice of shopping at Target and then joining an exclusive private club, or buying discreetly designer clothing that only insiders would recognize as such. There's ambiguity about the appropriate symbols of status and wealth, and the best ways to win the game of one-upmanship. And as we said in the Anxiety Overload chapter, around the bend of ambiguity is more anxiety. In fact, status anxiety has become an American social condition, an obsession even.

What is it exactly? That gripping sense that you're not doing as well as the people around you. In his 2004 book *Status Anxiety*, philosopher Alain de Botton says we're beset by stories of the self-made millionaires and left feeling inadequate: "The anxiety is provoked by, among other elements, recession, redundancy, promotions, retirement, conversations with colleagues in the same industry, newspaper profiles of the prominent and the greater success of friends."[34]

Especially plagued by this anxiety are young Americans in hot pursuit of the great American dream, which nowadays means big houses, big cars, and big debt. Pop culture images of young adults on sitcoms like *Friends* also depict a paradoxical lifestyle: Struggling actors and unemployed chefs live in expansive New York City apartments, they're dressed in the latest fashions, and they seem to have plenty of disposable income. There's never talk of making the rent or paying down debt. Coupled with these unreal images of the real world are a constant barrage of taunting advertisements that offer instant gratification through endless lines of credit for anything one's heart desires.

America is a culture that likes to shop and to indulge. Timothy Garton Ash in the *Guardian* says there's "a relentless commercial pressure to spend, spend, spend, which has given the United States its lowest average personal savings rate since 1959, and one of the lowest in the developed world."[35] And according to *US Banker*, this "spend, spend, spend" mentality is most prevalent among a generation that has little sense of thrift: "Young singles find themselves entering the job market with increased levels of existing debt—both student loans and consumer credit—than previous generations. Their resistance to adhering to a budget based on current income contributes to the continued waning influence of traditional or 'Puritan ethos' financial values."[36]

What's Next? A Counter Push to Simplicity

Trend watcher Gerald Celente says we're entering a long-term trend of downsizing and making do without: "In this new age of a threatening real estate bubble, a tepid stock market, rising interest rates, major business bankruptcies and a growing scarcity of solid jobs with high pay and healthy benefits—'less' will be 'more' for Simplicity Hip Americans."[37] Already Oprah has instituted a "Debt Diet," asking Americans, "Are you overcharging, overleasing and out of control?"[38] Part of the plan is to "find your Latte Factor," which means tracking every penny and then diverting dollars spent on "fancy cups of coffee" and the like to debt reduction. Simplicity will be voluntary for some and involuntary for others, but ultimately it may mean a little let-up on the anxiety factor: Watch as stretching a dollar becomes as fashionable as spending one.

Next: Latin Importance and Identity

There's already a digital divide that marks the lines between generations and how they adapt to and adopt new technologies. The next great American generational gap will be centered on accommodating a rising Latin landscape. In 20 years, children will wonder how their grandparents got by without speaking Spanish.

Between the 1990 and the 2000 Census, the U.S. Hispanic population rose by 58 percent (although higher rates of self-identification may account for some of the jump), becoming about equal in number to America's black population.[39] Their numbers continue to increase fast: From mid-2004 to mid-2005, the Census Bureau reports that the Hispanic population grew at more than three times the rate of the total U.S. population.[40] In 2006, Hispanics were 41 million strong and comprised 14 percent of America's population. How we adapt to the Latinization of American culture in all its forms is a big next.

Latin culture infuses American life in the form of music, styles, and food, but its influence extends far beyond the pop culture images of J. Lo and Mark Antony. "Today Los Angeles and California are quietly exporting their people and their way of life eastward across the continent," writes Pulitzer-prize winning journalist Hector Tobar in his book *Translation Nation*. "The city is the starting point of a new identity that is at once Latin American and—though it may not be immediately apparent—intertwined with North American traditions, with Jeffersonian ideals and the civic culture molded in the United States over the past two centuries."[41]

Issues related to Spanish as a second national language, immigration laws, taxation, and civic opportunities are at the heart of heated debates about the Latinization of America and the immigrant experience. Tobar tells *The Progressive*, "Other cities and towns across the continent have undergone the same pattern of response to the creeping advance of Latinization: denial, anger, acceptance."[42] How Americans come to terms with what Tobar calls a "Latin Republic of the United States" will be central to shaping generational ideologies and norms.

Watch also for new, more blurred notions of race and identity in this merging of North American and Latin American cultures, an idea we also touch on in the chapter "It's All a Blur." A report by the Pew Hispanic Center called "Shades of Belonging" notes that while a little more than half of Hispanics picked one of the standard race categories (mostly white) on the 2000 U.S. Census, some 15 million, or 42 percent of the Hispanic population, marked "some other race."[43] (The U.S. Census considers Hispanic identity as separate from race, and asks respondents both to specify race and to indicate whether they are "Spanish/Hispanic/Latino.") "Hispanics take distinctive views of race," the report observes, "and because their numbers are large and growing fast, these views are likely to change the way the nation manages the fundamental social divide that has characterized American society for 400 years."

How this immigrant story fits into America's melting pot character and history will give rise to the next big questions about race, integration, belonging, history, and national identity. As we confront these issues, we will find the Latinization of America informing all aspects of our political and personal life, from legislation to language.

Next: Attitude Toward the Environment Is Unsustainable

In his 2006 State of the Union address, President Bush touched on the issues of overdependency on foreign oil by saying, "We have a serious problem: America is addicted to oil, which is often imported from unstable parts of the world."[44] That's not news to any Americans who drive gas-guzzling SUVs or pay through the nose to heat their McMansions. But while we may be admitting some of our environmentally shortsighted addictions, we're not doing much to change them. Sustainability is simply not an American mind-set.

In fact, while the United States accounts for only 4 percent of the world's population, it contributes a quarter of the carbon dioxide emissions, according to the BBC News.[45] Redefining Progress, a sustainability policy group, says that the average American's environmental footprint—the amount of the earth's surface that it takes to provide everything a person consumes—is about 60 percent larger than the footprint of the average inhabitant of Italy. As Redefining Progress Executive Director Michel Gelobter notes, "If everyone lived like the average American, we would need 5.3 planets to support us."[46] America is a culture defined by consumption and waste.

> Every week the average American uses the equivalent of 300 shopping bags filled with natural resources for food, shelter, energy, and transportation, according to a report by the World Resources Institute in Washington, D.C., and three international research groups.[47]

We throw away everything from paper towels and plastic plates to computers and cell phones. And now it's the technology that we love and depend on that's becoming an Achilles heel. Electronic waste, or e-waste—computers, monitors, TVs, cell phones, DVDs, and other electronics that are considered at the "end of life"—is the fastest-growing waste stream in the world.[48] By 2010 we will have as many as 1 billion surplus computers and monitors, reports Computer Recycling for Education (CRE), an environmental consulting group; already California generates 6,000 surplus computers a day.[49] Within five years, one computer will be discarded for every one purchased, according to CRE, a tally of tens of millions annually.

That's a lot of waste, and it's a lot of materials, including lead and mercury, that are hazardous to humans and the environment, and costly to clean up. In the case of electronics, recycling doesn't solve the issue, it only turns America's waste into someone else's problem. Equipment that's donated is shipped overseas to developing countries; most of it is too outdated or inoperable to be used as is, and much of it is intended for recycling. So people strip the parts for scrap, leaving behind a mountain of dangerous waste. *The New York Times* reports that soil and water tests in the e-waste processing town of Guiyu, China, found levels of chromium, tin, and barium many times higher than what's allowed in the United States.[50]

One solution is to mandate that computer manufacturers reduce their use of toxic materials, which the EU has done, but America is behind in regulations. The Environmental Protection Agency maintains no formal standards for e-waste recyclers, but states are taking action of their own. California, Maine, Maryland, and Massachusetts have e-waste programs in place, and in 2006 Maine became the first state to require makers of computer monitors and TVs to pay for their own e-waste recycling.

Abroad, America is seen as a self-serving environmental glutton. In 2005, the United States was widely criticized by the international community for refusing to ratify the UN-sponsored Kyoto Protocol, which requires participating countries to reduce emissions of carbon dioxide and other greenhouse gases linked to global warming. "This is the American position because it's right for America," said President Bush at the time.[51] The rationale is that the protocol puts the burden entirely on industrialized countries and does not seek to limit pollution from developing nations.

Americans get the environmental evil eye from the rest of the world and as the junk piles up, watch for even more pressure at home and abroad to start abiding by the call to reduce, reuse, recycle, and regulate.

Next: Americans Have a Love-Hate Relationship with Voting

There's a lot of build-up to voting in American elections. Candidates spend millions on ad campaigns to entice us out to the polls, and public service announcements encourage us to go out and "rock the vote." But Americans don't. About 60 percent of voting-eligible Americans have turned out for presidential elections in the last few decades—compare that with turnout above 80 percent in developed nations like Italy, Sweden, Belgium, and Australia. Do Americans hate to vote? Hardly.

In fact, Americans have a thing for voting: After all, people enthusiastically weigh in from their phones and computers when it comes to choosing favorites on *American Idol* and *Dancing with the Stars*. (And nearly 22 million people tuned in to *American Idol* in February 2006 to find out who won the slots for the next crop of contestants.)[52] As Hua Hsu writes in the *Village Voice*, we love to vote, as long as it's for the absurd: "We vote on competing but really conspiring blends of Coca-Cola. We vote on who we believe will win the World Series or whether a given coach bungled a crucial third down. We vote people to the zenith of prefab pop stardom, often over the objections of bona fide talent scouts. We vote on issues of other people's matrimony and during the commercial breaks, Internet providers and cable music video channels mainline election-year imagery and jockey for our 'votes.' We are quizzed in the streets, on the Web, and on television for our views."[53]

Then what's the disjunction when it comes to politics? Disillusionment and a disconnect with politicians. People simply believe politics are controlled by special interests, according to a California Voter Foundation statewide survey on the attitudes of infrequent voters and eligible voters who are not registered.[54] For two-thirds of those surveyed, that was a big disincentive to vote. The average American perceives themselves having more personal power as a consumer than as a member of the electorate.

What's next in courting disaffected voters? *Time* reports that both parties in the 2008 elections will use technology to make their appeals feel more personal, more one-to-one. Republican National Committee chairman Ken Mehlman tells *Time* writer Josh Tyrangiel, "From now on, a smart candidate will reach you through your cell phone, your friends, the organizations you belong to and the Web sites you visit." Democrats hope to similarly galvanize their base: In the piece, Simon Rosenberg, president of the New Democrat Network, an advocacy group that introduces Democrats to new-media strategies, says, "Intel and Yahoo! are introducing technology that will allow every DVR to record video from a Web site the way it records ESPN."[55] That would keep campaign costs down and the candidates speaking directly to voters.

What's the logical (or illogical) extreme when it comes to engaging voters who'd rather choose pop stars than politicians? A Senate aide who works for a 2008 presidential hopeful tells Tyrangiel that the campaign has discussed the idea of a reality show centered on the candidate. Reasons the aide, "The obvious danger is that it would have to be warts and all to be credible, and you'd have to give up some control. The upside is people get emotionally invested in the candidate."[56] The 2008 political elections could well play out like a reality series as campaigns pull out every stop to keep voters actively engaged till the end. Just imagine the overly dramatized reality-style promo: "Two candidates. One White House. Who'll be sleeping in the Lincoln bedroom? You decide."

Ads for the 2006 satire *American Dreamz* asked viewers to "Imagine a country ... where more people vote for a pop idol than their next president." The movie envisions a collision between politics and *American Idol*-style reality TV when the president serves as guest judge on America's favorite weekly talent show.

What's Next? Social and Political Consciousness

Voter turnout may be low, but amazingly enough, no one seems to be able to get through a dinner without a political discussion—even the stereotypically self-absorbed 20–30-year-old group. People are volunteering for campaigns and organizations, and talking about things like how to use consumer power to institute responsible business practices.

Next: Them vs. Us at Home and Abroad

Enemies are confusing again. We're engaged in a war with an abstract enemy—terror—that doesn't draw clear lines or boundaries. The national instinct after 9/11 was to retaliate, but doubts still loom large about the targets of our revenge. This is not the era of Cold War conspiracies, with Russia at the center of our fear. The rules of the game are more complex and certainly more ambiguous. This is a time when we struggle to clearly define "them."

There are questions about how Saddam Hussein and the Taliban became linked. Following the attacks on the World Trade Center and the Pentagon, polls revealed that close to 70 percent of Americans believed Saddam was personally involved.[57] In his January 2002 State of the Union address, which focused on coping with the aftermath of 9/11, President Bush said, "Iraq continues to flaunt its hostility toward America and to support terror."[58] But no link to 9/11 was ever demonstrated, and Saddam's weapons of mass destruction prove to be more myth than menace. Nonetheless, America and its coalition partners are mired in an ongoing war in Iraq that, like Vietnam, is fracturing the United States into an us and a them—with everyone paying lip service to supporting the troops but one faction supporting the president's actions and the other ferociously opposing them.

We're also fractured when it comes to a national consensus on distinguishing friend from foe. Consider the storm over America's proposed deal with Dubai Port World, owned by the United Arab Emirates (UAE), which was to manage the security of six ports across the Eastern seaboard. Did the volatile reaction—consistent across party lines—reflect an unfounded intolerance against any and every Arab country? Writing in the *National Review*, CNBC host Larry Kudlow argued, "The brouhaha . . . has nothing to do with homeland security. Allow me to give this episode its proper name: Islamophobia."[59] Proponents of the deal noted that the UAE has offered public cooperation in the American war on terror: It's a friend. Those opposed charged that the UAE has long supported the

Taliban and other forms of radical extremism, and that handing our ports over to a country even vaguely tied to terrorist activity would be a grand-scale threat to national security: It's a foe.

The debate underscores America's unprecedented internal strife. It goes back again to the Constitution. As a new nation, America was fearful of impending attacks from Britain, Spain, and the native Indians; in response, the Constitution called for the country to "provide for the common defense." There was an understanding of cooperation against clear threats. Today, we're divided on how to tackle our enemies and even on who exactly they are, where the real threats come from. And we're split down the middle when it comes to supporting the current approach: Half of Americans (53 percent) disapprove of the way President Bush is handling terrorism, as of an April 2006, poll by CNN/*USA Today*/Gallup.[60] What's next for America? A call for clarity for the sake of security and our common defense.

Next: Americans under a Global Microscope

As it struggles with spreading democracy, staying ahead in a changing global economy, and grappling with bipartisan in-fighting at home, America is under scrutiny around the world. And it doesn't help America's image that there's widespread focus on controversies that cast the United States in a poor light—everything from prisoner abuse scandals and refusal to participate in environmental agreements to cultural insensitivity in Iraq.

A Pew Global Attitudes study from 2005 indicates that anti-Americanism in Europe, the Middle East, and Asia, which surged as a result of the war in Iraq, shows little signs of slowing.[61] "The magnitude of America's image problem is such that even popular U.S. policies have done little to repair it," notes the study. "President George W. Bush's calls for greater democracy in the Middle East and U.S. aid for tsunami victims in Asia were well received in many countries, but only in Indonesia, India and Russia has there been significant improvement in overall opinions of the U.S." Is it the American culture, the American people, or the American government that they're "anti"? Pew reports that in its Global Attitudes studies dating to 2002, the rest of the world has held the American people in higher esteem than it has held America as an entity. Skepticism seems most deeply rooted in the institution of government.

Around the world, there's also a perceived arrogance to the way America has approached Iraq, extending to the very evidence that seemed to justify the go-ahead for war. The U.S. government undeniably mishandled intelligence, a mistake magnified by an insistence on defending the events, even when many

Americans recognized the government was simply wrong. As the international community sees it, the United States went blindly into Iraq on false information, taking its partner countries with it. The United States, however, almost never admits mistakes and instead projects an image of always being on top of things, confident, and in control. It's a recipe for disaster.

The war also engendered charges of cultural insensitivity, as Iraq's national heritage suffered major casualties during the American invasion. Richard S. Lanier was one of three White House cultural advisers who resigned from his post in protest, claiming there was a blatant failure of U.S. forces to prevent the looting of Iraq's national museum, home to invaluable artifacts dating back 10,000 years. He saw in the invasion a "total lack of sensitivity and forethought regarding the . . . loss of cultural treasures." Martin Sullivan, head of the President's Advisory Committee on Cultural Property for eight years, likewise argued, "It didn't have to happen. In a pre-emptive war that's the kind of thing you should have planned for."[62]

In the Arab world, the bungling in Iraq has only added to fears of "Westoxification," a term used to denote non-Western societies' dependence on Western money and absorption of Western culture. Popularized in the 1970s by the writings of Jalal Al-e Ahmad, the leftist son of an Iranian cleric, the word reflects a growing distaste for American policy and influence. Many also see recent events in the Middle East as a product of America's hegemonic financial and military power.

The relationship between Arab and Western culture is a key issue of our times. America is seen as a bully, indiscriminately imposing its will on the world. "We hope Americans will learn from [the war in Iraq] and listen to reason and the advice of experts before toppling regimes here and there in the world," writes political science professor Ibrahim al-Hadban in Kuwait's *Al-Ra'y Al-Am* in November 2005, according to the BBC, which monitors editorials and comments in Arabic-language newspapers.[63]

Even traditional allies are starting to size up America with a different eye. In the Global Attitudes study, Pew notes that "Americans and Europeans continue to take very different views of the transatlantic alliance."[64] In fact, all the countries in Western Europe feel they should follow an approach independent from America's on issues related to security and diplomacy; by contrast, two-thirds of Americans think the United States and Western Europe should remain as close as always. Europe has also revealed a hostility toward America on many issues, from its political institutions and their impact on Europe to the speed of American life and its affect on the rest of the world. Europeans have even taken offense to the American style of eating—as a backlash against fast food, Italians started a movement in

1986 known as Slow Food, which eschews industrialized, processed meals in favor of fresh, local dishes.

What's Next? America, Owned and Operated by . . .

The 2006 debate about an Arab company that nearly made a deal to operate U.S. ports highlights a great next: Foreign capital, including Arab capital, owns more and more of America. Consider the Essex House in New York City (owned by Dubai Investment), Caribou Coffee, and Church's Chicken (both owned by a Bahrain-based investment group). America finances its whopping trade deficits by borrowing more than $2 billion per day from foreigners, and already half the U.S. government's publicly traded debt is owned by foreigners. But this is a just the beginning; we ain't seen nothing yet.

Next: Americans Look Inward to Find Method in the Madness

When the world seemingly goes mad, we search for a foundation on which to build some kind of order or control to combat the chaos. And America has endured a lot of chaos in recent years. So we're looking within to self and country for stability. But reassurance is hard to find, a lesson that Hurricane Katrina made clear.

Shortly before the winds and water of Katrina devastated New Orleans, Americans had opened their arms and wallets to victims of the Asian tsunami. Looking at a death toll of nearly 1,300 and an estimated $200 billion in property damage, Americans reached out to provide relief. Tales of ordinary citizens from health care workers to homemakers picking up and heading south inspired us on the national news. But as we focused on what went wrong, the national mood became defined by the "blame game," a maddening way to make sense of the literal and metaphorical mess—a way to seek stability. There has been tremendous discourse on the roles and responsibilities of city, state, and national governments. Who should have driven efforts to mitigate the disaster? Who is responsible for rebuilding?

As the levels of government feuded and fumed, New Orleans residents were left to fend for themselves from New England to California, with only FEMA-issued debit cards as seed money for starting over. The onus was on the individuals to rebuild and tend to their own patches, wherever they may have ended up. Self-reliance was assumed as a defining national characteristic. Former FEMA

Director Michael Brown said the debit card was a way for people to "make their own decisions about what do they need to have to start rebuilding their lives."[65] The clear message: Americans must take their fate in their own hands, make their own consumer decisions with the $2,000 that couldn't make up for civic short-comings at all levels of government.

The idea of consumer control is seeping into conversations about everything from health care to Social Security, with more talk of personal accounts than national accountability. It's seen as a way for people to make their own decisions, with the government staying out of the way. But while control can be empower-ing, times of trouble point to the need for cohesive collaboration between citi-zens and government at every level.

Next: What Happened to the Pursuit of Happiness?

Fundamental to American rights is the pursuit of happiness, and a lot of people in the United States are making good on their privileges. The epitome of our frenzy for fun is the booming lure of Las Vegas. According to the Las Vegas Convention and Visitors Authority, the city is setting new records for number of visitors each year (there were 38.5 million in 2005; 39.1 million were projected for 2006).[66] Las Vegas attracts all types, takes all kinds. It's at once a family-friendly destination that offers cheap buffets and thrilling theme parks and also the ultimate destina-tion for debauchery, a promise of complete freedom to be as base as one wants without regret. After all, as the city's ad campaign promises, "What happens in Vegas stays in Vegas." Perhaps some of Las Vegas's popularity is influenced by the success of *CSI: Crime Scene Investigation*, the number one Nielsen-rated scripted show for four years running? The original *CSI* was set in none other than Vegas. It's in Sin City that the average American can indulge himself for the weekend, or just spoil the kids with some good, clean fun. There's a tinge of American opti-mism at play, too. Vegas offers the opportunity for reinvention and new possibil-ities. There's the attraction of the city's wild side, but there's also the hope that the next roll of the dice or pull of the slot machine will be "the one." It's an acceler-ated shot at the American Dream, a quick win with a big return.

And Therefore Next

With turmoil on the domestic front—from port security and Katrina clean-up to ethics scandals in all branches of government—America is refocusing on taking care of business on the home front. Some see a corresponding downsizing of global ambitions: Lawrence Korb, a former Reagan administration defense official, told the *Christian Science Monitor:* "Because of continuing problems in

Iraq and now the attention and money demanded at home after Katrina, the Bush administration is going to take a much more patient approach to solving the world's problems. No more axis of evil, no more grand transformation of the Middle East."[67]

As America approaches the 2008 presidential election, pundits and PR from both parties will be pointed at domestic issues. But Americans are burned out by the behemoth of national government, skeptical about its competency and feeling let down by its poor performance. Instead of actively engaging in the political process, voters will turn a deaf ear and instead look to effect change through consumer choices more than anything else. Think debit card as the key to a new future—in this climate, plastic will be more prime than ever.

Section II

Cultural Nexts

chapter six

big next: blended and blurred reality

Fifty looks like 30, men primp like women, women complain about their stay-at-home spouse's lack of earning power. In the business sphere, art blends into commerce, with products integrated fully into entertainment. The unknowns mingle with the stars on reality TV, which in turn catapults average people to worldwide celebrity. Some of us simply imitate celebrities by making ourselves over in their image. Technology has created a continuum of the virtual and the real.

Lines are less clear as we travel through life's stages in far less predictable ways, upending traditional roles and reinventing familiar hallmarks of identity. Our vision is blurred as we gaze across a landscape where the old thresholds of identity and meaning have been upturned. We're living in an age-defying, gender-bending time, a trick-of-the-eye culture where authenticity and reliability are in question. Perception is the new reality.

Take Martha Stewart: She's a divorced woman serving as the archetype of the happy homemaker. She's among the highest-paid entertainment executives in the United States, and her ethos is do-it-yourself, with her branded goods sold at Kmart. She was locked up for months but sustained high visibility. She's a brand who crosses across all media and speaks to multiple generations—she's over 60 while her fan base is 30 years younger.

Is there a downside to the blur? Mixed messages can be disorienting and even unsettling. How real is that "reality" on TV, and how legitimate are the celebrities elbowing for attention? Consumers can spot fakery. There will be a rise in competitive authenticity, because when anyone can get famous, we try to separate the forgettable many from the special few. In our book *Buzz*, we make the point that all effective "grassroots" marketing requires the aura (if not the reality) of authenticity to have any chance of working. Even half-baked authenticity in the form of a really good fake will do. After all, looking younger is almost as good as being younger—what's important is how well you keep people guessing.

What's Next? Blended Puppies

Blended puppies continue to grow in prestige and stature—think goldendoodles ad schnoodles and others, all bred expressely because we've learned that pedigree isn't as sturdy as a lovely blur.

Next: Gender Is the New Medium for Self-Expression

There's a mounting blur in our expressions of gender and sexuality. It was American sex researcher Fritz Klein, a psychiatrist, who asserted that sexual orientation is fluid and can change over time, that the black-and-white labels "straight" and "gay" are too simplistic. In his 1978 book *The Bisexual Option*, he introduced the Klein Sexual Orientation Grid as a new way to view sexual orientation.[1] While most discourse on sexuality points to polarities with limited emphasis on the middle, Klein's ideas are gaining some momentum. At the least, as Stephanie Fairyington writes in *The Gay & Lesbian Review*, bisexuality teaches that "we live in a world whose reality is more complicated than the simplified binaries of our language and understanding."[2]

People are becoming more aware of that, acknowledging that there's a continuum of degrees of masculinity and femininity. There's growing acceptance of those who mix both natures.

In recent years, women have become much more open to exploring bisexuality (or, at any rate, they're now more comfortable reporting such activity). Whereas in 1995 just 4 percent of women 18 to 59 said they'd had at least one sexual experience with another woman, a decade later 11.5 percent of women 18–44 claimed a bisexual encounter in a Centers for Disease Control and Prevention survey. And for women in their late teens and 20s, that figure was at 14 percent in the 2005 survey.[3]

There's even a movement among asexuals, people who claim not to experience sexual attraction at all. The Asexual Visibility and Education Network, which claims 6,000-plus members worldwide, explains that "asexuality is an intrinsic part of who we are. Asexuality does not make our lives any worse or any better, we just face a different set of challenges than most sexual people."[4] There's some debate as to whether people can really be asexual; some experts think it's a matter of choice, although at least one study suggests that about 1 percent of the population may be asexual.[5]

The transgender community views the simple two-gender system as more harmful than helpful, a once-obscure notion that's filtering into the everyday realm. Felicity Huffman, known to many as one of the *Desperate Housewives*, was nominated for an Oscar in 2006 for portraying a male-to-female transexual in *Transamerica*. The role drew new mainstream focus to the complexities of identity, the blurs between male and female, gay and straight.

The 2006 teen movie *She's the Man* epitomizes our mixed-up notions of male and female identity. It may be based on Shakespeare's *Twelfth Night*, but its gender-bending confusion seems altogether 21st-century. The film's tagline: "Everybody has a secret. . . . Duke wants Olivia who likes Sebastian who is really Viola whose brother is dating Monique so she hates Olivia who's with Duke to make Sebastian jealous who is really Viola who's crushing on Duke who thinks she's a guy."

At a time when pop culture so easily plays off gender bending concepts, gay life is more than ever being depicted as mainstream. *Will & Grace* and *Queer Eye for the Straight Guy* have been on the air for years already, and the idea of a team of gay men making over a straight guy no longer seems novel. "Among lesbians," writer Andrew Sullivan notes, "Ellen DeGeneres's transition from closeted sit-com star to out-lesbian activist and back to appealingly middle-brow daytime talk-show host is almost a microcosm of diversifying lesbian identity in the past decade."[6] What does it take to raise some eyebrows? Turning the ultimate American icon of the cowboy on its head by introducing homosexuality into Marlboro man terrain, as Ang Lee did in his Oscar-nominated and much-debated (and even parodied) film, *Brokeback Mountain*.

As gender and sexuality become less compartmentalized into discrete categories, rituals are also converging between the sexes. Many bachelor and bachelorette parties, for example, are now joint events. The wedding Web site The Knot names the combined party one of their "seven favorite trends" for bridesmaids, noting that "with all your friends around, both male and female, it's sure to be a blast."[7] As change sweeps in, some cling to conformity and tradition. There's a rising advocacy among some sectors in society for a return to traditional gender roles, but there's no going back altogether.

Next: A Female Take on Entrepreneurship and Identity

There's a monopoly on the classic tale of American business success. The stories usually feature a male hero at their center, and the entrepreneurial ingenuity of

Henry Ford, Sam Walton, Bill Gates, and Jeff Bezos is legend in the canon of business school case studies. But since the mid-1980s, the stories have slowly been changing. Women are moving to the foreground, and the likes of Oprah Winfrey, Martha Stewart, and Anita Roddick, founder of The Body Shop, have paved the way for a crop of eager businesswomen. Women are blurring the traditional face of business.

More women around the world are embarking on entrepreneurship. Women headed up nearly 30 percent of nonfarm businesses in the United States as of 2002, according to a Census Bureau study released in 2006, representing about 6.5 million companies; another 2.7 million business were equally male/female-owned.[8] "Women-owned businesses are growing at twice the rate of all U.S. firms," noted U.S. Secretary of Labor Elaine L. Chao during a Women's History Month celebration in March 2006, "and as entrepreneurs, women are creating jobs and strengthening our economy."[9]

> The Canadian Imperial Bank of Commerce estimates that 1 million Canadian women will own a small business by the year 2010 and that the number of women-owned businesses is growing 60 percent faster than those run by men.[10]

The number of women entrepreneurs has increased more than 200 percent over the past 20 years—and those 821,000 women annually contribute in excess of $18 billion to the economy, which makes them Canada's fastest-growing business sector. That's according to a study by the prime minister's task force on women entrepreneurs, which also found that approximately 20 percent of these women were pushed to go into business for themselves because of negative employment circumstances.[11]

The gender revolution that launched more women into self-employment is affecting all areas of society. It has "radically" redefined the role and status of women, says Australian social researcher Hugh Mackay, and is gradually prompting men to reexamine their own roles. "In turn, that has reshaped the institutions of marriage and the family, the life of the neighborhood, the nature of shopping, the landscape of politics, and the dynamics of the workplace," observes Mackay.[12]

The birthrate is dropping, although science is certainly adjusting the rules of racing against the biological clock. With the help of advances in fertility, for example, some women are having children well into their 40s and, occasionally, their 50s. Birth rates among women 35 to 39 and 40 to 44 are at the highest levels for those age groups in more than 30 years, according to a 2002 report by the Centers for Disease Control and Prevention.[13]

Society is slowly growing more accepting of women who choose to marry later—or not at all. (Role model Oprah, for one, has never tied the knot.) Women in midlife, especially, "don't necessarily need men like they used to," says *San Francisco Chronicle* writer Jane Ganahl, author of *Single Women of a Certain Age*. "They've achieved a degree of mastery in their lives. They travel alone, have their children, care for their pets and their work, and have huge amounts of satisfaction that relationships can't touch."[14]

There's clearly an evolving set of rules for what's socially acceptable for women. For some, these changing roles bring security and happiness. But the inclination to relegate women's work to narrow parameters persists, along with a myopic view of the female sensibility. And many women are still struggling with how to merge gender with persona and identity as they make inroads into traditionally male-dominated universes. Some have dropped the demure screen only to adopt the worst of male behavior.

In Britain, for example, there's the rise of the "ladette," described by *The New York Times* as a young woman trying to be one of the lads by "drinking to excess, shouting four-letter words and, if necessary, belching."[15] This blur of clichéd gender-based behavior sparked a British reality show, *Ladette to Lady*. Ten of these uncouth, uninhibited women check into a finishing school to be transformed into "stylish, well-mannered ladies," as described by the Sundance Channel (which imports the show). These 21st-century creations are taught the old-time arts of flower arranging, gourmet cooking, and polite conversation.

There are high expectations for women today. Women are under extreme pressures to fill several roles, and it takes a real high achiever to maintain a career, a family and a marriage, several friendships, close ties with one's family, and a fit physique all at the same time. In a hundred years society will wonder how early 21st-century women coped with all the stress.

What's Next? Lifestyle Helpers

An increasing demand for lifestyle helpers who are there both for the entrepreneur in the house and also for child-minding, kitchen coordination, and so on. As female entrepreneurship rises, watch women hire other women (and men) in roles that once might have perfectly defined the duties of the COW—the corporate officer's wife of the 1970s and 1980s.

Next: Mom Is the New Powerhouse

What's next for women? Roles will shift even farther along the continuum, and more women will become the primary family breadwinners. In Britain, a study by the Centre for Economics and Business Research describes women as the new "financial powerhouses." Within 20 years female millionaires will outnumber their male counterparts in the U.K. and, the study estimates, women will own nearly 60 percent of the nation's personal wealth.[16]

The new face of motherhood will be the "alpha mom," a well-informed, strong, decision-making multitasker who wields great personal and consumer power. The modern mom is confident and in control.

Today, however, as many as 70 percent of mothers feel companies aren't doing a good job speaking to them, says Maria Bailey in her book *Marketing to Moms*. While women tend to have distinct spending, saving, and investment habits, banks and investment companies rarely dedicate resources to these differences.[17]

The new Alpha Mom TV channel is for "mothers seeking excellence."[18] The brainchild of Isabel Kallman and Vicky Germaise, the channel airs nationally on Comcast's free on-demand service, offering nuggets on parenting from professionals and moms themselves.

Writing about the channel, *New York* magazine suggests the alpha mom is a modern variant of Betty Crocker, that pervasive model of domesticity, only "better, stronger, faster."[19] Randall Patterson writes in the magazine: "To all the best-selling scolds who say that Mother should slow down, that we expect too much of her, the new, improved Mama says, if anything, the goalposts have been set too low. With the right planning, resources, and work ethic, you can, too, be a perfect and fulfilled woman, raising a perfect and happy child."

The reality behind that ethos is the topic of the sitcom *Alpha Mom*, a pilot NBC was planning for its 2006–2007 season. It centers on a 30-year-old lawyer trying to balance kids, a stay-at-home husband, and her career, the "journey of a modern mom who would die for her children, and may die trying to raise them," according to press materials.[20]

> Moms are now including baby in their pampering: Think indulgent "mommy and me" spa excursions. Susie Ellis, president of travel and marketing company Spa Finder Inc., notes in *The New York Times* that five years ago there were no such baby programs. After a slew of requests for spas that welcome tots, Spa Finder started a Mommy and Baby category on its online spa guide.[21]

Next: The Modern Father Redefined

As mom acts more like the stereotypical dad, fathers are acting more like mothers. Western dads are increasingly spending quality time at home, rather than face time in the office. A study of 3,020 Gen X (b. 1965–1977) and baby boomer parents in the United States showed that 48 percent of Gen X fathers spend three to six hours per day on child rearing, versus 39 percent of boomer dads. And 47 percent of Xers wish they could spend more time with the kids, compared with 36 percent of boomers, according to the research by Reach Advisors, a marketing-strategy firm.[22]

Men are showing a much greater interest in emotional intelligence—they want to really take part in raising the kids, to be close to them. As one young Gen Xer from London told us, "Men in offices I know seek flex time urgently, working through their lunch breaks so that they can rush home at 5 on the dot to be with their families and experience their children growing up."

Why the change in attitudes? Perhaps it's that men want to be different from their fathers, who were constantly working. Some feel they were neglected by both parents. An article by Newhouse News's Laura DeMarco on the changing role of fathers notes that Gen X parents represent the first generation in which large numbers of kids were raised by single parents; about half had working moms and almost one-third had divorced parents, according to Yankelovich research cited by DeMarco, compared with 13 percent of boomers. "Before they were labeled slackers, they were latchkey kids," she writes.[23] (As the article points out, Gen Xers are raising more than half of all children under 18 in the United States.)

Some Generation X dads are leaving the office behind, choosing to work from home in order to be more active parents, or dropping their careers altogether to become full-time parents. The number of fathers caring for children at home while wives work has risen 70 percent since 1990, according to an analysis of U.S. Census data by Ajilon Finance.[24] The stay-at-home dad is such a pervasive idea it was dramatized in a plotline on *Desperate Housewives*.

> In Australia, family law is moving toward the assumption of a "share care" arrangement between divorced parents that more equally divides parental responsibility. Previously, laws generally favored mothers taking on the majority of the parenting role, with fathers seeing the children on alternate weekends.[25]

Next: There's More Than One Dating Game in Town

The rituals of romantic relationships are changing, evolving; courtship has been reinvented. In the era of rapid change, we're looking for love in new ways. We've become so accustomed to the many choices of a consumer-driven culture that we now want to maximize all of our options when looking for a partner.

With so many demands on our time, dating has become one more item on our to-do lists. As Judi James, Match.com's relationship expert, says in the *Guardian*, "Searching for a partner has to fit in with existing demands so we can no longer afford to be random, which is why online dating is so effective."[26] The Internet, with its huge databases of dates to be mined, helps streamline the process, making it simpler, faster, broader.

> The Pew Internet and American Life Project says 9 percent of the people who go online use dating services.[27] In the U.K., a NetRatings survey showed that Internet dating and personals Web sites drew more than 3.5 million people a month in 2005.[28]

Does online dating and all its infinite choices increase the odds of romantic connection? The *Guardian* reports that Match.com shows that 88 percent of its subscribers were likely to be attracted to someone they met through an online dating service, while only 52 percent were likely to be attracted to someone they met in a bar or nightclub.[29]

Speed dating provides an array of choices in a time-efficient format; it's mini-dates in minutes. A prescribed number of participants pair off for anywhere between four and eight minutes; at the sound of a buzzer or bell, they move on to the next potential match. When the session ends, they check off the names of people they want to see again, and organizers provide contact information if interest is mutual.

It's this expectation of choice that's changing the long-standing cultural traditions of arranged marriages. Western influences on the importance of choice are infiltrating Eastern mores through the media and certainly the Internet. While many Eastern youth are not ready to relinquish the traditions of arranged marriages, they want more options. As *The New York Times* notes, "Purely arranged marriage has morphed into a new culture of what might be called 'assisted' marriage. Parents are now free to arrange all they like, allowing their sons and daughters choice among a roster of nominees."[30]

Next: Changing Attitudes about Marriage

Today's parents approach the task quite differently than their own parents did, and they're looking at marriage differently, too. New twists on marriage and alternative options abound. People aren't under the same pressure to beat a path to the altar, then stay together and tough it out; maybe they decide to remain solo, perhaps they marry, break up, then have children with different partners. It's an open playing field, with people following divergent paths—or going down the traditional path but at different stages of life.

The numbers show fewer married people, more cohabiting couples, and more people living alone. In the United States, the annual number of marriages per 1,000 unmarried adult women dropped by nearly half from 1970 to 2004, according to a report by Rutgers University's National Marriage Project.[31] In England and Wales, the number of people getting married is estimated to drop by 10 percent over the next 25 years. The proportion of married men will fall from about 53 percent in 2003 to 42 percent by 2031; married women will decrease from 50 to 40 percent. And the number of people who've never married will rise by 11 percent, according to the Government Actuary Department.[32]

In 1960, the median age at first marriage in the United States was 20 for women and 23 for men; in 2004, that had increased to 26 and 27, respectively.[33]

The Rutgers report attributes the decline partly to people postponing marriage, as well as to the ever-increasing rise in unmarried couples living together. From 1990 to 2004, the number of American cohabiting couples of the opposite sex jumped by about 78 percent.[34] (The phenomenon isn't strictly limited to the young: The U.S. Census Bureau reported in 2000 that the number of men and women 65 and older who live together had almost doubled in a decade.)[35] In Australia today, three-quarters of couples live together before marriage, compared with 16 percent in 1975.[36] And due to the nation's property boom, young couples are buying instead of renting together, seemingly more willing to commit to a mortgage than to a marriage.

As people around the globe and across age lines gravitate toward cohabitation, watch for more legislation geared specifically to unmarried couples and specialized services like estate and financial planning. Advocacy groups like the Alternatives to Marriage Project in the United States, which argues for "equality and fairness for unmarried people, including people who are single, choose not to marry, cannot marry, or live together before marriage," will become more prominent.[37]

In Europe, cohabitation isn't just what couples do before they decide to marry and have kids—rather, "marriage is no longer considered an indispensable preliminary to welcoming a child," according to a French parliamentary report cited by the *Christian Science Monitor*.[38] Nearly one in three babies is born to an unmarried couple in Europe; in some countries it's almost half of babies (France) or even more than half (Sweden). Cohabiting couples generally do marry eventually, though in France (which gives unmarried couples the same rights as married ones when it comes to inheritance and parental rights) only about a third do so, according to the Office for National Statistics in the U.K.[39]

Some committed couples even stop short of domestic partnerships, opting to maintain their own homes. There are 2 million people "living apart together" in the U.K., according to the Office of National Statistics; that's three in 20 people ages 16–59.[40] For some, it's a practical issue, as they build careers in different cities or even countries; cheap flights, Webcams, and free Internet phone calls make long-distance relationships easier to maintain. Some who have gone through divorce are cautious about uprooting their children or giving up their lives in case of another failed relationship. And in other cases—including that of actress Helena Bonham Carter and director Tim Burton, who live next door to each other—it's simply about having your own space and not putting up with someone else's dirty socks.

For Generations X and Y (b. 1975–1984), marriage is all about finding happiness in a quality relationship, whereas boomers entered into marriage with a commitment to its stability and a firm belief in the institution. Having grown up surrounded by divorce and accustomed to a world of accelerating change, X and Yers prefer to postpone commitment and keep their options open.

Western youth today spend a tremendous amount of time learning who they are so they can contribute to and benefit from a happy marriage. But they're also frightened that the more complex and self-reliant they become, the harder it will be to find one person who sates all their needs. It's why the dating sites are so compelling, even offering the help of complex algorithms and a "scientific approach" to matchmaking, as in the case of eHarmony.

In some cases, there's an inclination to jump into marriage with an overly romanticized idea of what it can be, resulting in the "starter marriage." Pamela Paul, author of *The Starter Marriage and the Future of Matrimony* and editor at *American Demographics*, notes that these unions last five years or less and don't involve children.[41] Paul contends that some Xers are "blinded to the reality" of marriage, looking for a fairy tale and the promise of personal fulfillment. Noting that they're rarely talked out of these notions, Paul posits that, "Perhaps our parents, embarrassed or ashamed by their own unhappy marriages or divorces, feel they're in no position to guide their children."

> As fewer straight couples marry, more gay couples are seeking the financial rights and legal equity that marriage provides, seen in the rising number of cohabitation agreements that clarify rights and status.

Next: The Skin You're In

The reality show *Black.White*, which premiered on the FX network in early 2006, aimed to show what it's like to live in someone else's skin by having two families literally trade races and places (in the spirit of John Howard Griffin's 1961 book *Black Like Me*)—a white Southern California family that was made to look black, while an African American family from Atlanta was made over as white. Of particular interest, notes columnist Clarence Page in the *Chicago Tribune*, was how the younger generation seemed to bridge divides of color more easily: "The youths, typical of a generation that can't even remember when Michael Jackson didn't have a nose job, are a lot more relaxed than their elders about the old racial rules. In the age of white rappers like Eminem or black golfers like Tiger Woods, it's not as big of a deal as it used to be for today's teenagers to cross racial boundaries. Some of them are doing it every day."[42]

Nonetheless, race is still a defining characteristic that's loaded with implications—both good and bad—about how people are perceived and how they perceive themselves. The Pew Hispanic Center analyzed 2000 Census data and found that about 42 percent of the Hispanic population (about 15 million people) marked "some other race" instead of picking one of the government's five categories.[43] (Hispanic identity is a separate question from race on the census.) Forty-eight percent of respondents marked white and 2 percent black. The report says, "The Latino experience demonstrates that whiteness remains an important measure of belonging, stature and acceptance. And Hispanic views of race also show that half of this ever-larger segment of the U.S. population is feeling left out."

We tend to define entire cultures in terms of single labels of ethnicity and even race, but the issue of identity is as complex and as potent as ever. Notably, 2000 was the first year the U.S. Census allowed respondents to claim more than one race, from among six categories (white, black, American Indian and Alaska native, Asian, Native Hawaiian and other Pacific Islander, and "some other race"). That works out to 63 possible combinations. About 2.4 percent of the population (6.8 million people) chose more than one race.[44]

Mixed Media Watch (mixedmediawatch.com) describes itself as "a blog that monitors representations of mixed people, couples, families and transracial adoptees in film, television, radio and print media." Its co-editors also host a biweekly podcast called "Addicted to Race."

Hurricane Katrina put a spotlight on race, highlighting the vast racial divide in New Orleans and stirring debate about whether race played a role in the federal government's slow response. The topic became even more contentious after rapper Kanye West's bitter comment at a live telethon for storm victims that "George Bush doesn't care about black people." Six months after the hurricane, at the 2006 Academy Awards, the surprise winner for best picture was *Crash*, the film that explores some of the complexities of race and class in L.A. As of this writing, it was being developed for a TV adaptation, a show that would surely stir some further national conversation. Perhaps the most interesting television-programming conversation relates to the popular show *Survivor*, which announced that its thirteenth season would segregate "tribes" by race and ethnicity. This declaration created a firestorm and resulted in the defection of several advertisers. The experiment was suspended after two episodes, without comment from the producer.

Next: Product Placement, or Where Art and Commerce Meet

Nowadays art and commerce are so tightly woven together, it's hard to distinguish the artist's message from a well-placed product endorsement. And the blur is getting increasingly sophisticated.

On Visure Corp.'s evisure.com, viewers can track down exactly which products popped up in a TV show or movie—the Mini Cooper seen on *Alias*, the phone featured on *Commander in Chief*—then find links to conveniently purchase the items. Or fans of *Desperate Housewives* can go to ABC's online store to buy items worn by the women on recent episodes. Everything can be identified and commodified.

Next up are more twists on branded programming. One new take was BET's co-branded promotion with Infiniti, the luxury division of Nissan, which included 30 minutes of original programming in the spirit of an infomercial and images of new Infiniti models, which were never explicitly named. Part of the channel's Black History Month lineup, *In Black* showed five African American artists talking about elements of design, the same artists featured in Infiniti's "In Black" campaign (its first directly targeting African Americans). "We've pushed the format of the presentation to meet the depth of the dialogue, so that one becomes the other," noted creative director Christopher Davis of The True Agency, which came up with the program, in *Adweek*.[45]

There's a lot of money to be had in the art of product placement and endorsements. As more programming becomes available in every conceivable medium, the next big discussions will be centered not only on more branded programming that blurs content and commercial lines but also on customized placements that cleverly embed the pitch in the program. With digital video recording becoming more pervasive, TV ads as we know them will change, becoming intertwined into storylines. *Maclean's* writer Steve Maich observes that, "The sell is embedded—part of the experience rather than a distraction from it. Consumers tell marketers what they're interested in, and advertisers control how they send their messages and to whom." Because the message is a part of content people seek out themselves, Maich says, these pitches appear to generate a better response than commercials.[46]

The art/commerce blur will only become more pervasive now that the EU is relaxing rules on product placements; a draft directive allows for product placements in all shows beginning in 2009. The "Television without Frontiers Directive" updates standards from the late 1980s, when there were many fewer channels competing for ad revenue. European officials are hoping to make their own television industry more competitive, reports the *International Herald Tribune:* "They are conscious of growing revenue in the United States, with some studies showing that product placement advertising there has been rising by an average of 21 percent annually since 1999."[47]

Next: The Twists and Turns of Fame

Once upon a time, celebrities were people famous for their high-profile jobs, their significant achievements, or even just their birthright: politicians, actors, athletes, artists, royalty. Now virtually everyone and anyone who has had sustained media exposure counts as a celebrity by virtue of being recognizable to millions of people.

The concept of celebrity has blurred and shifted: Celebrity is no longer about status, it's about familiarity. And it's morally neutral, so whether fame is "deserved" or not is irrelevant; so too is distinguishing between celebrity based on good or bad deeds. It's purely about face and/or name recognition, and the acid test of being able to draw a crowd.

More and more, we're seeing nobodies wrangle a moment in the spotlight— and then hold on to it for astonishing lengths of time. Think Rob and Amber, whose 15 minutes of *Survivor* fame was substantially extended by *The Amazing Race*, which was followed by their televised wedding on CBS. With the proliferation of "all-star reunions" and such shows as *The Surreal Life*, the more memorable members of this crowd could be around for a very long time. (Watch for even more standout behavior as reality stars compete to avoid sinking back into normality once their shows are finished.) And you thought you were sick of Paris Hilton *now . . .*

The upside here is that programs such as *American Idol, Project Greenlight* (in which aspiring screenwriters and directors vie to be selected for a movie project), and *Project Runway* (the Bravo contest to find America's next great clothing designer) give some talented novices access to wide audiences and professionals in the field. HBO's first *Greenlight* series received in excess of 7,000 original script entries. It's also true that new technologies are democratizing entertainment in ways never seen before, giving poets, novelists, cartoonists, and visual and performance artists of all sorts of access to audiences around the world at a low cost.

Regardless of talent, celebrity is a coveted calling. People go out of their way to mimic the stars, sometimes going to extremes to attain knockoff celebrity.

Think MTV's *I Want a Famous Face*, which follows young adults who use plastic surgery to look like their celebrity idols. Celebrity Cruises both spoofs and capitalizes on this mimicry, promising travelers "The Celebrity Treatment" in its ads, which show average midlifers assuming the roles of stars on the ship. In one TV spot, a middle-aged guy sports a white tux and his best Sean Connery accent for a taste of the 007 life; in another, a boomer woman stands atop a staircase, presumably on her way to the buffet, and delivers a Hollywood-style acceptance speech in which she thanks her agent—her travel agent, that is.

> "Kelly is an extremely outgoing 26-year-old who is absolutely infatuated with Jennifer Aniston, whom everyone says she resembles. She buys clothes to match Jennifer's and owns all her movies. Kelly just divorced her husband and really wants to find a new man and start fresh with a new, 'hot' body. She hopes that having rhinoplasty, a breast lift and augmentation, and extensive liposuction will help her finally be comfortable in her own skin."
>
> —MTV's summary of *I Want a Famous Face*, episode 204[48]

Real celebrities, meanwhile, are finding it harder to maintain the illusion of perfection. *Us Weekly* magazine regularly features unflattering pictures of stars acting "just like us," and we're increasingly aware that glamour is a team effort. Oscar night, notes *The New York Times'* Alessandra Stanley, is now "about viewers deconstructing celebrity—abetted by a cottage industry of stylists, dermatologists, surgeons and trainers who reveal the fakery behind even the most seemingly natural beauties: celebrity with a dehumanized face."[49]

In the long run, it's authenticity that will give celebrities edge and depth of appeal. Unapologetically real personalities such as Kate Moss and Angelina Jolie will prove more enduring than rent-a-smile brand endorsers who are more benign.

> For those who feel celebrity mania has gone too far, there's the LOTPAU Web site (lotpau.com), which celebrates the "Lifestyles of the Poor and Unknown." The site asks, "Are you tired of dopey actors getting paid millions of dollars to appear in really bad movies? Are you tired of people being famous just for being famous?" The site showcases "Cribs and Rides of the Poor and Unknown," virtual tours of an everyday person's home and car. LOTPAU wittily skewers celebrity-centric lifestyle shows like VH1's *Fabulous Life Of . . .* and MTV's *Cribs*, both mocking the modern idea of celebrity and celebrating "all the real people out there."

Next: Pass Me that Wrench—I'm a Celebrity

Being an expert is an increasingly common route to celebrity. There are the experts who supply instant news analysis, the stock-pick professionals, security specialists, even climate-change experts who we see over and over again so that eventually they're celebrities in their own right. It's become such a cliché that *The Daily Show* has a coterie of fake news experts with titles like "senior political ana- lyst analyst" (an "expert on the experts").

Chefs have achieved high visibility as we become more obsessed with food and cooking. People like Wolfgang Puck, Jamie Oliver, and Nigella Lawson are powerful brands and influencers, and they're parlaying that into other areas of the consumer mar- ket, producing cookbooks, videos, lines of cookware, restaurant chains, and more. Emeril has even come out with a line of food-inspired toothpaste in what's described as "kickin' " flavors (Cinnamon Rush, Fresh Citrus Breeze, and Extreme Herbal Mint).

Interior design is another area that's booming for the celebrity brand. Ty Pennington, the hunky carpenter from the hit ABC show *Extreme Makeover: Home Edition*, now has his own line of furniture at Sears. Oprah Winfrey's design guru, Nate Berkus, who appears on her talk show and contributes to *O: The Oprah Magazine*, has his own home line in partnerships with Linens 'N Things.

Styling the stars is now a springboard to stardom as well. Rachel Zoe, stylist to teen queen Lindsay Lohan and Nicole Richie, is now a regular on TV shows and quoted in print. L'Wren Scott, Nicole Kidman and Renee Zellweger's stylist, became a tabloid celebrity as the leading lady in Mick Jagger's life.

What's Next? Almost Real

While many viewers loved Greg Brady when they were growing up, he was never more than a TV character; in the past decade, the immortalization of *Sex and the City*'s Carrie Bradshaw as the woman to copy has changed women around the world. Like "truthiness," almost-real is a quintessentially now concept.

> Celebrities are reversing the equation by leveraging their reputations to showcase off-camera areas of expertise and interest. Paul Newman (although his motivations are different since he organized as a nonprofit) may have pioneered the trend with his line of salad dressings, counting on the public to show a proclivity for a celebrity version of balsamic vinaigrette. The new incarnation of this is bigger and bolder. George Clooney is involved in the design and development of a Las Vegas hotel, and Lenny Kravitz, meanwhile, has launched a commercial interior design firm.

Next: Walking the Line between Real and Virtual

We've talked about all kinds of new ambiguities, things blending and blurring together, lines crossing. The ultimate overlap is where the real and the virtual meet. Increasingly people are turning to the virtual world for everything from entertainment and personal fulfillment to military training and college degrees.

Note how the virtual universe of massively multiplayer online games meets the U.S. Department of Defense's real-world training. Crews from around the world participate in simulated war exercises like Virtual Red Flag, which took place in February 2006, at an American Air Force base. In this virtual reality, tasks and information were tailored to specific geographic factors, maps, weather, and enemy forces. "The simulators do everything but burn gas and pull G-forces," boasted an Air Force press release.[50]

The government is also using a high-tech system with components from popular games like *Full Spectrum Warrior* to treat war veterans suffering from post-traumatic stress disorder. The virtual world simulates the real world of combat: "The soldier being treated wears VR goggles and headphones. Using a tablet-based interface, a therapist can activate or remove the sounds of gunshots or the sight of smoke, depending on a patient's reaction."[51] The idea is that painful memories become less traumatic when a patient is gradually reintroduced to the triggering experiences.

As more people get addicted to online fantasy games, real life gets more complex. Players are paying actual money for valuable virtual commodities such as gold pieces and more powerful characters. It's known as "gold farming," and it profits the real-life seller and the buyer's virtual self. NPR cites Internet reports that "there are individuals and groups in Asia and Eastern Europe where people are paid a very low wage to play characters for long hours—with the sole purpose of making virtual money that will later be converted into real money."[52] This economic exchange between "worlds" is bringing up new issues as people actually make a living dealing in synthetic economies. "From a standpoint of tax policy, there just isn't a line there between fantasy and reality," says Edward Castronova, author of *Synthetic Worlds: The Business and Culture of Online Games*, in *Computer Gaming World*, questioning whether the IRS will one day tax these transactions.[53]

China is so concerned over the growing number of its citizens addicted to online fantasy games, the country has not only imposed a five-hour limit on online role playing but intends to enforce it. As NPR also reports, "Your life as a magician or warrior will be interrupted with the warning: 'You have entered unhealthy game time. Please go offline immediately to rest.'" Failure to do so sets you back in the game.[54] Think of it this way: People who spend too much of their real life in the virtual world receive warnings from their real government that ultimately result in punishment of their virtual personas. It's a postmodern patchwork of blurred actions and consequences in wholly unique spaces.

And Therefore Next

The worlds of the real and the virtual are evolving, crossing, and blurring in complex economic, government, social, and personal spheres. New laws and codes of conduct will try to keep pace and make the lines more clear. Or we may simply come to accept that we live in parallel universes, enabled by technology, one real and one, well, kinda real.

The real issue here is that all of our conventional touch points for understanding exactly where we stand, what matters, how we keep score in terms of life achievements are coming into question. What we suspect will be the next great struggle of human identity is to see whether these markers really matter, if we can do better without them or if we're content to just live—the signposts be damned.

chapter seven

big next: ages without stages

In *Next*, we suggested that "demography was dead," replaced by the numerically agnostic "lifestage."[1] Today, this has become a mainstream, global reality. Age is now ambiguous. We're living in a generation delay: The ages at which we do things are getting higher—it's taking longer to lose our virginity, get married, have kids. Today we see much less emphasis on age as the barometer for when accomplishments and milestones should be met. As author Gail Sheehy puts it, "There's a revolution in the life cycle."[2]

We also made the point in *Next* that the indelible age of "youth" was 36—the age at which both Princess Diana and Marilyn Monroe died. Today, we'd be tempted to push this age up by perhaps as much as a decade.

The age shuffle is one more manifestation of blurring. Teens have become mini-adults, while adults wearing ripped jeans and sneakers swap MP3s with their kids. We're following Oprah's philosophy: "Whether you're 28 or 88, you've probably stamped yourself with a label," she says. "Look at the label that comes with your age, then replace it with one that reflects the reality of your life."[3] It's no longer a matter of lying about your age, it's a matter of recreating the reality of your age—changing expectations and turning the tables for what you want to do and how you want to do it.

More than ever, we're trying to look younger than our years, but with longer life spans and medical breakthroughs that can help us age with grace and virility, we're also starting to associate age with experience and wisdom. With Mick Jagger still a sexy rock star in his 60s, why fear 50, 60, and up? Rather than let her 50th birthday slip quietly by, Oprah turned it into a rallying cry for the benefits of midlife and beyond. "All these years I've been taking lessons from life experiences and feeling like I was growing into myself," she said at the time. "Finally, I feel grown. More like myself than I've ever been."[4]

Next: Teens Are Less Childish

On MySpace, the phenomenally popular social networking site, teenage girls build personal pages with pink, heart-patterned backgrounds, photos of friends goofing off, lists of favorite things, odes to heartthrob celebrities and favorite bands. It's a digital scrapbook, a collage of ephemera the girl decides is most representative of her true self. But there are hints of the gulf between today's teens and those of generations past. Check out one profile from a 16-year-old girl in Myrtle Beach who lists her sexual orientation as "not sure" and includes photos of both her boyfriend and her girlfriend; or another from a 17-year-old who has her own band and offers free downloads of her songs to MySpace browsers. Their blogs recount tales that are both refreshingly familiar and startlingly grown-up. They self-publish and promote. They are the kings and queens of their own domains.

Kids are increasingly sophisticated at a younger age, behaving more and more like grownups. According to a Mintel survey of nearly 6,000 children, 74 percent of girls ages 7 to 10 wear lipstick and 56 percent use perfume.[5] Teen Research Unlimited notes that 10 percent of teens are in possession of one or more credit cards, and another 20 percent have expressed interest in obtaining one.[6]

Teens are spending like their elders, with a sense of entitlement that's only spurred by such shows as VH1's *The Fabulous Life* and the MTV reality shows *Rich Girls* and *My Super Sweet 16*, along with the designer gowns showcased in *Teen Vogue*. Their buying patterns are becoming more reflective of the culture at large. Girls are amassing shoe and handbag collections that would make *Sex and the City*'s Carrie Bradshaw jealous, while boys are funneling their funds into techno gadgets, gaming devices, and plasma TVs. At a panel held by trend researcher WGSN in Los Angeles in 2005, teens were asked to name something they had recently bought with their own money. Responses included a Marc Jacobs necklace, a TV for the car, a Sony PSP game player, and a Motorola RAZR cell phone. "Materialism is way up this year," said Jim Taylor of market research firm Harrison Group in late 2005.[7]

Next: The Disappearing Generation Gap

It's no surprise that parents are increasingly treating kids more like peers. "PEERents" work through issues together with their children and share experiences candidly in a form of "collaborative parenting."

Teens and parents are talking much more freely about dating and sex. Four in ten teens say they talk with their parents about sex often, girls more so than boys, according to an NBC News/*People* magazine poll from January 2005.[8] Teenagers who are having intercourse are somewhat more likely to speak with their parents about sex. While teens learn about sex from various sources, a majority are well-informed by their parents: Seventy percent say they have gotten some or a lot of information about sex and sexual relationships from parents, with a little over half saying the same about friends, school, and TV and movies.

And though teenagers may still give their parents a hard time, the fact is that parents top the list of teen role models in a recent Junior Achievement Poll. More than a quarter of teens polled identified parents as the best role models for teens. (Next came teachers at 11 percent, and third was President Bush at 6 percent.)[9]

One over-the-top example of the disappearing generation gap is the MTV show *Date My Mom*. Three mothers each go out several times with a handsome young man and try to persuade him to choose their daughter for an intimate date. In between dates, the daughters and moms might chat about the guy's body or speculate on the size of his manhood. On one episode, a mother tells her daughter that she mentioned their "six inches rule" to the dater. The daughter playfully slaps her mother as they tell the camera how they love to talk about sex together.

Next: Adultescence Is the New Life Stage

When parents are more like peers, and times are tough anyway, why leave the cozy comforts of home? Many of today's late teens to late twentysomethings have settled at the crossroads between autonomous living and relying on the 'rents, stuck in a new life stage dubbed "adultescence." The stay-homes are variously called yo-yos or boomerangs; they're mammismos in Italy, where parents love having their grown children around so much that they pay them to stay, according to London School of Economics research.[10]

"It has happened quietly, and it's here to stay," says David Morrison, president of market research firm Twentysomething, Inc. "The stigma of depending on your parents is gone."[11] For many that means saving money by staying at home. More than 18 million Americans age 18 to 34 live with parents.[12] And according to a *Time* cover story, that means one in five 26-year-olds is still in a parent's home.[13]

Writer Rick Montgomery notes that the adultescent phenomenon is an international one: "Their numbers are multiplying worldwide: Germany calls them nesthockers, or nest squatters. Italy has charted a 50 percent increase since 1990 in mammones, or people who won't eat anywhere but mama's. In fast-growing Asian nations, living with the folks is the custom."[14] Canada's 2001 census revealed that 41 percent of twentysomethings were living with parents, a 27 percent increase since 1981.[15] In Australia the figure is similar: 36 percent of 20- to 29-year-olds live at home.[16]

These helicopter kids hover around the parental home for a variety of reasons: They're in debt from student and credit-card loans, and they can't afford to buy or even rent. They may have split up with a partner, or they may be delaying marriage, which isn't something you rush into anymore. As MSNBC puts it, "A seismic shift has occurred: A growing number of young adults are reassessing their lifestyles and mimicking the frugal habits of their Depression-era grandparents."[17]

Watch for more multigenerational households with adult children and their parents, or elderly parents who move in with their children and grandchildren. It's not so much a desire to return to the notion of extended family as a practical issue. Rising house prices mean we'll have to club together to buy or rent suitable homes, and a rapidly aging population will require taking more care of our nearest and dearest. In the United States the Census Bureau has already recognized this by adding new categories to its household questionnaire, including parent-in-law and son/daughter-in-law. Builders in the United States and Europe are constructing homes complete with annexes to provide some privacy either for older parents or boomerang kids.

Next: Adults in Name Only

"Real life," these twenty-somethings might find, is surprisingly similar to adolescence: Older adults now tend to enjoy the same media as teens and twentysomethings, dress similarly, and not really think of themselves as decades older. There is little difference between the lives of some people in their late 30s or 40s and those in their early 20s. In a *New York* magazine story on "Why nobody wants to be an adult anymore," TV writer and producer Michael Rauch talks about a slightly surreal visit to an undergraduate NYU class: "It was terrifying how much we had in common. I'm looking at these kids who look about 12, and we're all going to the same movies and watching the same TV shows and listening to the same music. I don't know if it's scarier for them or scarier for me."[18]

Similarly, *New York Times* shopping columnist Michelle Slatalla writes of being "a 44-year-old mother of three [who] looked in the mirror and saw a person impersonating one of her daughters."[19] Think also of Amy Poehler as the youth-obsessed mom trying to be one of the teens in *Mean Girls*. And when clothing chain Talbots took a detour from its conservative looks for older women and came out with rhinestone-embellished jeans, the youthful style proved to be a best-seller. "The 50-year-old woman today thinks of herself as 40," observes Talbots chief executive Arnold Zetcher in the *Boston Globe*.[20]

And 40 has lost some of its scare factor. It used to be that anyone in his or her 40s who hadn't settled into some form of genuine adulthood risked ridicule. Now, it's less a dreaded milestone marking the far edge of youth and more of a gateway into one's most productive, meaningful years.

"I'm 40 fucking 5 and proud of it."—Samantha on *Sex and the City*

Having long been overlooked—typically lumped in with baby boomers, even though their formative years did not overlap—today's fortysomethings are starting to feel their own distinctiveness as an age cohort. In some ways, however, they're behaving more like traditional thirtysomethings: still partying and dressing provocatively, looking young and glamorous, having babies in some cases, traveling, and saving next to nothing. (Whereas more thirtysomethings now have the worries of traditional 40-somethings, fretting about retirement, mortgage payments and life insurance.)

Forty and up is increasingly the norm as populations grow older. By 2000, the median age in Japan was 41, and in Europe it had reached 38.[21]

While the mass media is still overwhelmingly populated by those under 35, that's also slowly changing. *Sex and the City*'s Samantha hardly looked over the hill, and certainly lived it up like a twentysomething. Sharon Stone, now in her late 40s, reprised her risqué *Basic Instinct* role in the 2006 sequel, still playing a sexy seductress. Four of the five leading ladies on *Desperate Housewives* are over 40, all looking nothing like yesterday's notions of the middle-aged woman.

What's Next? Childhood Reigns

In Sweden and Finland, singalongs and sledding are becoming the new activities of choice for hip adults. Innocent simplicity is the order of the day.

Next: How Old Are You *Really?*

Age has increasingly become elusive, harder to detect, and there's more emphasis than ever on perpetuating that ambiguity. "Keep them guessing" is the crux of Crest's campaign for its Whitestrips Renewal product. "A lot of things can give away your age, especially your smile," says the promotion for the "Age Defying Strips." The strips can make teeth look brighter by removing up to 20 years of stains, Crest promises: "That way, when people wonder about your age, you can keep them guessing." A game on the Crest Web site has players try to match photos of women with the cultural markers of their age groups based on how old they look. For example, "In high school, I rocked out to . . ." is paired with generational answers like "heavy-metal hair bands," "hip-hop rappers," and "new wave bands." (Of course, the age gap between the women looks to be only about five years.)

There's also RealAge, a consumer-health media company, that posits a new way of thinking about age: "Your RealAge is the biological age of your body, based on how well you've maintained it."[22] Members can take an assessment test that balances the factors prematurely aging them with the things they're seemingly doing right and then yields an indication of biological age. The company promises to then teach you how "to look, feel, and actually be many years younger—to Live Life to the Youngest." RealAge also markets a series of books authored by doctors, from *The RealAge Workout* to *Cooking the RealAge Way* ("Turn back your biological clock with more than 80 delicious and easy recipes").

What's significant about the process and the mind-set is that age is touted as a conquerable biological condition. It can simply be modified with the right action plan. And when someone inquires about your age, you can qualify your response by offering your "real age." That way, as Revlon suggests with its line of anti-aging beauty products, you "don't lie about your age," you "defy it."

Next: Waging a War on Aging, Inside and Out

We may embrace the wisdom and advantages of age, but we're also desperate to appear more youthful. Defying the physical effects of aging is now a priority for all age groups, and we're willing to spend on the fountain of products and services that promise help. For some of us that means shelling out for anything that will reduce the appearance of wrinkles and fight the signs of aging, and for others, notably aging boomers, it's more about anti-aging products that promote health rather than merely affect appearance.

The beauty industry has undeniably tapped into and perpetuated the myth of eternal youth, and we're eating it up. Nearly 90 million American consumers are using or have used products or procedures to reduce their visible signs of aging, the National Consumers League reported in 2004.[23] What's hot now is over-the-counter products that claim to provide the benefits of plastic surgery at a drugstore cost. Oil of Olay's Regenerist Serum, for example, invites consumers to "Have Work Done" courtesy of a formula that "regenerates skin's appearance without such drastic measures as chemical peels, cosmetic surgery or laser."

And now you can pick up an at-home microdermabrasion kit along with your groceries. Supermarkets mirror department-store trends, says Kat Fay, an editor and consumer analyst at Mintel International, so they're stocking up on these DIY kits, along with a wider selection of anti-aging products.[24]

There are also the new cosmeceuticals, which boast "biologically active" ingredients that purport to do everything from preventing wrinkles and sun damage to diminishing skin discolorations and acne. Cosmeceuticals already represent a $12.4 billion market, one that's projected to grow 11 percent annually through 2008, reports *NutraCos*.[25]

While there may be simpler options, we're clamoring for the results of more extreme makeovers nonetheless. The number of people undergoing cosmetic surgical and nonsurgical procedures jumped 444 percent between 1997 and 2005, according to the American Society for Aesthetic Plastic Surgery. The Society reports that Americans spent almost $12.4 billion on the 11.5 million procedures performed in 2005.[26] The most popular procedure was Botox injections, and the most common surgical procedure was liposuction.

Also significant is the rise in the number of medical spas—which offer cosmetic care under a doctor's supervision—which doubled to 600 in the United States in 2004.[27] There's laser hair removal, scar and wrinkle reduction, medical microdermabrasion and acne treatment, Botox injections, and more, so that the new spa experience gives procedures as much weight as pampering.

Who's getting this work done? Both young (sometimes very young) and old, women and, increasingly, men. Teenagers are now asking for and getting breast implants or liposuction as graduation presents. The number of girls 18 and younger who got implants nearly tripled from 2002 to 2003, to more than 11,000, according to the American Society for Aesthetic Plastic Surgery.[28] Meanwhile, men are becoming just as paranoid as women about fighting off the pesky signs of aging. The American Academy of Facial Plastic and Reconstructive Surgery has seen a 60 percent increase in men getting nonsurgical cosmetic work since 2000 (versus 30 percent among women).[29]

The most common nonsurgical procedures that men choose: Botox injections, fat injections, and hair removal.[30]

Among boomers in particular, there's an intense concern with internal well-being as a way to turn back the clock. There's been a rise in clinics that specialize in anti-aging care, dispensing megadoses of supplements as well as controversial drugs like HGH, under the theory that the regimen helps preserve internal organs and stave off the aging process. *Business Week* notes that doctors can get certified by a professional group called the American Academy of Anti-Aging Medicine and quotes one mantra of practitioner Dr. Ron Rothenberg: "We are not prisoners of our destiny."[31]

Prescribing HGH for anti-aging purposes is illegal (pharmaceutical versions are intended largely for children with growth problems as well as some adults with serious medical issues), but "age management" doctors appear to be doing it anyway—and their patients are sometimes paying many hundreds of dollars out of pocket for the stuff. The substance has been linked to low blood sugar levels, and other possible side effects include heightened cholesterol levels and blood pressure. This brings up challenges for companies like Pfizer, which bought an HGH drug called Genotropin as part of an acquisition of Pharmacia in 2003.

In the push to prevent aging, more attention and money is going into the field of gerontology, the study of aging. One prevalent theory is that contrary to popular belief, humans are not biologically programmed to become decrepit and die; our repair and maintenance systems evolved to work hardest during the early years of life, but there is no "active mechanism for death and destruction," says Thomas Kirkwood, co-director of the Institute for Ageing and Health at Newcastle University in England.[32] "The aging process is malleable," according to Kirkwood. He explains that scientists are trying to discover how to enhance the body's protection systems in order to slow the accumulation of "unrepaired faults" in cells and tissues.

Until researchers make real breakthroughs, the manipulation of science as a solvent to aging bodies is only going to get more complex, and potentially more dangerous. After all, no one ever thought we'd happily inject ourselves with growth hormones or even diluted food poison, in the form of Botox.

Next: Seniors—Just Like Us!

As the population ages, the face of old age is changing. Senior citizenship ain't what it used to be. Seniors are looking less and less like the stereotypical images of old people and they are raising expectations of what getting old can be. After all, the Rolling Stones (who once sang, "What a drag it is getting old"), are still strutting the stage for stadium crowds: At their Super Bowl gig in February 2006, the youngest member of the band was 58. And they're not alone: David Bowie (who turns 60 in 2007) and Led Zeppelin's Robert Plant (in his late 50s) are among the aging but active rock 'n' rollers.

In most of the developed world and many parts of the developing world, the average 60-year-old grew up listening to rock 'n' roll. Many of the baby boomers who came of age in the late 1950s and 1960s identified closely with rebellious icons like Elvis Presley and then the Beatles, the Rolling Stones, and Bob Dylan. Those who did so were hugely influential, and set the tone for their age cohort and for the following generations. Today's seniors are still listening to rock 'n' roll, and loud, irreverent music is just a part of the youthful attitude they're taking into their 60s and beyond. In fall 2006, Bob Dylan's *Modern Times* is a best-selling album in the U.S., and the Rolling Stones are touring, attracting multiple generations to sold-out stadiums and concert halls worldwide.

When they were young, this generation expected to remake the world and its rules. They nurtured the notion that youth is a heroic condition and that middle age—never mind old age—represents dreary surrender. "I hope I die before I get old," sang The Who's Roger Daltrey some 40 years ago. But in his early 60s he's still around (and still performing), and many of his generation have likewise refused to surrender to old age.

> The global profile is increasingly old. People 60 and over represented 1 in 12 people alive in 1950 and 1 in 10 alive in 2000; by 2050, they will account for 1 in 5 people alive, to reach nearly 2 billion, according to UN figures.[33] And while there were just three countries with more than 10 million over-60-year-olds in 1950, there will be 33 by the middle of the 21st century; five countries will have more than 50 million seniors (China, India, the United States, Indonesia, and Brazil). Europe has the biggest proportion of over-60-year-olds, at around 20 percent of the population. More than a third of its population will be over 60 by 2050.

Of course, not all seniors are hell-bent on "growing old disgracefully." But many are redefining what is considered normal and even possible for the 60-plus group, exercising their taste for the wild side by snowboarding, going on adventure vacations, or riding Harleys. In the United States, the average age of people who buy the legendary bikes is 47.[34] Switched-on seniors buy into the expression "You're as old as you feel" in a big way, set on showing that calendar age is just a number, one that doesn't necessarily correlate with "real age."

> Now in her late 60s, Chickie Rosenberg was once a New Jersey high school teacher but for well over a decade she's worked as a snowboarding instructor in Vermont. "I don't have any nose or eyebrow rings," she told the *New York Times*. "But all my young friends look like that."[35]

The older demographic has plenty of money to indulge in sexy cars and new hobbies. Previous generations raised in tough times were inclined to fear the worst and spend cautiously. By contrast, today's swelling ranks of seniors have mostly known times of plenty, and they're not inclined to sit at home counting their money. They intend to make the best of life, even if that means "SKI-ing"— spending the kids' inheritance.

> Older folks are getting hip to online gaming: The 60-plus set is actually playing online games almost as much as their younger counterparts. About a third have played a game online, according to a survey by the Pew Internet & American Life Project.[36] Seniors are enjoying digital versions of old staples such as cards, chess or checkers, writes John Reinan in the *Star Tribune*.[37] It's not only a way to pass the time, but a means of keeping the mind active: In Japan, a Nintendo game called Brain Age, which presents a series of quick mental workouts, has sold more than 3 million copies, notes University of Minnesota Medical School assistant professor Anne Murray in the *Tribune*.

What's Next? Hen Lit One-ups Chick Lit

Chick Lit has provided literary mentoring for young women making their way in the world and figuring out what it means to be a woman today. But older women are interested in the plot as it evolves beyond chick-dom into the mature years of hen-dom.

Next: Love at Any Age

Senior seems to be sexier now. In the words of their generation's Marvin Gaye, boomers are still getting it on. A National Council on Aging study found that 71 percent of men in their 60s and 57 percent in their 70s engage in some kind of sexual activity at least once a month. The women aren't doing too badly either: 51 percent in their 60s and 30 percent in their 70s are active once a month.[38]

The magic blue pill, Viagra, has helped put swing back into the 60s and swagger into the 70s. Like the Viagra Web site suggests, "Because an empty nest is the chance to fall in love all over again. Because reading the Sunday paper doesn't take all day." Erectile dysfunction aids (Cialis and Levitra, along with Viagra) have made sex into something that's possible at any age. Men need now look only as far as Hugh Hefner to entertain a *Playboy* fantasy well into old age.

Older women too are more openly sexual these days. Gail Sheehy came out with *Sex and the Seasoned Woman* in 2006, telling women that "it's not over at 45."[39] Jane Juska got lots of buzz with her book *A Round-heeled Woman: My Late-Life Adventures in Sex and Romance*, in which she writes of what happened after she wrote a personal ad declaring, "I would like to have a lot of sex with a man I like" as she approached her 67th birthday.[40] Her latest book, *Unaccompanied Women: Late-Life Adventures in Love, Sex, and Real Estate*, continues the theme.

> "Viagra and nursing home orgies are frequent topics for Frank Kaiser, a Florida journalist whose column, 'Suddenly Senior,' is featured in 56 newspapers. His equally bawdy Web site of the same name gets more than 5 million hits a month."[41]

The dynamics of the relationships are changing too: Women are trending younger in selecting partners. England's *Yorkshire Post* reports, "While the sugar daddy is far from extinct, in these more emancipated times, a corresponding creature is on the rise: the sugar-mummy."[42] The new "yummy mummies" are giving older men a run for their money. A recent AARP report shows that a third of women over 40 are dating younger men.[43] And more May-December romances are becoming part of the mainstream: *The Chicago Daily Herald* notes the likes of Demi Moore (43) and Ashton Kutcher (28), Susan Sarandon (59) and Tim Robbins (48), Cameron Diaz (34) and Justin Timberlake (25); and gossip reports linked Diane Keaton with Keanu Reeves, 20 years her junior, in an off-screen version of their on-screen romance in *Something's Gotta Give*.[44]

What's behind this shift? Sex therapist Laura Berman, the talk-show host, tells the *Chicago Daily Herald* it's a boost in confidence: "Much of this trend shift can be attributed to the fact that women are much more independent than in years past. Not too long ago, older women were made to be uncomfortable with their sexuality."[45]

> Some swinging seniors are foregoing safe sex: The Centers for Disease Control and Prevention reported that seniors are one-sixth as likely to use condoms and one-fifth as likely to get tested for HIV as the younger generations[46]; in fact, HIV/AIDS cases among Americans over 50 quintupled since 1995.[47]

Just like their kids (and grandkids), many mature singles are turning to the Internet for potential dates. "Baby boomers are seeing their children use online dating, and watching their success at finding mates. They're seeing that it's not such a crazy concept,"[48] says Yahoo! Personals spokeswoman Rochelle Adams. The Yahoo site includes a column for those over 50, offering tips on etiquette and sexual health.

What's Next? More Demi-Ashton-Style Mergers

With women building their careers first and having kids later, if at all, "older woman marries younger man" is no longer so unusual.

Next: Redefining Retirement for
Love and Money

Getting older no longer means it's time to pack it in, both in terms of lifestyle and career. "Forget that dot-com-era idea of cashing out at 55, the wonks advise. Let 62, Social Security's 'early' retirement age, pass, and its 'full' retirement ages, too. Seventy is the new 65," writes Paula Span in *The Washington Post*.[49]

Dot-comers cashed in their soaring tech stocks and welcomed early retirements. But that was a unique economic bubble. More people now are actually postponing retirement: They want to stay in the game, and they want to keep their incomes, too. It's about meaning and money. "Their perception of themselves as forever young is tied to having a job," observes Sara Rix of the AARP's Public Policy Institute. A Roper Starch Worldwide survey found that as many as 80 percent of people 45 and older plan to continue working in their "retirement" years; more than a third of those said they'll stay on for the pure enjoyment of work.[50] With the prospect of longer, healthier lives than past generations, many will simply need more cash. And as senior citizenship approaches, many don't have it. According to Rix, "Maybe a third to a half are on track to maintaining their living standards. The rest we should worry about."[51]

Next: Global Push to Beat Poverty
in Retirement

Will the retirement years ever come? Says Liz Pullman on MSN Money, "Social Security's in trouble. Pensions are biting the dust. America's savings rate is abominable. And every time you turn around, some pundit is warning that if you haven't already put aside some vast sum—the number changes, but it's always immense—then you have no hope of ever retiring."[52] More people will certainly linger in the job market, but for those unwilling or unable to keep working, the financial strain of retirement will have an economic impact across the generations.

Many of us around the globe will be lucky just to make ends meet. According to a study conducted by Virgin Money, more than 8 million British workers have no pension provision. The situation is so dire that Virgin Money capitalized on the business opportunity by offering a "free for a year" program to anyone who opened a pension plan, and the company made a contribution to the plan. The promotion, said chairman Richard Branson, was intended to "spur more people into taking action now to avoid falling into pensioner poverty later."[53]

As the United States grapples with how to revamp the Social Security and Medicare programs, these mainstays have become tenuous and uncertain. What's next? A U.S. Census report shows that the fastest-growing segment of the population is age 85 and older, and by 2030, nearly one in five Americans, or 72 million people, will be over 65.[54] Watch as more companies, in the spirit of the Virgin Money offer, balance compassion with commission and start offering products and services that help seniors pinch their pennies.

Next: Sandwich Generation Feels the Squeeze

It's not just older folks who will be drained of cash but the generation taking care of them as well. For the sandwich generation, the children are only just moving out when Grandma moves in.

According to the AARP Public Policy Institute, an estimated 44 million Americans are providing unpaid assistance to elder parents, aunts, uncles, grandparents and other adults with disabilities who need support.[55] Elder care is becoming a cultural phenomenon, and it's only going to grow; in just about ten years, there will be "78 million demanding, sassy, aging baby boomers," as *The Seattle Times* calls them, commanding their families' care and attention.[56]

Elder care will become a huge drain on people's pockets. Most boomers will barely have saved enough to cover their own care when the time comes for them to cash it in. The physical and emotional strain will take a major toll on caregivers' patience and stamina, too.

In response, watch for a new emphasis on care for both the elderly and the caregiver. To give those tending to relatives a break, a growing number of U.S. states have initiated tax breaks and support programs with services such as in-home respite and private aids. Companies will need to find ways to help employees distracted by elder care issues, such as expanding family-leave policies to include time off for caregivers. One of the next big public health topics will be the strain of the sandwich generation, stretched between child care and elder care.

Businesses will work hard to tap this market via products and services that help to ease the pain and pressure for caregivers. Comfort Keepers, for example, ranked by *Entrepreneur Magazine* as one of the top 500 franchises in 2006, offers seniors non-medical care, companionship, meal prep, light housekeeping, and even recreational activities—services that give the stressed-out sandwich set a much-needed break.[57]

And Therefore Next

What do "ages and stages" all really mean today? It comes down to a quite traditional adage whose time has come: Age is just a number. And the number continues to become less relevant, except to those who ply monetary advantage from making sure that it remains just so and cater to a whole new set of demands from the "forever young."

chapter eight

big next: new identities

We live in a world of constant change. Borders are broken, and cultures are crossed; the world is a pastiche of this and that. We talk in terms of makeovers and renovations and being born again and reinvented. There used to be clear markers of identity like nationality and religion that left little room for ambivalence, but today identity is evolving, in flux, and how we define it is becoming more a matter of choice. (In fact there's so much choice now that stealing someone's identity is common practice, if only for economic gain.)

In 2005, there were 8.9 million cases of identity theft in the United States alone, according to the Better Business Bureau.[1]

At the root of the concept of identity is the idea of a core self that remains the same even under varying conditions. But now, identity is more tenuous. English sociologist Zygmunt Bauman proposes that we live in "liquid modern times," an era of rapid change in which our identities undergo regular transformations. Identity, he says, has become transient and precarious. It's no surprise that we're inventing new ways of defining ourselves if you consider that today jobs can change and become obsolete at the whim of the market, seemingly permanent relationships come to abrupt ends, boundaries are constantly evolving, sexuality is shifting, and we live in both online and offline worlds that blur together. It's adaptation, a survival mechanism.

Essentially, our identities in all spheres—from politics and culture to sexuality and nationality—are taking on new forms. We're no longer readily defined as either one thing or another but are often two things at once, sometimes many at once: traditional but also modern, sophisticated yet simple at heart, all-American yet steeped in other cultures, too. Consider the appeal of organic farmer MaryJane Butters, who landed a $1.35 million deal to write for "the farmgirl in all of us."[2] The idea tugs at the dilemmas and dualities of the modern urban woman, trying to be a homemaker and breadwinner at the same time.

Identity shifts across age groups, with different generations defining themselves around evolving life priorities. The boomer's life has tended to revolve around work, with family sacrificed for career; it's a generation that started working in the days when jobs were for life, then had to adapt to economic instability. Generation X arrived to unstable work conditions and has constantly grappled with how to balance life and work. For Generation Y, home and family are central to identity—while work is important, it has to fit with one's values and priorities, not the other way around.

There's also a rising sense of regionalism, driven by a sense of common identity and common interests, which presents new complexities. People united by geography may well have different cultural and/or religious affinities (Muslim Indonesia vs. the Christian Philippines, Hindu India vs. Muslim Pakistan and Bangladesh, the Anglo-Saxon United States and Canada vs. Hispanic Mexico and Central America). There are even red states and blue states. On the largest scale, nations in big geographical regions are coming together: Southeast Asia, North America, Europe, Africa, the Caribbean. On a smaller scale are such groupings as the Nordic countries and several nations in South America. At the smallest end of the scale are regions that are asserting their identities and interests within the larger political entities to which they belong: Scotland and Wales in the U.K., Corsica and Brittany in France, and Catalonia and the Basque country in Spain.

Also born out of the quest to find commonality and meaning in precarious times are new subcultures of identity. Take the notion of Desi culture, a term used by many diasporic South Asians to define themselves without specific reference to a state or nation. While their nations and cultures are quite diverse and clearly distinguished at home, these Indians, Pakistanis, Sri Lankans, and others choose to identify as Desi abroad as a way to bind themselves together as countrymen. Desi is about finding similarities and maintaining meaning as the cultures of East and West mix and mingle. It's diversity with homogeneity.

Perhaps it's just because it's what we do, but we can't help thinking that brands will also become a more important part of what we use as identity. They seem to say something about the user (in a language the rest of the culture understands). The more times change and the world changes, the more we'll choose to invent and clone new identities to help us preserve our self-interest and our sense of self.

Next: Name Changing Is an Identity Game

People personalize their stakes in identity through their names. And in "liquid times," with identity more a matter of choice than anything else, more people and businesses are choosing to change their names.

Corporate name changes were up 12 percent between 2004 and 2005, according to *Business 2.0*, largely as a result of companies that needed a cleaner image (WorldCom changing back to MCI, for example) or mergers and acquisitions. "Suddenly, renaming has become a big priority for many companies," observes the magazine.[3]

And these days, more women are inclined to buck the feminist trend and adopt their husband's name. In 1990, 23 percent of college-educated women kept their birth names, but in 2000 the number was down to 17 percent. It's a trend that's been ongoing: Only about a third of female Harvard grads kept their birth names in 1990, compared with 44 percent in 1980, according to research by Harvard's Claudia Golden cited in Maureen Dowd's book *Are Men Necessary?*[4] There's clearly a keen interest in taking on a new identity, although debate continues about the reasons behind it, whether there's a resistance to being tagged an "old-school feminist" or a desire to show that one is off the market.

Nicknames, too, have become more prevalent. Mark Jacob, a *Chicago Tribune* editor, notes that 2005 was a year in which " 'Deep Throat' was exposed, 'God's Rottweiler' became pope, and Joey 'the Clown' Lombardo went on the lam." The U.S. president is often referred to simply as Dubya, and he has his own penchant for renaming and nicknaming, referring to Russian President Vladimir Putin as "Pootie-Poot" and columnist Dowd as "Cobra." To Jacob, the colorful names signify "a healthy civilization that views people as fascinating characters, not just as census statistics."[5] Nicknames also reflect the rising importance of individual identity—not surprising when you consider the blurring lines of reality and celebrity and how quickly an average Joe can ascend to stardom. It's identity invention and brand building on the part of the name caller and the recipient.

Nicknaming and renaming are ways to mask or enhance old identities and create new ones. People accept these changes and are drawn to the possibility of redefinition. Brands that perpetuate this ideology will be more in than out.

Next: Modern and Traditional Identities
Meet in the Middle

Where we are born and the times in which we live may be out of our control, but how we choose to interpret meaning in our surroundings is more a personal decision than ever. At play in the essence of our identities is a mix of the modern and traditional so that we embrace the momentum of the future while encapsulating the traditions of the past.

Queen Rania of Jordan is an über-model of mingled values. She chooses modern mores to express herself and approach her role, but stands firm in her fidelity to the traditions of her Arab nation. She does not wear a veil but, notes *Psychology Today*, she is "quick to point out that this does not diminish the strength of her faith in Islam."[6] Al Jazeera makes note that she's one of the world's best-dressed women, among a list of other accomplishments. Queen Rania may not wear the Muslim woman's traditional garb, but she stands as a powerful figure in the Middle East. By heritage a traditional Muslim, she opts to self-define with the symbols and styles of a modern Western woman, drawing attention to herself as a woman, a queen, and a fashion plate.

While Madonna is often cited as the ultimate shape shifter and image inventor, there's another singer and performer who's playing with identity in a way that's perhaps even more postmodern. Deeyah, a Norwegian-born Muslim pop star, is making dramatic waves with her open-minded, Western take on the modern Islamic woman. Dubbed the Muslim Madonna and the Asian J. Lo, Deeyah endured death threats for a video featuring the faces of women who died in honor killings projected onto her bare back. More controversial: She also strips from burka to bikini. Even her name defies pigeonholing. On her Web site, a frequently asked question is whether she's Hindu; the response is that while Deeyah is traditionally a Hindu name, "she was born to Muslim parents. It is ridiculous to assume that she must have an Arabic name to be considered Muslim."[7] Deeyah is at work reconciling herself between the worlds of the modern and the traditional, a place marked by a blend of extreme dualities.

In response to the backlash against her video, Deeyah was defiant: "I am amazed to find that most people seem drawn to the final scene where the burka drops and I enter the pool. . . . The images of hangings, shootings and brutal executions seem to have been decidedly ignored by many in the South East Asian community. I guess they find skin is a bigger sin than murder."[8]

The tug between these worlds is also evident in the rise of an American simplicity movement. It's a harkening back to the land and the pesticide-free basics of organics and rural living. In our modern technological society, we yearn to recreate simpler times. It's why MaryJane Butters received such a sizable advance to write about her brand of basic living. As *The Oregonian* says, Clarkson Potter, her publisher, was banking not on the rural buyer but on "downtown—a critical mass of urban women, and maybe a few men, willing to buy into the romance of an organic and environmentally satisfying country life. Butters—or at least Clarkson Potter—is selling a dream."[9] This is not a small demographic that's looking for the calm and plain pleasures of country life. Americans feel consumed by their own consumption and fantasize about shedding the trappings of modern existence for a back-to-the-roots rural life.

MaryJane's Ideabook, Cookbook, Lifebook is a mix of stories and domestic-arts lessons on old-time essentials like tending chickens, making butter, planting a garden, and chopping wood. Sociologist Bernard Beck, a professor at Northwestern University, says the theme has tapped a need in these future-forward times: "It's a . . . message going back to the founding of America. Go back to your land. It's a life of simplicity, of human scale. . . . It also shows a dissatisfaction with the way things are going. In recent years, there's a retro culture, a sense that things used to be better, a yearning to return to an earlier time."[10] The notion that we can learn something from the past is also evident in the title of Butters' latest book, *MaryJane's Farmgirl Wisdom*.

A dual American identity is emerging: We want to keep moving ahead but not be blind to where we came from. High speed but able to slow down. Complex and sophisticated, but simultaneously plain and simple.

Next: Identity through the Ages

There's real potency in the possibility of reinventing ourselves at any age. Teenagers today tend to be characterized by a positive attitude, compared with the trademark apathy of the grungy Generation X before them. They're outward- rather than inward-focused, interested more in politics and culture than consumerism. And they're hungry for social change. A study on generational differences in political attitudes by Frank N. Magid Associates, a research-driven consulting group, indicates that today's youth are "more likely than other generational groups to favor specific governmental policies to reduce economic differences in America, ameliorating social and economic conditions as a way of dealing with crime, and to tolerate or even endorse alternative lifestyles such as same-sex marriage."[11]

What's also significant is that the size of this group, defined as "transitional millennials" (ages 18–22) and "cusp millennials" (23–28), will make it a political powerhouse. "The generational political differences we've uncovered will likely become more pronounced over the next 10 years as millennials take their place as the largest generation . . . and therefore potentially the most politically influential generation in history,"[12] notes Jack MacKenzie, senior vice president of Frank N. Magid Associates.

Their generational identity is framed by an outlook that achieving great things is possible in all spheres: political, economic, social, technological. In particular, identity is very tied to community, which will mean technological advances that will give people more ways to connect with one another. After all, this is the generation most keen on social networking sites like MySpace and Facebook. This group also encourages the expression of individual identity. Respect is now sought and accorded on the basis of creative aspirations and personal projects.

It's the "me and you" generation. For Western youth at least, family and friends are crucial to their sense of self. They live in urban tribes, or communities of peers, consisting of a rotating network of friends and acquaintances with whom they keep track and keep in touch, if only through online networks. There's a recognition that friends and family offer something real and meaningful, a desire to define oneself as part of that network rather than through work. And since this generation was weaned into a world of second and third marriages, donor insemination, single parents, and new takes on the family unit, there's an especially keen interest in forming and maintaining tight bonds, no matter how they're defined.

Contrast this with the boomers, whose sense of self seems to be in flux. As the Magid study points out, they "tend to take more extreme positions on most issues, but cannot be typecast as either liberal or conservative across a broad range of issues currently facing America."[13] That may be because they came of age politically during the turbulent 1960s and 1970s, notes the study, but what's clear is that boomers are also polarized in their worldview. They're looking forward and they're also looking back.

At midlife, boomers are rediscovering the simplicity of their youth. There's nostalgia for comfort foods and home cooking. Many of the recipes requested on the Food Network site, for example, are from Paula Deen, a midlifer who prides herself on good old-fashioned comfort food served up Southern-style.[14] Nostalgia is big business. "From child-oriented snack products to high-end fashion, retro brand licensing is producing some interesting partnerships," according to *In Store* magazine.[15] These co-branded efforts include such partnerships as the one between traditional shirt maker Thomas Pink and MGM's Pink Panther character. *In Store* notes that for boomers, the character lends a sense of old familiarity, while their kids appreciate its vintage cool. Diane McGrath, global head of licensing at Reckitt Benckiser, says, "A lot of people born before 1964 have these characters active in their minds. Secondly, the whole retro thing appeals to a younger generation—in many ways these characters are simpler and nicer than contemporary ones."[16]

The boomer identity is future-forward and backward-looking, a duality personified in boomer music. Look at the longevity enjoyed by the likes of the Rolling Stones and Paul McCartney, now all in their 60s; their staying power has even earned them coveted halftime spots at recent Super Bowls. (Interestingly enough, it was during the two years following Janet Jackson's infamous "wardrobe malfunction"—perhaps the gun-shy networks thought that guys with a bit more maturity, not the mention the imprimatur of the MBE, would be a safer bet.)

These classic rock acts allow boomers to relive youthful pleasures. Michael Hill at *The Baltimore Sun* writes, "A Stones concert might be a high-priced oldies show, nothing more than a nostalgia wallow for well-off baby boomers. Or it might be a trip to an incredible museum, displaying some of the works of rock's golden age, the years 1965 to 1975, when the Stones were at their best."[17] Boomers may be focused on a golden future, but they just can't take their eyes off the past.

Next: Transcending Real and Virtual Borders

The Internet presents any number of dualities: It's a source of infinite information, but it's muddled with misleading facts and untruths; its users can explore free of limits and border constraints, but they're prone to crossing boundaries where they shouldn't; it promotes diversity, but people end up in homogenous clusters (like looks for like).

Walter Humes, education professor at Scotland's University of Aberdeen, offers the theory that the Internet and its dualities play an important role in notions of personal identity. In the 19th century, identity was perceived as "relatively fixed," Humes writes. "This can be seen in the great novels of the period in which characters may sometimes lose their way for a time but eventually find their 'true selves.'" He observes that "20th century writers, influenced by Freudian psychology, offer a much more fluid and elusive view of human character and indeed often present the search for identity as a never-ending quest."[18] In this century, Humes suggests, the anonymity of the Internet allows this quest to enter new territory, giving us the means to explore aspects of ourselves that normal social situations never allowed: People can "set up multiple screen names, create fictitious profiles of themselves and enter chat rooms where they can present themselves in ways that their friends and families might not recognize. In a sense, they can become whoever they want to be."[19]

According to a Pew Internet & American Life Project survey on how Americans use Instant Messaging, a third of IM users have posted a profile for their screen names that people not on their buddy list can see.[20]

Modern identity is all about choice, and the Internet serves as a fluid and open medium in which to express one's identity—or even identities. There's a world of people and information available to the masses that has certainly helped to expand worldviews and understanding or, at the very least, has opened lines of communication. "Now, any 18-year-old with a modem is just a click away from a universe of fellow travelers, and to me, that's a good thing," commented author and cultural critic Mark Dery at a *Time* magazine panel on trends most likely to affect our future.[21] But Esther Dyson, the digital-technology entrepreneur, cautioned that identity is similar in any realm: "The Internet is like alcohol in some sense. It accentuates what you would do anyway. If you want to be a loner, you can be more alone. If you want to connect, it makes it easier to connect."[22]

Discussion at the *Time* panel centered on virtual and geographic boundaries and how they affect who we are. The lack of borders opens minds to the new and novel. With the growth in low-fare airlines like JetBlue and Southwest, the rise in travel across real boundaries has made discovering the uniqueness of places from Milwaukee to Montreal a common experience. The same is true in Europe, where easyJet has made Athens, Cannes, and Geneva readily accessible. And that's led to "new geographical identities," as author Malcolm Gladwell says. "Many working people today travel who never could have in the past, for meetings and conferences and all kinds of things, and this is creating another identity for them." Some interesting twists on modern life and identity evolve from all this travel, including a rise in transnationalism, noted Gladwell: "There are pockets in Queens [N.Y.] that maintain active ties with home in Mexico. If you extrapolate, I don't think foreign policy or any kind of politics can be practiced the way it is now in a country where enormous numbers of people genuinely have dual identities and reinforce them by flying back and forth to their adoptive countries for nothing."[23]

The blending of cultures has created significant opportunities for new forms of expression. Or as Gladwell says, "We're talking about the multiplication of identities so that in addition to the strong national identities, you start to construct new ones." As we grapple with who we are and manage our dual identities and split personalities, the brands we use to define ourselves will be more important than ever as markers of meaning in both our virtual and real lives.

And Therefore Next

Of all the factors in modern life that are subject to the upheavals of change, perhaps identity is the most significant—it is, after all, who we are (or, at least, what we want to project as who we are). And today, when we can change identities with the same frequency and facility with which we change our clothes, we may be hard-pressed to choose precisely what we want to wear. With so many choices (all a mouse click away), the permanent is becoming mutable. The question becomes, Will *they* know who we are? Do we care?

chapter nine

big next: our branded universe

Like the features of a landscape or the buildings of a cityscape, the brands in a brandscape meld together to form a unified whole with just a few standout features: Picture the thousands of colored packages that crowd the aisles and shelves of any modern store, the advertising pages of magazines, the streets of most modern cities, and the head space of anyone who lives in any modern consumer society. (And if you're living in an emerging market, buckle your seatbelt, because the deluge of brands has only just begun.)

For better or worse, brands and branding are among the most fundamental features of modern consumer societies. The names will vary by country—although big global brands are almost everywhere now—but whatever part of the connected world we're in, an important part of our lives takes place within the vast brandscape. You can tell how connected people and societies are with the wider world by how they think about brands. And while a person may or may not be a fan of international brands like Coca-Cola, Nike, McDonald's, Toyota, and Apple, someone who has never heard of any of them is either living in the back of beyond or has been on a self-imposed retreat for a few decades.

Imagine that Americans have upward of 800,000 to 1 million registered names in their personal brand vocabulary, and many more pop up every day: TNS Media Intelligence reckons it adds some 400 to 700 brands to its tracking list daily—yes, that's every 24 hours. Overall, it tracks around 2.1 million brands.[1] The brandscape evolves almost overnight, and as we reflect on the original *Next* a decade after its first publication, in many ways it seems the brandscape we confronted then, and the "infrastructure" on which it was built, were a kind of "third world."

> In India, which only recently opened up as a free-market economy, the number of advertised brands jumped fivefold from a little under 15,000 in the late 1990s to about 76,000 by 2003, according to *The India Times*. New brands advertising in TV and print skyrocketed from just 3,800 products to 20,000 in 2003.[2]

What's significant about this new technology is that it's fulfilling our vision of an instant-gratification universe. A decade ago, we saw the beginnings of this mind-set and the development of a fundamentally new view of time:

> Having made new technologies a part of our lives, we want everything faster than ever before. Anything that's not immediate is s-l-o-w. Same-day delivery. Instant news. Nuked meals. DirecTV. PC banking. Increasingly, we have no patience for products and services we can't access right NOW. And, of great commercial significance, our satisfaction with brands increasingly is defined by immediacy rather than quality of service. In North America, in particular, retailers are discovering that customers aren't willing to wait till the store reopens at 9 a.m. to buy a quart of milk. We want it now—and we'll get it, whether via a competitor that stays open late or a 24-hour convenience store. The result is a burgeoning number of 24-hour retail establishments, from bookstores to copy shops to doughnut shops.[3]

Still, back then we were in the nascent days of the Internet, and dial-up modems were the norm—we'd just advanced to a 56.6 kbps world. Today, we are much closer to living in a true real-time, on-demand world. The one element most responsible for modifying our view of the brandscape since we wrote *Next* is the simple notion of time and speed.

> What's in a brand name? Consider this: Branding site TippingSprung.com reports that 79 unlucky patients in the United States who were meant to receive either Zyrtec, an antihistamine, or Zyprexa, an antipsychotic, ended up taking the wrong drug because the two bear such similar names. Eli Lilly is now labeling its drug as ZyPREXA, with the letters highlighted in yellow.[4]

Next: Branding—The Bigger Truth

Branding is deceptive. The vast majority of people who think about brands and branding think of them as being part of the paraphernalia that marketers use to sell more stuff. Ask most people about brands and branding, and they'll talk about logos, jingles, advertising, and catch phrases. There's no arguing with that; it's true, but it's one part of a bigger truth.

Ask people who make their living from brands and branding, and you'll get broader, deeper, and more varied views. It's a topic that has exercised many fine minds for many years. Amazon returns more than 6,400 books with "brand" in the title, sometimes used multiple times, like Philip Kotler and Martin Lindstrom's *Brand Sense: Build Powerful Brands through Touch, Taste, Smell, Sight, and Sound* and *How Brands Become Icons: The Principles of Cultural Branding*, by D. B. Holt. And while what they all say is also true, but it's still only part of a bigger truth.

Here's the bigger truth: Branding started out as a part of the commercial world and was peripheral to most people's worldview, but it has become a fundamental part of how we think about modern life. The idea of branding has infused every aspect of our world—think, for example, of how Darwin's notion of evolution applied only to biology when it was put forward in the 19th century but has since become a standard way of understanding how organisms and organizations change over time.

Similarly, as we explain here, the notion of "brand" is now applied not only to tangible consumer products but also to companies, places, people, and political parties, and even to intangibles such as Web sites and concepts. The widespread use of a marketing term, "brand," for such things shows just how far the terminology of free markets has shaped the thinking of society as a whole. At the risk of wheeling out an overused buzzword, brands and branding are part of a new paradigm in thinking about identity.

Next: Branding Is the Language of More than Business

The modern branding mind-set is new, but it has deep roots. People have long used symbols and patterns to identify themselves. In Scotland, the clans wore distinctive tartans (plaids) that are still instantly recognizable. Knights developed coats of arms, later passed down through families; military regiments had their "colors"; and nations developed flags. One of the earliest commercial logos was devised by the Medici banking family of Florence, arguably *the* proto-capitalists; starting in the 13th century, they could be instantly identified by the "palle" (balls) that distinguished their family emblems. And, as many branding texts have pointed out, the word "brand" itself comes from the practice of marking cattle using a distinctive iron (or "brand," meaning a flaming torch).

Identity and symbols of identity have been with us for a long time, but it's only in the last decade or so that it has become commonplace to think of them in terms of branding. Maybe it's a result of the inexorable spread of free markets since the fall of the Soviet empire in the late 1980s. By 1997, management guru Tom Peters was urging people to think of themselves as brands: In "The Brand Called You," an article that appeared in *Fast Company*, Peters argued that we're all CEOs of Me, Inc.[5]

The branding bug has also bitten nations and their leaders. During its first flush of enthusiasm, the government of Tony Blair set about updating crusty perceptions of the U.K. with a rock-and-design image-building campaign to update Brand Britain. With tourism a major global industry, countries around the world have seized on branding as a way to highlight their distinctive appeal (New Zealand, Australia, South Africa, Spain, and Ireland to name but a few). And, in the aftermath of 9/11, President Bush appointed advertising veteran Charlotte Beers to tackle the daunting task of rebranding America—the first of several people to take on that challenge.

Next: Branding Is Identity

So while branding is still about business, it's about much more, too. It's how we look at one of the oldest and most basic issues facing individuals and groups: identity. Branding is the "now" way of thinking about crucial questions such as "Who am I?" and "Who do I belong with?" Or "How do I show who I am?" and "How do I tell the difference between Us and Them?"

What distinguishes "brand" from other ways of talking about identity (gestalts or concepts, for example) is that it implies a transactional relationship: buying and selling. It may be buying and selling in a literal sense, or—increasingly—it may be "buying into," as in buying into what Brand America or Body Shop stands for. Thinking in terms of Me, Inc., is essentially about packaging and presenting oneself in the most advantageous way so as to attract attention and engage in transactions with others; it may be as a prospective co-worker or consultant, or as a potential lover or spouse. The implications for free agents are astonishing, and they will become more so in the near future: Imagine having to understand your essence and develop a tagline around it to stay in the game and win.

What's Driving the Branded Universe?

Next: Living With Strangers: Social mobility and the decline of stable communities have undermined old pillars of identity. People used to live in the same area, work in the same organization, and attend the same place of worship their whole life. They knew each other from school and work. Everyone in the area could identify others by subtle markers such as where they lived, where they shopped, and the way they dressed. Now that's increasingly less the case. People change jobs and work with strangers, they move to cities where they know nobody, and they are quite likely to share neighborhoods with people of very different cultures and backgrounds. Shared means of identification are weakened or gone, but thanks to the media, people are learning new shared ways of thinking about identity. And those new ways take their cues and their techniques from branding.

Next: Mass, Borderless Media: Brands have been around for a long time, but the modern discipline of branding is the child of mass media and mass markets that may be far from the brand's home. Branding has evolved as the standard approach for an entity (product, service, corporation, and so on) to project and establish an identity among strangers and to influence their perceptions of that entity. As people participate in markets, consciously or unconsciously they absorb the branding mind-set. They become "marketing literate." Brands are now a lingua franca, the common language of the consumer universe, and branding is the grammar of that shared language. When it comes to creating and projecting individual identities, branding is the natural route for people educated by consumer media and markets.

Next: Dealing with Crowds and Hyperchoice: Brands help people find their way in a crowded, complex world full of bewildering choices. The more economies evolve—from providing a basic selection of unpackaged commodities to offering a complex range of packaged products from far and near—the more strongly companies must rely on branding to differentiate their products. In the old Soviet economy, goods were scarce and brands were irrelevant; people stood in lines for hours to buy whatever new supplies became available. In the post-Soviet economies, and even more so in the new China, people have many more choices and are embracing brands with a passion.

Mobile phones are one story. In Beijing, Shanghai, and Guangzhou, not a single local brand penetrates the top five, despite price points 50 percent (or more) below Nokia, Motorola, and Siemens. Cell phones represent a revolution in personal communications. They are also the most powerfully public means of projecting individualism. A young person's "cool" is more than tangentially correlated with his mobile phone "badge." It is a personalized calling card, both literally and figuratively.[6]

Next: Competition for Business and Attention: Increasingly, people need to differentiate themselves from the competition in much the same way that brands do. When people had stable jobs in stable organizations, they could rely on their co-workers to know who they were and what they were capable of. Their career did not necessarily rely on standing out from the crowd. But with corporate downsizing and workers jumping (or being pushed) into becoming "free agents," people are vying for attention and assignments, and turning to branding to create a memorable professional identitiy.

Financial reward and career success are not the only things motivating people to stand out from the crowd. In our all-pervasive celebrity culture, many people hanker for recognition of their own, for acknowledgment, for acclaim, and here, too, branding is the natural reflex.

Next: Affordable Branding: Until very recently, only corporations with deep pockets had the resources to do serious branding. Only they could afford the services of graphic designers and marketing professionals, and the high cost of media placements. The Internet has removed that barrier, allowing individuals and small companies to project their brands globally at very little expense. Anyone can have a Web site, whether it be to showcase one's services, sell products, or just share a hobby. And it's not even necessary to have a site of one's own: People can rent space on blog sites and social networking sites to establish their brand. With the Internet now part of the fabric of everyday life, the question is shifting from "Do you have a Web site?" to "Why don't you have a Web site?"

This doesn't mean the world has become filled with polished, coherent, and compelling brands. As with corporations, so with individuals and small companies: A few brands are hot (or cool), professional, and together, but many are cobbled together on the fly, with little thought and even less understanding of how other people see them.

Next: The Brand Called Me

In the same year that Tom Peters wrote "A Brand Called You" for *Fast Company*, Dan Pink, a contributing editor at the magazine, spread the notion of the "Free Agent Nation," which subsequently became a successful book. Free agents are arguably creating an alternative to the classic notion of a capitalist society, as laid out by the father of communism, Karl Marx: Workers (or labor) create wealth by operating the means of production, which are owned by the bourgeoisie (or capitalists), who profit from the surplus value (the difference between the cost of workers and machinery, and what they sell the products for). Now, free agents control some of the means of production.

During the 1980s and 1990s, when many corporations started cutting costs by downsizing, also known as "getting rid of people," many of the key tools of business were dropping in price and becoming accessible to ordinary people. Workers who had been ousted from corporate life, or who opted to leave, could readily equip themselves with the tools of their trade (that is, the means of production)—computers, fax machines, copiers, sophisticated phones, and so on— and do much the same work outside corporations as they had done on the inside.

The upside is that some free agents now may even be better equipped with the latest "means of production" than their corporate counterparts, with the added advantage of being able to set their own fee levels and plan their days more flexibly. The downside is that free agents can't depend on the corporation for branding, marketing, and getting in front of hot prospects. They have to market themselves.

Fortunately, the tools for doing so are now readily accessible: There are plenty of freelance HR people and recruitment consultants keen to advise fellow free agents on how best to present themselves. There are plenty of freelance graphic designers and Web site builders out there to help free agents put together the basic materials. And there are numerous ways to get the word out: Monster.com, for example, acts as a virtual employment agency, allowing members to post a personal profile and a resume online so that employers can seek them out. Offline networking is proliferating, with breakfast meetings, lunches, briefings, seminars, and retreats for people keen to project their personal brand.

> "You don't 'belong to' any company for life, and your chief affiliation isn't to any particular 'function.' You're not defined by your job title and you're not confined by your job description. Starting today you are a brand. You're every bit as much a brand as Nike, Coke, Pepsi, or the Body Shop."
>
> —Tom Peters, "The Brand Called You"[7]

Next: Brands at Hyperspeed

How long does it take for a brand to become a serious force? There's no standard answer, but savvy brands can now do it very fast—certainly a lot faster than they used to, a trend we expected to see more of in 1997:

> When we consider brands for the future (a.k.a. millennium brands), it's clear to us that, whether classic or newly minted, these brands will share a capacity to be reinvented, reinterpreted, and reoriented at an extraordinary rate. Rather than be motivated by a chameleonlike hypocrisy, such change will be an extension of the brand's guiding force.[8]

Globalized markets, globalized media, and interactive technology have made it possible for brands to shoot from nowhere to everywhere in very little time. It took McDonald's decades of bricks-and-mortar franchising and expensive marketing to get to the point where young kids instantly recognize the trademark golden arches. It has taken Google much less than a decade to become the automatic first point of call for schoolkids researching a class project or their latest idol.

It's because the Internet takes branding into completely new territory, both literally and metaphorically. It facilitates much more intense relationships between consumers and those brands that know how to really use the Web.

Compare the Internet with television. The brand of the TV set itself has little impact on the viewing experience, and viewers generally tune out the branded messages pushed at them by commercials. Occasionally an advertiser finds the alchemist touch and turns the base metal of a "buy this product" message into the gold of a commercial that people really enjoy and take to heart. But in most cases, the only brands to build a truly intensive bond with consumers through television have been program brands, especially cult shows (*The X-Files, The Simpsons*, and so on). TV is an environment where most commercial brands are unwelcome intruders.

Online, consumers (that's you and us, and everyone all of us know) actively seek out brands such as Google, eBay, Yahoo!, Monster, Match.com, and Amazon. These are facilitator brands that serve a specific function for consumers. People interact with them for many minutes, even hours every week, and this enables them to evaluate the brand's performance moment by moment. Brands that live on the Internet or through the Internet achieve a hands-on, eyes-on, brain-engaged level of intimacy with consumers that is unparalleled in most of the offline world.

This is not surprising when you consider that in the space of barely a decade the Internet itself has gone from nowhere to everywhere, from a practically zero share of attention to a major share of attention in hundreds of millions of homes and offices across the world. The Internet is a communication channel where access is cheap—there is little cost to hosting a Web site, and while one can pay for position on search engines, there's no cost for inclusion. And with a powerful "word of the Web" referral network that's only growing stronger, it is a truly open platform on which anyone can play.

In the global brandscape, the Internet is the fast track for brands that are "Internet fit." But it's not the only interactive technology that's setting the new hyperspeed standard: Mobile phones, text messaging, interactive TV, and self-service touch screens have all contributed to the expectation that it's normal for things to happen just about instantly. They have set the pace even for traditional brands and for the traditional medium of TV.

When the total brandscape is evolving fast, brands that are sitting still risk looking out of touch and out of energy. Though for some brands, being traditional, a stick-in-the-mud, and even a little clunky can be a virtue. Harley-Davidson and Triumph motorbikes and Leica cameras are much less high-tech and gimmicky than the Japanese brands that dominate those markets—a big plus for their target demographics, which value old-fashioned solidity and continuity. But it takes a brave brand with lots of self-belief and deep values to go at its own slower pace. For most brands—whether in technology, media, entertainment, packaged goods, or household products—slow is dangerous.

Next: Mixing, Mashing Our Brand Choices

Marketers used to be able to assume that a consumer buying into the values of Brand A would be amenable to other brands with similar values. That's no longer the case. The brandscape is now much more densely populated, and with a lot more choice, consumers are fickle. They feel no loyalty to shop in the same place or buy the same type of brands.

For most people it's no longer possible or even desirable to have a stable relationship with a few trusted brands in a few product categories. The number of product categories and sub-categories has exploded with the arrival of so many new technologies (think MP3 players, GPS equipment, cell phones, digital cameras, camcorders, Web sites) and new takes on familiar categories (think microbrew beers, low-carb foods, low-cost airlines). And in this hyperspeed environment, brands arrive out of the blue and quickly become ubiquitous. Compared with a decade ago, the average consumer faces a much wider range of brand choices across a wider range of categories.

This gives us plenty of incentive to mix and match brands according to our needs and financial resources. The high-low approach to consumption means people are all over the map with the level of products they choose: A BMW owner might use an old, simple cell phone. A clotheshorse may be decked out in designer clothing but wear discount-store underwear—or vice versa.

Our brand choices will have their own internal logic, but our overall selection will look haphazard and inconsistent—at least in the eyes of traditional marketers. And even in our own eyes, our choices won't add up to a consistent, coherent point of view; they're the result of a series of ad hoc choices that may have no larger meaning—a hotchpotch. The exception is the more brand-savvy consumer who goes a step further and selects brands with the intention of assembling a distinctive, idiosyncratic style, a deliberate fusion with its own underlying point of view.

Next: Brand Promiscuity and Brand Sluts

Another increasingly prevalent attitude toward brands is a certain gleeful promiscuity that has given rise to the half-joking label "brand sluts." The term was coined by marketers including Marian, who took it public to a Dutch audience, mostly marketing types, at the end of 2005, only to have their faces move from

"Huh?" to "Wow!" as she described our ever-more-wanton consuming styles. The line of thought is as follows: Some people feel strong emotional ties to certain brands, buying them consistently and faithfully, come what may; they're loyal through thick and thin, just like a faithful spouse or partner who snubs any tempting offers. Then there are the people who flit from one alluring brand offer to another with no sense of fidelity to any one of them—these are "brand sluts."

Theoretically, brand marketers value their faithful very deeply. They talk about rewarding loyalists and trot out figures showing that it costs less to keep established customers than to acquire new ones. But in practice, most brands want to grow their market share, so to pull in new customers, they do everything they can to reel in brand sluts.

While the connotation is negative, brand sluts are actually smart people who make informed consumer choices about what's available now. Many people are brand sluts in some area of their life, even the sort of primly dressed twentysomething woman who was overheard discussing her new cell phone:

> "I'm getting my new mobile next week . . . a Sony-Ericsson, like my old one."
> "You like Sony-Ericsson? Is that the brand you prefer?"
> "Oh, no, I don't care, really. It's the one they're offering as the free upgrade. As long as it does more stuff than the old one, the brand doesn't matter to me. It also has to be the right design and color, of course."

There are five "what's nexts" pushing consumers to be promiscuous.

What's Next? Commoditization

A product—whether it's a T-shirt or a microprocessor—may enjoy a brief spell of being new and different and special, but the market quickly finds a way of making a similar item that's cheaper and better. The more widespread products become, the more they're regarded as commodities. And commodities don't command loyalty. Only the most innovative and aggressive brands (Intel and Apple, for example) manage to fend off the legions of knockoff merchants. That's why someone who wants a portable digital music device is more likely to choose an iPod (brand) despite the higher price than one of the many MP3 players (commodities) crowding the shelves. And let's not forget that Microsoft is joining the fray with its release of Zune, a digital media player, and an online store, Zune Marketplace. And that's why Intel CPUs have managed not only to corner the lion's share of the market for computers running the Windows operating system but to get into Apple computers, too.

What's Next? Outsourcing

When production is contracted out, what does the brand mean, anyway? Once upon a time, companies made the products that proudly carried their logos, but now most brands outsource manufacturing to far-off places where labor is cheap. And today's promiscuous consumers are well aware of this. They know that similar products bearing different brands may actually come from the same factory in China or some other low-cost country.

What's Next? Brand Inflation

Thousands of new brands spring up every year, many of them making similar moves and using similar techniques lifted straight from "Marketing and Branding 101," and often creating nothing but a lot of brand noise. There were close to a quarter-million U.S. trademark filings in 2004 (up 9 percent from 2003), the third highest number in U.S. trademark history.[9] In 2005, the World Intellectual Property Organization received a record number of international trademark applications: 33,565.[10]

There's a lot of competition out there, a lot of brands clamoring for our attention and money. So it is inevitable that we form superficial emotional relationships with many brands and behave like brand sluts: Easy come, easy go.

> "The increasing difficulty in differentiating between products and the speed with which competitors take up innovations will assist in the rise and rise of the brand."
> —Gillian Law and Nick Grant, *Managemen*[11]

What's Next? Rapid Innovation

In the hottest new product areas, rapid innovation has become the norm. In traditional product areas, such as alcohol, there is limited scope or need for innovation, so business continues much as usual, and people stay attached to their preferred brands. But with products that evolve constantly, it may make no sense to stay with a brand—especially when the underlying technologies are commodities. As with sex, so with brands: as more attractive options come along, the less appealing the idea of loyalty. Why should we stick with one brand when others have great new features?

What's Next? Abundance of Consumer Information

The fifth factor that's fostering brand sluts is the huge increase in access to information, largely thanks to the Internet. For the growing numbers of people with online access, the Web is the first source of information when they want to buy a vacation package, a computer, a car, or virtually any other product. Figures from Miniwatts Marketing Group show that about 204 million Americans use the Internet,[12] and according to Nielsen/Net Ratings, online searches rose from about 4.1 billion in January 2005 to 5.7 billion in January 2006.[13] The way we shop and the range of our shopping is changing.

A brand used to be an important guarantee of a certain level of quality in times when manufacturing standards were patchy. But today, intense competition, consumer watchdogs, and consumer legislation have raised quality benchmarks and removed much of the risk from our purchase decisions. Many brands are now simply about cosmetic allure—the emotional packaging of the underlying product. And by way of online product reviews, expert evaluations, and comparison sites, it's easier than ever to see beneath the packaging and make really informed choices, deciding for ourselves what is on offer for our money.

"The Web enables total transparency. People with access to relevant information are beginning to challenge any type of authority. The stupid, loyal and humble customer, employee, patient or citizen is dead."
—Kjell Nordstrom and Jonas Ridderstrale, *Funky Business*[14]

What's Next? What's in It for Me?

Today's consumers aren't just in on the game, they're also in on the act. Everyone feels they're playing a part in this great big media world, and they're coming to the table with ever-longer lists of demands. The audience has decided to make marketing participatory.

Next: Think It, Source It (from Wherever), Brand It

In the old logic, a product came first, then its brand. That's no longer always the case. Now that the branding mind-set is so widespread, an astute entrepreneur is just as likely to devise the brand first and then figure out what products fit the brand—the tail wagging the dog. In fact, one successful beverage brand in the U.K. was conceived first as a brand with specific attributes, then registered in the country most appropriate to the brand's values, and then marketed as being made according to a local recipe.

Originally a brand was a guarantee of a product's origin and authenticity. Now, in the vast majority of cases, there is no fixed link between the geographical home of a brand and where its products are produced. Fashion brands such as Dior, Gucci, and DKNY may be French, Italian, and American, respectively, but who knows where their products are actually made? And perhaps more to the point, who cares?

It matters very little that Apple's iconic iPod is manufactured in China, possibly just across the road from a factory making no-brand dishwashers or disposable

T-shirts. And provided product quality is maintained, it would matter very little if Apple switched production to another far-flung place. As is the case with fashion brands, the essential "iPod-ness" doesn't derive from where it's made. What matters is that it looks cool and works properly, and that's what the Apple brand signals to people who buy it.

There are still a few brands that are deeply tied to their place of origin and make great play of it in their marketing. For example, Jack Daniels whiskey has been telling us for many years about its home in Lynchburg, Tennessee. Other "origin guaranteed" products such as Champagne and Parma ham derive much of their value from their place of production—it's an essential part of the brand. But such brands are increasingly rare.

Origin may be losing its importance, but it's still important for global brands to create local identities. In *Next*, we thought the blurring of global and local, merging into "glocal," would be crucial for future brands:

> It seems to us that achieving a balance between global and hyperlocal will be of increasing importance to both people and brands in the years ahead. For people, hyperlocal ties help us to partition the world into manageable chunks. I may not know how to solve the problems that may arise from Europe's new single currency, but I can create a workable budget for my homeowners' association or chess club. . . .
>
> As brands consider the implications of going global, it's important that they to recognize, too, the enormous draw of hyperlocal connections. Forging hyperlocal links with consumers is a must for tomorrow's brands—no matter how global. In fact, we can safely assume that tomorrow's mass-appeal brands will share three commonalities: global relevance, hyperlocal desirability, and strong ties to multiple niches.[15]

"Glocal" brands still rack up disproportionate success.

Hot Brands and On-the-Radar Brands

If you're looking for official lists of top brands, there are some definitive, high-metric sources out there, and they generally come up with a pretty consistent list: the likes of Coca-Cola, Microsoft, IBM, GE, and Dell. Beyond the usual suspects, the potential list is wide, wide open, especially if you include "place brands" and "people brands."

The following are a few that have caught our eye—especially because they also represent another kind of what's next: what's next, trendy trendy.

Iceland and Estonia: Right now the world is going crazy about four huge countries summed up with the acronym BRIC, standing for Brazil, Russia, India, and China. They are geographically vast, and they have big populations. Yet as these giants occupy endless tracts of media and mind-space, a couple of much smaller and less populous countries are steadily emerging as very hot place brands.

Iceland is the coolest, hottest place brand. Stuck out in the middle of the North Atlantic, just south of the Arctic Circle, it has clawed itself up from one of the poorest countries in the world to one of the richest in terms of GDP per capita. Deforestation and overgrazing took it to the brink of ecological disaster, but now Iceland's 300,000 people have become ecological pioneers, and there's a growing eco-tourism industry. The country gets a lot of its electricity from geo-thermal sources and is now committed to being the world's first hydrogen econ-omy by 2050, which means getting all its energy without burning fossil fuels.

Icelanders share their Nordic cousins' reputation for efficiency, honesty, and healthy living, but perhaps unlike the Swedes, Danes, and Norwegians, they're also known for their eccentricity and party-animal tendencies.

Estonia is a tiny country of around 1.3 million people on the eastern shores of the Baltic Sea. After coming free from the stifling grip of Soviet Russia, Estonia raced to turn itself into a free-market economy, and it has been showing impressive growth. The country pioneered a flat-rate tax for both individuals and corporations (originally 26 percent, it's being gradually lowered), and has become a focus of interest from abroad and a hotbed of entrepreneurial activity.

Skype and VoIP: The technology to make voice calls through the Internet—Voice over IP, or VoIP—has been around for a few years, but it was Skype that turned VoIP into something that anyone can access and use. Skype released its first free downloadable version in July 2004, allowing users to speak to each other through their computers for free. Skype also allows calls from the Internet to land line or mobile numbers ("SkypeOut") or vice-versa ("SkypeIn") at low cost.

Not surprisingly, it tracked 1 million users online concurrently in October 2004, 2 million in February 2005, 3 million in May 2005, and 6 million in March 2006, all through word-of-mouth and editorial coverage.

In September 2005, eBay announced it was buying Skype for $2.6 billion, plus an additional $1.5 billion if Skype hits certain performance targets in com-ing years. In a sure sign of brand power, "to Skype" has quickly become the verb for making calls through the Internet ("I'll Skype you tomorrow"). And by the way, one of Skype's main offices is in Tallinn, the capital of Estonia.

Toyota: For most of its 70-odd years, Toyota has been the epitome of corporate Japan, with its relentless pursuit of quality improvements, manufacturing effi-ciency, and market share. Its cars have a legendary reputation for reliability, but neither the cars nor the brand have ever really rivaled industry leaders for status, let alone desirability.

Yet thanks to "The Toyota Way," the company is poised to overtake GM as the world's biggest car maker by volume. And in 2006, it was the first foreign brand to make it into the top 10 on *Fortune*'s list of America's Most Admired Companies.[16] While its conventional models will never enjoy the cachet of a Porsche or a Jaguar, its hybrid, the Prius, propelled by celebrities, has made it the brand to watch in the coming wave of more environmentally conscious vehicles.

Of all the long-established automotive brands, Toyota looks to be the one most likely to achieve a fundamental change in image and desirability.

Samsung and LG: South Korea has been amazingly successful as an economy, but it hasn't shown much in the way of branding savvy until recently.

Korean champion Samsung has undertaken a brand-building campaign that's paying off handsomely. While Japanese consumer electronics brands such as JVC and Toshiba have rarely seemed to pose a real threat to the preeminence of Sony, Samsung is now looking like a serious rival that's all the more distinctive for not being Japanese. It helps that Samsung is pushing hard in the hottest area of consumer technology, mobile phones, where change is a constant. It also helps that Samsung is the sponsor of Britain's Chelsea Football Club, which has rocketed to success under Portuguese manager José Mourinho.

Like Samsung (and GE), the LG brand fronts up a conglomerate (Chaebol) operating in many product areas but most visible in consumer electronics, especially mobile phones. ("LG" came from combining the group's two main businesses: Lucky Chemical Industrial Co. and Goldstar Electronics Co.) Although the logo is smart and increasingly visible around the world, LG doesn't yet have the brand sophistication of Samsung—but it's learning fast.

Google and eBay: It feels like cheating to include these two, but it would be negligent not to. Like Skype, these Brands Next are entirely inventions of the Internet age.

eBay achieves the remarkable feat of appealing to Net-savvy people as well as to many who might otherwise ignore the Internet. It's the world's garage sale, where anyone can buy or sell, where anyone can experience the thrill of an auction, and where (increasingly) low-cost vendors are setting up shop to sell fixed-price items. It's so instantly understandable and widely recognized that a TV show or movie could make a throwaway reference to it ("You should put that on eBay") and most of the global audience would get it.

Google already looms very large in the lives of most people who use the Internet, and it keeps on rolling out new ideas. With its relentlessly innovative culture, its two distinctive founders (Larry Page and Sergey Brin), its media-savvy headquarters (the Googleplex), and its quirky, playful spirit, Google is a brand that's got what it takes to get even bigger. There's even a Flash short called "Epic 2014" that charts how Google merges with Amazon (to become Googlezon), defeats Microsoft, and ends up ruling the Internet. The fact that the scenario is plausible shows just how powerful the Google brand has become.

In-flight meals are dabbling in the world of brands and will definitely be what's next—anything from TGI Fridays, Einstein Bros. bagels, Cinnabon, even Wolfgang Puck- and Hard Rock Café–branded meals are on trays now or in the works. The big question: Does this strengthen the airline brand and the food brand, or just make for a slightly less obvious tray in the sky?

What's Next? Peeping Toms and Tinas

Thanks to *Big Brother* and its progeny, we've developed a taste for voyeurism, and we want more—lots more. Marketers have barely scratched the surface of how to put this public appetite to best use.

People Brands on the What's Next Radar

Sporting achievements are a classic foundation for people brands. That was the case with Swedish tennis player Bjorn Borg, who went on to found an apparel business. Golfer Tiger Woods certainly has the makings of a long-term brand beyond the greens. And soccer star David Beckham clearly has business intentions beyond his playing career.

There's a major cross-media industry dedicated to creating a certain type of people brand known as the celebrity. But celebrities who owe their fame entirely to the media are like straw fires—they burn quickly and brightly, but they don't last long if there's no substance. So for our purposes, we're making a clear distinction between celebrities and real people brands.

In an era when getting a makeover, a Web site, and a personal image consultant is a snap, anyone can regard themselves as Me, Inc., and behave accordingly. But as in the world of corporate brands, so in the world of people brands—there are millions of wannabes and just a few really strong contenders. The essential criterion of a strong people brand is that it must be about more than thinking up a series of sound bites, publicity stunts, and photo opportunities.

For all her well-publicized shortcomings, Martha Stewart is clearly a strong people brand. She has embedded her personality, values, and spirit into a business that bears her name. Steve Jobs and Richard Branson are both celebrities and the people at the heart of their brands (Apple/Pixar and Virgin). In the movie industry, Steven Spielberg's spirit animates DreamWorks, while on the other coast of the United States, business gurus Tom Peters, Faith Popcorn, and Seth Godin have built businesses around their styles and thinking.

In the entertainment industry virtually everyone is a brand, even if most stick strictly to their core arena. Few manage to branch into other areas of activity in the way that rock singers Bono and Bob Geldof have parlayed their values and personalities into charitable works (War Child, Debt Relief) and business ventures.

It's probably easier for artists to infuse their brand spirit into different ventures. Picasso was arguably the original artist brand, with his own distinctive signature and style in different media. Andy Warhol had a deep, instinctive understanding of "Me, Inc.," and was able to turn his personal brand into an art production line.

Modern politicians have been accused of being too concerned with marketing and personal branding. But for better or worse, there are clearly some strong personal brands out there seeking to influence and persuade. Italy's former Prime Minister Silvio Berlusconi was a very successful businessman before he went into politics, and his personality (like it or loath it) shows through in the party he founded, Forza Italia (Go, Italy). Former bodybuilder and movie star Arnold Schwarzenegger leveraged his personal brand into getting elected governor of California. And what are political dynasties if not personal brands that hold good through time? Think the Gandhi family in India, and the Kennedy, Bush, and Daly dynasties in the United States.

Elected politicians face a lot of pressure to pursue short-term personal branding initiatives, whereas royalty can—and should—take a much longer-term, more strategic view. In the Netherlands, Queen Wilhelmina established a relatively down-to-earth, unstuffy brand personality for the Dutch royal family that has continued for three generations. Contrast that with the U.K., where the British royal family has stuck to a stiff, aloof image that was at odds with two of the women (Diana Spencer and Sarah Ferguson) who married into it and divorced out of it.

Matt Groening, creator of *The Simpsons*, knows a thing or two about personal branding. He reckons that a strong personal brand (at least in cartoons) needs to be immediately recognizable from its silhouette, and on that basis all of the Simpson family pass muster. In the Middle East the same might be said of the late Yasser Arafat, who built a powerful personal brand. It might also apply to Osama bin Laden, who as the personal brand at the heart of Al-Qaeda must now be the best-known Muslim alive. And in the what's next category, we note that with such powerful personal brands dominating the brandscape in the Arab world, it will be increasingly hard for more moderate figures such as King Abdullah II of Jordan and his wife, Queen Rania, to gain traction locally despite their stature in the rest of the world.

What's Next? Brands Front and Center

It may well be that the advertising industry has had an entirely wrong take on celebrity. Advertising is supposed to make brands and products famous: turning them into celebrities. Yet all too often advertising uses celebrities to endorse products—fattening their bank accounts and helping them stay in the public eye without doing much for the brand. Putting brands back in the spotlight will take a lot more than clever product placement.

What's Next? There's No Hero Like a Dead Hero

After so many of our heroes have taken nosedives off their pedestals—think O. J. Simpson, José Conseco, Michael Jackson—we've come to find that no one can be considered reliable until he's six feet under. Advertisers will increasingly cherish those who have passed over to the other side, since they're no longer apt to make mortal mistakes.

Next: In the End Was the Brand Spirit

The more people become used to interacting with the outside world through technology, the more they become comfortable with things existing as concepts or virtual entities rather than as tangible objects.

Nobody now thinks it's at all strange to have a conversation with a stranger who is thousands of miles away, thanks to the telephone. It's totally normal to watch strangers pretending (that is, acting) to fall in love, to fight, or to hang out together making jokes, thanks to the movies and to television. And it's increasingly normal to receive and to spend hundreds or even thousands of dollars/pounds/euros without actually seeing any of it in bills and coins, thanks to credit cards, telephone banking, ATMs, and Internet banking. And, at the more extreme end of things, millions of people devote many long hours of sweat and adrenaline to battling against computer-generated adversaries.

The same applies to brands. Brands and branding originated in the very physical world of red-hot metal being applied to hide or wood, and modern brands are in many cases still strongly rooted in physical products that embody and express the brand. BMW's Mini, Intel's Pentium chip, Canon's cool Ixus camera (Elph in the United States), and the iconic Absolut vodka bottle are all thoroughly modern and very physical. Yet increasingly brands can be abstracted from the products that embody them; their essence can be distilled into an idea, a spirit that retains its power across product categories.

> "The idea that business is just a numbers affair has always struck me as preposterous. For one thing, I've never been particularly good at numbers, but I think I've done a reasonable job with feelings. And I'm convinced that it is feelings—and feelings alone—that account for the success of the Virgin brand in all of its myriad forms."
> —Richard Branson[17]

Apple co-founder Steve Jobs has proved the power of brand spirit by very successfully branching out from computing into digital music. But that's just a small stretch compared with what Richard Branson has done with the Virgin brand. He has used it to set up a music retail chain and recording label, an airline, a radio station, a cola brand, a train company, a mobile phone company, a financial services company, an Internet ISP, a publishing company, and a space-tourism company. Although Branson has sold several of the companies, they continue to bear the Virgin name and retain some of the Branson-Virgin energy.

Both Jobs and Branson developed consumer brands that were closely tied to their own personal brands, but with different outcomes. Jobs was ousted from Apple in 1985, and the company and brand floundered until he returned as interim CEO in 1997. By contrast, Branson has a record of setting up successful companies and moving on, leaving them buzzing with Branson spirit.

This raises a crucial question for brands that have larger-than-life personalities at their core: Can the spirit and the brand continue after the personality has gone?

And Therefore Next

The numbers surely suggest that in modern life, brands win. Branding is now a fundamental part of how people think about everything. Brands are now companies, places, people, political parties, and intangibles such as Web sites and even concepts. Increasingly, in an economy that's about opportunities rather than careers, we all really need to sell ourselves, and branding is how we'll do it.

Section III

Personal Nexts

chapter ten

big next: extended family trees

There's a new continuum for what defines a family. There's the conventional mother and father and baby makes three, but that's a limited way of thinking these days. In the era of the blended family, there are half-siblings, step-siblings, step-parents, and everything in between. As the *Irish Independent* puts it, "In just three decades, we have single parents, stay-at-home dads, gay couples, stepfamilies, interracial families, mixed-religion families, surrogate mothers, in vitro fertilization and the genetic technology to create a child with two biological mothers."[1] The demographics are shifting, and new definitions of family identity are emerging.

> Tradition paints a holiday picture of harmonious gatherings replete with the nuclear family around a festive table. But with changing families come changing conventions. Step- and half-families are trying to craft new holiday rituals, says psychotherapist Irene Shapiro. Shapiro notes on secondwivescafe.com that there are more than 20 million stepparents in the United States, of whom almost a third have stepchildren who live in the household: "For these kids, who said it's a happy holiday season? They often wish they could be split in two!"[2] More families are negotiating new family dynamics with new holiday traditions.

Next: Fertility Costs, but Eggs and Sperm Sell

It costs a lot to raise kids, but these days it also costs a lot to *make* kids. Money talks when it comes to conceiving children. Women can freeze a batch of eggs harvested from their ovaries and later fertilize them with sperm for about $10,000. Donated sperm can be ordered for $150 to $600 per sample. Capital One even has a Family Fee Plan loan option for people who don't have the cash to conceive: "We offer loans from $1,500 to $25,000, giving you a flexible range of funds to help pay for fertility treatment options like Clomid, PCOS treatment, IVF, IUI, ICSI, surgery, tubal ligation reversals and donor eggs."[3]

In today's world, you can break the sperm bank making babies. Spending has ballooned to an estimated $3 billion a year in the United States on an industry that includes eggs, sperm, and fertility drugs and procedures. And that's just what's regulated. In the commerce of conception, everything has a price. As the *Chicago Sun-Times* says, the fertility industry is "practically a microcosm of the entire global economy. It includes the manufacturing of fertility hormones, harvesting of renewable natural resources (sperm and egg collection), international trade (foreign adoptions), expert services (IVF and other high-tech medicine), and even rental real estate (surrogate mothers) and long-term storage (embryo banks)."[4] And when costs are prohibitively high, people start looking elsewhere, going abroad to find lower prices for sperm and eggs.

> "Advertisements in campus newspapers and on websites plead [for egg donors] daily. 'Egg Donors Needed. $10,000,' says one in *The Daily Californian*, the student newspaper at the University of California, Berkeley. The ad, from a San Diego broker called A Perfect Match, seeks women who are 'attractive, under the age of 29' and have SAT scores above 1,300."
>
> —Jim Hopkins, *USA Today*[5]

As with any economic force, regulation becomes inevitable and essential. Harvard Business School professor Debora L. Spar, author of *The Baby Business*, compares the fertility industry to the unregulated Web: "As with the early Internet, where people were high on the lack of rules and eventually wanted protection against scammers and online pedophiles, I think we'll eventually want rules protecting the health of the women and babies."[6] While conversations about conception tend to get personal and emotional, the next big baby talk will be about balancing between choice and reproductive freedoms with market rules and regulations.

Next: Mommies Going Solo

More mothers are going alone into the role of parenting. The number of babies born to unmarried American women ages 30 to 44 increased almost 17 percent between 1999 and 2003, according to the National Center for Health Statistics.[7] Known as "single mothers by choice" or "choice mothers," these women have children through sperm donor insemination (DI), or they adopt in the United States or abroad. Single Mothers by Choice, a 25-year-old support group that boasts chapters in most American cities, took in nearly twice as many new members in 2005 than it did ten years before, according to *The New York Times*.[8]

Single Mothers by Choice says the majority of its members are professional women with the means to support a child on their own. Choice mothers have made conscious, well-informed decisions about their path, and the group says as part of its philosophy that these women "have chosen not to be in a relationship rather than be in one that does not seem satisfactory."[9] Going it alone may be better than just going along, says Jennifer Egan, writing for *The New York Times:* "More than a third of American marriages end [in divorce]; often there are children involved, and often the mothers end up caring for those children mostly on their own, saddled with ex-spouses, custody wrangles and nagging in-laws. Considered this way, single motherhood would seem to have a clean, almost thrilling logic—more than a third of the time, these women will have circumvented a lot of pain and unpleasantness and cut straight to being mothers on their own."[10]

Many new images of the single mother are entering our cultural consciousness. Angelina Jolie has become a model of modern single motherhood by adopting two children from different countries, then conceiving a child with boyfriend Brad Pitt. Television shows are spotlighting single mothers as strong central characters, notably Showtime's *Weeds*, about a widow selling marijuana to support her family. Notes Joseph P. Kahn in *The Boston Globe*, "*Weeds* is hardly the only example of a TV show or movie of recent vintage that reflects, if not drives, changing attitudes and demographics concerning single mothers. A few years ago, when *Friends* still reigned supreme, Rachel's out-of-wedlock pregnancy was a major plot device, the stuff of one-liners, not scandal or shame. Other TV shows featuring strong single mothers include *Desperate Housewives, Gilmore Girls, Judging Amy, Surface, Living with Fran* and *The Suite Life of Zack and Cody*."[11]

It's a very different media landscape than back in 1992, when Vice President Dan Quayle rebuked the sitcom *Murphy Brown* for "mocking the importance of the father" by portraying the title character as a single mother by choice. The cultural majority has certainly cast a more favorable and tolerant light on the single mother. To some extent that's because being a single woman—mother or not—now carries far less of a stigma than it used to. Take *Sex and the City*, which offers up a host of options for women: Miranda has a child out of wedlock, and she and the father initially decide to raise the child together separately (they eventually get married); Charlotte divorces, remarries, and adopts a child from China; and Samantha, who has no interest in children, dabbles with a lesbian relationship before finding happiness with a much younger hunk. All kinds of choices are seen as acceptable and "normal." (Not all countries take the same approach: Sweden and Italy ban single women from participating in IVF programs or using anonymous sperm.)

What's Next? More Paternity Leave

How can men play an active and more equal role in parenting when so much parental-leave legislation is slanted toward women? Indeed, Germany's minister for family affairs is advocating that fathers be required to take at least two months of paternity leave—at least, if the mother is to receive her full maternity benefits. It's one idea to stimulate the birth rate in a country that has one of the lowest birth rates in the world. One reason for this is that working mothers are frowned upon, dismissed as *rabenmutters*—"raven mothers," or women who put their careers over their children. "The question is not whether women will work," says Ursula von der Leyen, the family affairs minister, in an interview with *The New York Times.* "They will work. The question is whether they will have kids."[12] She would like to shorten parental leave support to one year from two and link payments to income. That provides higher-income families with more incentive to have kids and gives women more reason to return to the labor force sooner. And with benefits tied to paternity leave, mothers will be assured of some help.

Next: Donor Insemination Means New Family Trees

With an entire generation conceived through donor insemination coming of age, new kinds of family connections are forming between siblings raised in different households. People conceived through DI are looking to find and identify with their DI siblings as a way to develop closeness and commonality; it's a way to combat the feeling that, as they sometimes describe themselves, they're "half adopted" or "lopsided." Amy Harmon writes in *The New York Times:* "While many donor-conceived children prefer to call their genetic father 'donor' to differentiate the biological function of fatherhood from the social one, they often feel no need to distance themselves, linguistically or emotionally, from their siblings."[13]

Siblings are now looking for each other through online networks like the Donor Sibling Registry, which was started by a single mother and her DI-conceived son in 2000. Since "no public outlet exists for mutual-consent contact between DI relatives," the site explains, it offers "the logical next step to making those connections."[14] What's interesting to note is the primacy of the search for siblings over the biological father as a way to find a meaningful shared identity, and how common it's going to become.

The search, though, can be almost endless, since a child of a popular sperm donor may well have several dozen siblings. (The *Guardian* quotes one sperm donor—a man who donated twice a week for four years before there were rules governing the number of women who could receive sperm from the same donor—as estimating that he may have a hundred or so children.[15]) Several siblings who have met describe a surprising sense of familiarity. These newly introduced brothers and sisters are building a definition of family that both rests on biology and transcends it.

> Sperm bank officials estimate the number of children born to donors in the United States at about 30,000 a year, but hard numbers are elusive because the industry is largely unregulated.

The Donor Sibling Registry also provides a way for mothers to meet and bond. *The New York Times* reports, "Many mothers seek out each other on the registry, eager to create a patchwork family for themselves and their children. One group of seven say they, too, feel bonded by the half-blood relations of their children, and perhaps by the vaguely biological urge that led them all to choose Fairfax Cryobank's Donor 401."[16] There's a shared sense of identity among the women that comes just from selecting the same sperm.

Perhaps one day fathers will be part of the mix as well. In the United States, some donors agree to be contacted by their offspring when they turn 18. In the U.K., however, any adult conceived through DI has a legal right to know the identity of his or her donor, according to a law passed in 2005. The result is that far fewer men are now donating, especially the students who once enjoyed the financial payoff, and Britain's sperm banks now face a severe shortage.

> "'It's a bit unsettling,' one girl who recently discovered her half-siblings admits. 'I could have passed them on the street. I could have met and dated and even married my new half-brother Tyler, who is due to go to the same university as me next year, having no idea who he was. We have no idea how many more siblings we might have. . . . I would probably avoid dating a local guy who looked too much like me, because you never know.' "[17]

What's Next? Family Reunions around Dad's Donor Sperm

Shared genes will help to form the basis of long-term relationships. It's roots revisited, 21st-century style, as youngsters born of donated sperm track down their half-brothers and -sisters. What's the DNA version of "blood is thicker than water"?

Next: Chinese Adoptees Trace Roots

Another new type of ad hoc family is one being created by children adopted from China. China's one-child policy left a lot of children abandoned, especially girls, and when the country loosened adoption laws in 1991, many Westerners started the process. Since then the growth has been exponential. The trickle into the United States grew to 2,130 orphans who got visas in 1995, to nearly 8,000 in 2005, making China the leading country for foreign adoptions in America.

Now, a subculture is emerging that includes play groups and support groups, as well as group tours to China. More parents are working to preserve their children's heritage and help them assimilate at the same time via an extensive network that connects these families. A group called Families with Children from China, which has chapters around the world, helps with everything from finding bilingual schools and coordinating play dates to helping families recognize and resist racism. The goal is to "honor our children's Chinese and Chinese American heritage," says the group.[18] At the heart of the Chinese-adoption experience are issues related to race, culture, and identity. "As the oldest of the adopted children move through their teenage years, they are beginning—independently and with a mix of enthusiasm and trepidation—to explore their identities," *The New York Times* says. "Their experiences offer hints at journeys yet to come."[19]

Networks and support groups are so well connected that many adoptive parents are using them to find biological siblings among other adopted children through DNA registries and Web sites. One such site is Sister Far, which has about 100 members and is a starting place for families who think they may have found their internationally adopted child's sibling.

As these Chinese American youth come to terms with identity and connect through commonalities, watch for more support groups, social networks, and efforts to preserve the culture of this unique American demographic, among both parents and children.

What's Next? Reunions Become Big Business alongside Weddings

Weddings and reunions: Both are big events, laden with emotion and hopes. If everything works out as intended, a couple has only one wedding in their life but a load of reunions. The event with the bigger growth potential is clear.

Next: Family Plans for Singletons

As single mothers become more of a cultural norm, single women without children could be considered old news. Working women in their 20s and 30s who are not in any particular hurry to get married are no longer an anomaly. These days, pin-up singleton Bridget Jones is no longer a novelty and more a routine representation of the single woman. (It's telling, too, that as Bridget approaches 40 in Helen Fielding's serial saga in *The Independent*, she has become a single mother.)

We recently initiated a research project to discover whether there are common roots of singleton identity in diverse geographies (we targeted six cities, two in the U.K. and four in the United States). What we found is that friends and family—the connections of personal relationships—are central to singleton life. Singletons have gone from living within a set framework of family and school to living as free agents in an open-ended framework. With new perspectives, pressures, and lifestyles come new requirements for friendships and dating. So sooner or later they re-evaluate their relationships and determine which to keep and which to leave behind.

For singletons, mom is an especially strong force. The parent-child relationship is one of the most influential and significant in most people's lives, of course, but as these singletons grow into women, they increasingly view their mothers in a new light. They're now also seen as women, friends, wives. Regardless of whether mom has had a career, she's a valued resource. In fact, many singletons regard their mothers as their most important role models, examples of whom they hope to become. It's particularly important to them that their mothers accept their lifestyles and not try to railroad them into settling down and having children in a hurry.

Next: That's What Friends Are for

Friends are vital to singletons, too. Through their early 20s, singletons tend to find friends through their circumstances: living in the same neighborhood, going to the same school, hanging out with the same people. As more time and energy is taken up with career and other responsibilities, they have less time for maintaining friendships. One result is that singletons start thinking about the nature of friendship—what it means to them, what they expect from it, and what they're willing to do for it. These young women find themselves letting go of the more shallow circumstantial friendships and focusing on friendships based on true affinity.

Janice, a 35-year-old Londoner, says, "I have an address book full of friends, but if I haven't seen or heard from them in six months, then I take them out—I haven't got the time to focus on those on the periphery, so I'm focusing only on those I really care about." Singletons are picky about whom they call friends. They're looking for quality over quantity, for relationships based on a lot more than convenience and location. At this stage in their lives, friends are becoming a matter of choice, not of circumstance.

The singleton years are a difficult time for women to have male friends. Women are looking for more depth and intimacy in their relationships, and that can be difficult to maintain with men without sexual involvement. They still value male friendships, but for the real well of support and understanding they need as they invent their adult lives, it's female friends who feel closest and most supportive. As Carrie says on *Sex and the City* when Samantha is diagnosed with breast cancer: "Samantha is my friend. She's my family. My insides. She will be fine because she has to be fine. That's how important she is to me." There's no clearer statement about how friends form identity for this group.

Next: Distance Is No Barrier to Friendship . . . Or Love

All over the world, populations have been migrating as people seek better education, jobs, or other opportunities. And wherever living standards have improved, birthrates have fallen. The result is that compared with previous generations, family networks are smaller but more widespread, and family bonds are looser.

When family ties are weaker, people have more time and inclination to develop strong and enduring friendships. This is one upside of social upheaval and fragmented lives—a phenomenon dubbed "families by choice" or "families of affinity." It means, quite simply, that people are choosing to invest as much or more in long-term relationships with people they like as they are in relationships with blood relatives. Think *Seinfeld* or *Friends*.

Greater mobility, though, means that not only family but friends—and sometimes lovers—are often long-distance. Nearly 2 percent of European citizens live in an EU member state that is not their own, and 30 percent of those left their own country for love.[20] The growth of the Internet also means that friendships (and love affairs) can spring up regardless of distance; whether you're into quilting, an obscure 1980s pop band, or bungee jumping, there's a community of new virtual friends out there.

While younger women are getting choosier about their friends, teens are not—they collect them. According to a report in *The Dallas Morning News*, the average teen spends five and a half hours online a day, visiting chat rooms, instant messaging, or blogging, and parents are understandably worried about who their kids are meeting as they sit at their computers.[21] This is a genuinely "now" problem.

Next: Rethinking Relationships

It might be surprising, but nine out of ten British women think that one-night stands are immoral. Research conducted by the University of Sheffield found that even women who have had one-night stands themselves don't think it is a good idea, and they deem women who engage in them as desperate, needy, drunk, or on drugs.[22] As Emma, a 32-year-old Londoner says, "I've had quite a few one-night stands, but I've never been sober when I've done it. The morning after, the walk of shame home from someone's house to the tube is terrible."

Psychologist Sharron Hinchliffe, author of the University of Sheffield study, tells the *Daily Telegraph* that study results did not jibe with today's image of independent young women who have no qualms about finding sexual fulfillment outside of relationships: "It makes me question whether women have really gained all the sexual freedom they are supposed to have gained since the '60s," she says.[23] The study found that women in their early 30s are much more negative about one-night stands than women in their 50s. (Indeed, the number of sexually transmitted infections among the middle-aged has almost doubled in the last five years, according to the U.K.'s Health Protection Agency.[24])

New puritans are on the rise in the U.K.—that is, young people who do not have multiple sexual partners, binge-drink, smoke, buy big brands, eat junk food, subscribe to gossip magazines, or live to watch television. "Something very interesting, indeed radical, is happening to Britain," Jim Murphy, associate director of the Future Foundation, told *The Observer*.[25]

While women in their 30s may be veering away from the one-night stand, some singletons can rely on "friends with benefits" or the "faithful old fuck" (FOF), as it's sometimes known in the U.K.—a sex partner with no strings attached. As Penny, a 38-year-old Londoner, says, "All my single friends have an FOF. Mine is an old workmate who I'm very fond of and who I can call up if I feel in need of sex or a cuddle. He's lovely. We go out to the cinema or for dinner, and often there's no sex involved at all—but sometimes there is. But we couldn't become partners or anything, because we would just drive each other mad."

The Internet is also freeing up women to do more sexual exploring. As Adam McCulloch writes in the Australian *Sunday Telegraph Magazine*, "With the anonymity of chat rooms, women can reconstruct their body image and shake off the taboos and social stigma dictating the sort of sex they should enjoy."[26] Text, e-mail, and the Web are all changing the way people think about relationships. After all, it's now possible to have an amorous liaison of sorts that's even better than reality; says McCulloch, "There are no chores, dirty dishes or toilet seats online. Just a whole lot of what many feel is neglected in their real-world relationships: communication. The lower the chance of meeting, the more likely fantasy will be used to enliven conversation in place of the mundane truth."

While women in their 30s may be getting less promiscuous, that doesn't seem to be the case among some younger women. The *Journal of Sex Research* reports that coercion is a significant problem in college dating relationships—and in some cases, it's women who are the aggressors.[27] There is evidence that some women use threats to end the relationship or threats of violence to get sex, or they ply men with alcohol or drugs.

For teens, the pattern seems to be less intercourse but more sexual activity overall. David Brooks notes in *The New York Times* that teen pregnancy rates in the United States have dropped by about a third over the past 15 years, and while 39 percent of high school boys said they were virgins in 1990, now half of them do. Michael Resnick, professor of pediatrics and public health at the University of Minnesota, found that 47 percent of high school students reported ever having sexual intercourse in 2003, compared with 54 percent in 1991.[28]

American teens also seem to be redefining what constitutes intimacy. According to the Centers for Disease Control and Prevention, more than half of 15- to 19-year-olds are engaging in oral sex, sometimes with a regular partner, sometimes at parties, and sometimes with multiple partners.[29] Terri Fisher, associate professor of psychology at Ohio State University, tells *USA Today* that after the 1960s, oral sex was considered much more intimate than intercourse, but now, among the young, it's seen as a more casual act.[30] The teen dating scene is all about "hooking up," a deliberately ambiguous term that can mean anything from watching a movie together to oral sex or beyond. As Andrea Lavinthal and Jessica Rozler, authors of *The Hookup Handbook*, tell a reporter: "Maybe it's kissing, making out or getting to third base. One thing's for sure: It's not a one-night stand, it's not dating."[31]

Next: Who We Will Live With

As families are changing, so is the way we live with them. People cohabit, share with friends, yo-yo back and forth to their parents' place, or bounce between two parents' homes, in the case of divorced parents. And some are happiest all on their own.

More people than ever live by themselves. The trend is especially prevalent in Northern Europe: In Norway, more than 40 percent of households consist of one person only, and in Sweden, Finland, Denmark, and Germany, it's more than a third.[32] Increasingly, these are not the young singletons we associate with single living, but older people—and their numbers will rise. In the U.K., the Office of the Deputy Prime Minister forecasts that the number of married and cohabiting households will fall to 47 percent by 2026 compared with 55 percent today, and that older people will comprise the majority of single households.[33]

What's Next? The Gay-Wedding Industry

Whether or not gay marriage is legalized, the gay wedding industry is already booming in the United States. In 2005, on the same day that a law allowing same-sex civil partnerships went into effect in England and Wales, Elton John and partner David Furnish held an all-out star-studded bash to celebrate their union.

Next: Pets Are the New Family Fixture

As the family unit changes shape, with more couples opting not to have children and many more people living alone, pets have become a family fixture—and, in many cases, are even referred to as the owner's "children." Three-quarters of dog owners do literally consider their pets to be family members, at least according to an American Pet Products Manufacturers Association (APPMA) survey.[34]

Hurricane Katrina and even the war in Iraq highlighted the importance of pets and their equal weighting with people. "Every time a pet in jeopardy makes the news—whether it's the wretched-looking creatures stranded by Hurricane Katrina or the dogs wandering the Iraq war zone—Americans clamor to help," writes Jenifer Goodwin in the *San Diego Union-Tribune*. "Pet lovers send checks, arrange for chartered jets to fly the animals out of harm's way and volunteer to feed them, shelter them and love them forever."[35]

In September 2006, orphaned pets from Lebanon headed to the U.S.; abandoned cats and dogs—left behind when their owners fled the country during fighting between Hezbollah and Israel—were airlifted by Beirut for the Ethical Treatment of Animals and Utah-based Best Friends. Best Friends was also active in Israel, where pets were left stranded when their owners evacuated their homes in the north during the most recent war.

> In lieu of baby sitters, some pet parents find ways to keep pets occupied when they're out of the house. Dog can be left in front of the TV to watch *It's a Dog's Life* (or any of several competing products), a DVD filled with images of dogs playing that can run all day on a continuous loop. Another option is to leave the radio tuned in to DogCatRadio (dogcatradio.com).

Pets also serve to assuage some of our ever-accumulating anxieties. They're trusted companions and love unconditionally, and unlike children (apart from the yo-yos, of course), they won't leave home. When home life itself isn't a haven, a pet provides common ground, writes Guy Fiddell in the *Virginian Pilot*: "In some embattled homes in which family members tend to turn on one another, a rare peaceful topic is the family dog. The dog wigwags itself into the good graces of all members of the family circle."[36] It's the pet as peacemaker. And for people suffering a variety of illnesses, pets are literally therapeutic. Research by the UCLA Medical Center showed that among 76 patients visited by a dog and a volunteer, levels of anxiety dropped by 24 percent and blood pressure decreased by 10 percent.[37]

Next: Big Business Pets

The furry friends are certainly doted on like family. In the U.K., a country renowned for its love of animals, a dog owner will spend an average of £22,000 over the course of the dog's lifetime—more than half of what it costs to raise a child.[38] Meanwhile, Americans spend about $20,000 in the course of a cat's life, $18,000 on small dogs, and as much as $13,000 on rabbits and $12,000 on iguanas.[39] There are big financial sacrifices for tenderness.

We're clearly buying far more than the basics. In fact, the APPMA says eight out of ten dog owners will buy their pets gifts. That's just the beginning: In the United States in 2006, an estimated 9 percent of the country's 73 million domestic dogs had their own birthday parties.[40] We're not just indulging our pets, we're affording them the same luxuries to which we treat ourselves: faux-mink coats, lavish bedding, spa excursions, and specialized gourmet meals. "More and more companies traditionally known for human products are going to the dogs, cats and reptiles," reports the APPMA. "Big-name companies including Paul Mitchell, Omaha Steaks, Origins, Harley Davidson and Old Navy are now offering lines of pet products ranging from dog shampoo, pet attire and name-brand toys to gourmet treats and food."[41]

L. Phillips Brown notes in *Nutraceuticals World* that "the 'humanization' of pets is exaggerating consumer demand for products and services that are as good (and sometimes better) as those available for people themselves." Companies are responding, he says, with quality products that treat pets' "specific physiological (and even psychological) needs."[42]

Can you put a price on your pet's unconditional love? Many of us do. In 2005, Americans shelled out $36 billion on pet products and services, more than double the amount we spent just over a decade ago. And of that, more than $17 billion went to maintaining the health and wellness of our animals.[43] We spare few expenses when it comes to protecting our faithful friends, even if that means opting for the cost of pet insurance.

In the U.K., the pet insurance market expanded from 14 percent penetration in 2003 to 23 percent in 2005, says Suzanne Murray, senior campaign manager at Cardif Pinnacle Insurance.[44] Cardif Pinnacle makes the case for the cost of pet insurance by telling owners: "Our pets can't tell us what's wrong or where it hurts, so we rely on the skill and care of our veterinary practice team . . . implicitly! . . . But it can prove expensive."[45] Costs range from $10 to $80 a month for members of Canadian carrier Petplan, which offers illness and accident coverage, extended dental care, and sometimes even "behavioral therapies."

We'll also work hard to prolong the health and well-being of our pets. As people become more aware of what they eat, they are more attentive to their pets' diets as well. Bob Vetere, managing director of the American Pet Products Manufacturers Association, tells *The Wall Street Journal:* "If you see a human trend in food, you'll see it in pet food within six months now."[46] And as we try to minimize our own stress, we're doing the same for our pets. The market now offers Chill Pills, which contain amino acids that help with everything from motion sickness to everyday stress, and a Pet Organics No-Stress Behavior Modification Spray, intended to help reduce anxiety in cats and dogs. Of course, a canine massage at a pet spa is soothing as well.

Pet coffins are also big business—poffins.co.uk provides seven different sizes.

Next: Pedigree Push-Back and Mutt Mystique

Where pedigree pets were once the bastion of royalty and high society, the new status symbol is a designer mutt known as a hybrid. Think Labradoodle, spoodle, and puggle, all mixes of various purebred dogs. For example, there's the schnoodle, a mix of a schnauzer and a poodle, and the bullmatian, a bull mastiff plus a Dalmatian. The puggle even has a celebrity connection: After *The Sopranos'* James Gandolfini and other stars were spotted sporting their own, prices jumped from $200 to $2,000.[47]

People are willing to pay a pretty penny for these dogs, which are said to possess a better temperament than their purist cousins and are less likely to cause allergies. It was about 15 years ago that the first of these hybrids, the Australian Labradoodle, started the designer-dog trend. A cross between a Labrador retriever and a poodle, the breed was a good-tempered, hypoallergenic pet that had buyers spending almost $2,000 per puppy.[48] Many breeders, enticed by the prices, started creating their own new combinations.

The hybrids may be hot, but they're still second-class citizens as far as the American Kennel Club is concerned. The registry of purebred dogs does not recognize hybrids because with mixed breeds, it's hard to guarantee the size, type of coat, and temperament of dogs when they reach adulthood. Lisa Peterson of the American Kennel Club says, "What is the purpose of a puggle? They're not really breeds. Tomorrow, someone could breed a Great Dane with a mastiff and they call it a Great Stiff."[49] Many people, though, are happy to put ideas of puppy perfection aside—after all, who could really resist owning a peekapoo?

And Therefore Next

Perhaps family styles change more slowly than any other element of the culture. Where so much in our lives has gone through revolutionary development, we are struck by how little has substantially changed in this category. Two elements that have really developed are the businesses of sperm donation and adoption—while both were certainly around a decade ago, several factors have pushed these practices into the mainstream. We have a very different view on age and aging (in other words, the chronology of when parenthood is appropriate), and there's also an ever-loosening definition of "family unit"—today, we don't think twice about a single parent deciding to have a kid. As well, the Internet has evolved both practices to a much higher order. The ability to shop for sperm donors and to specify a myriad of desired attributes was not possible before the cataloging ability of the Web. Similarly, navigating the adoption business's multiplicity of possibilities while evaluating the seemingly endless requirements that vary from country to country is made far easier and more appealing by the accessibility of information online.

chapter eleven

big next: bringing it all home

It was in 1977 that historian and social critic Christopher Lasch described the home as our haven from a heartless world, but the idea is more relevant than ever for people living in hectic, fast-paced, anxiety-filled times. The harsher the outside environment, the more we yearn for a comforting place to escape. And so today we assign great importance to the place where we relax, wind down, and recharge our batteries.

This is not dissimilar to what we said in the original *Next*. "The function of the modern home is expanding, as well. In a wired world, it serves as both home and office. In an uncertain world, it has become a haven."[1] Of course, that was without the benefit of a post-9/11 perspective.

Consider the explosion in home-oriented media since then: Newsstands are glutted with home-themed magazines (and established magazines are spinning off home titles to capitalize on the trend, including *O at Home*, *InStyle Home*, and *Martha Stewart Living*), and the TV schedule now covers almost every aspect of home owning, from *Extreme Makeover: Home Edition* to *Trading Spaces* to *Flip This House*. And there has been a corresponding rise of "starchitects," idols of the architecture world. Our homes are our castles, and we're obsessed with finding homes, renovating them, decorating them, and even selling them so we can start the process anew.

The Web site for Home and Garden Television, hgtv.com, reports that it attracted more than 2.5 million unique visitors each month in 2005.[2]

To make the home a haven, we're bringing in amenities normally found in the outside world: theater systems, coffee bars, offices, professional kitchen equipment. In an online survey of young couples by Christopher Lowell Enterprises, the parent company of designer Lowell's television and design divisions, the majority of respondents said they take inspiration from public places like bars, restaurants, hotels, and spas when they decorate their homes.[3] Watch as homes in the next decade become fully equipped compounds that offer both comfort and entertainment—and very little reason to leave.

More time spent at home means more money goes toward improving it. Home improvement and home electronics are seen as a legitimate way to spend. Homes are designed to impress: You invite people over to wow them. Home one-upmanship is now on the rise. In the United States, home owners are hiring professional photographers to document their homes in detail. For some, a house isn't completely finished until it has been featured in *Architectural Digest* or *Elle Décor*, the home owner's equivalent of winning an Oscar. Less fortunate owners settle for featuring exterior shots of their recently purchased homes on customized greeting cards.

Most people fall into one of three types of luxury shopping pattern: personal luxuries (clothing, jewelry), experiential luxuries (travel, fine dining), or home luxuries (art, antiques). By the same token, some countries, such as France, "live on the street"—people spend first on cars, clothes, and jewelry—while in others, such as Sweden, you reflect who you are through your home. More people now want to make their personal statement through their home. A perfect home is synonymous with the perfect family life. Your home is also a way of showcasing your lifestyle and personality. Sophisticated shelving systems now commonly display ethnic touches—objects picked up on world travels—and tokens of culture (books and mementos).

Americans are looking to express the very essence of their national character through their homes. Davis Remignanti, lead design consultant at Furniture.com, says: "I'm finding that people want to define what it means to be American—who they are and what they believe in. And they want to see those beliefs reflected in the style of their homes' decor. The result is a new focus on bringing American design into our homes. The wonderful consequence, of course, is the diversity of looks we're seeing now, as each person defines being American in a very personal and unique way."[4] If Americans feel uncertain about their futures in a global marketplace or unclear about what it means to be patriotic in a partisan era, it seems decorating offers a manageable way to articulate a personal, national viewpoint.

In Asia, the home spa phenomenon is taking off: Once the kids have flown the coop, empty-nesters are transforming spare bedrooms into fitness suites and spas.

Next: Home Is where Your Office Is

Homes are becoming more adaptable to different needs and life purposes. And as more people work from home—be it corporate workers telecommuting or stay-at-home moms running small businesses—the office is increasingly an essential component of the home. It's the most popular room being requested in new home designs, with almost half of architects surveyed in August 2005 by the American Institute of Architects reporting an increased interest in home offices among their clients.[5]

In the home office, images of the bathrobe-clad worker at a makeshift desk are long gone. (Although bathrooms themselves are becoming work spaces in their own right.) The home office is high tech, resembling a small business office more than a simple room reserved for work. It is tricked out with tools like laser printers and networked computers, which are becoming more dominant in the home than televisions. (With TV shows now available for downloading, the focus is moving to a screen that serves two purposes.) And with a growing need for more gadgets, look for workers to push businesses to foot the bill. The technology gap between SOHO firms—meaning small offices with fewer than ten employees (SO) vs. income-generating home offices (HO)—will narrow in the coming years, reports market research firm IDC. It also projects some 23 million SOHOs by the end of 2009, and they will demand higher-end business technology for less.[6]

According to the U.S. Census Bureau, 55 percent of American households own at least one computer.[7]

Set up in our tricked-out home offices, we'll start to obsess about getting the atmosphere just right. A new genre of self-help products will spring up for home office set-up. AOL Coaches, a self-improvement Web site, offers business and career coach Jake Steinfeld to provide insights into starting a business and crafting the nuances of a home office. Home office aesthetics and decorating will be serious business. There will be plenty of chatter about harmony in the home as people try to draw a line between work and living spaces—think no-work zones and even more storage options to keep office clutter out of sight.

The *South China Morning Post* quotes Neal Zimmerman, author of *Home Workspace Idea Book*, on home-office basics: "Whatever the work and whatever the space, I've learnt that successful workplaces share three basic features: They balance home life and work life; they're well-planned and organized; and they have a personal spirit about them that stimulates their owners to do their best work."[8] And in the *Calgary Herald*, Ikea office planner Kim Farrelly advises people to "let your personality out; create a space that inspires you."[9]

Boomers will be big backers of the home office movement. In a survey run by Merrill Lynch, three-quarters of boomers said they anticipate working into their retirement years—and with more mobile technology, they plan to work from a home office, too spry to quit but too tired to tow the company line from the office.[10] Some of the more affluent boomers will have two home offices: Known as "splitters," these 50- and 60-somethings divide their time between at least two homes for family, vacation, and work-life reasons. Boomers want flexibility—and as their coffee-bar and home-theater-equipped homes satisfy ever more needs, there will be little incentive to leave the comfort zone.

That comfort zone now includes bathrooms with amenities like a steam shower/whirlpool unit that includes a standard hands-free phone. Indeed, the bathroom will be an extension of the home office in world where work is done at any time from anywhere. "The humble bathroom, long a place of refuge and solitude, is playing quiet host to more workplace transactions," writes Jon Weinbach for *The Wall Street Journal*. "Bathroom business has gone way beyond tapping out furtive e-mails on a BlackBerry. Lately, more hard-driving homeowners have converted their loos into virtual satellite workspaces, with retractable desks or waterproof touch-screen monitors."[11]

According to a Yahoo!-commissioned report by Forrester Research, 21 percent of homeowners with laptops and wireless broadband say they've checked e-mail in the bathroom.

Next: Home Is the Hot Spot for Entertainment

Going out is now about staying in. Home entertainment systems and dinner parties are the new theaters and restaurants. As we spend more money and thought on creating our havens, we're finding fewer reasons to head out for a good time.

A recent poll by ICM Research on changing leisure habits in the U.K. shows that three times as many people prefer to cook a meal for friends than go out on the town. And half the survey respondents said they're dining in more now than they were five years ago, with more than half hosting a dinner party once a month.[12] ICM calls this rising demographic SHEFs (Stay Home and Entertain Friends). Nationally syndicated chef Rachael Ray, for example, has tapped the market with her magazine *Everyday with Rachael Ray*, which offers a department called "Big Bashes, Small Get Togethers" that caters to the home entertainer. Many stay-at-homers are congregating, entertaining, and dining around televised events like the Oscars, the Super Bowl, and the World Cup.

The more people stay home, the more they invest in ensuring their comfort. Furniture retailers in the United States are working to accommodate the at-home crowd and also to design furnishings around the ever-increasing varieties of home entertainment technology. Recliners, for example, are still a mainstay of the middle-class living room, and now as the *Chicago Tribune* notes, "La-Z-Boy chairs and sofas recline, rock, swivel, lift, heat and massage. They also can contain computer hookups, phones and drink compartments."[13]

How will the leisure industry entice hunkered-down homeowners out in public? With ever-more inventive attractions, predicts ICM. And leisure outlets will have to upgrade to new levels of comfort and luxury as they compete with home amenities. Watch for even bigger and better stadium seating at theaters. Forget the drink holders: Think massages as you watch movies.

What's Next? Private Spaces Take Over from Public Spaces

Harvard economist John Kenneth Galbraith wrote about the phenomenon of "private opulence and public squalor" in 1958's *The Affluent Society*. His view was that privately owned spaces were generally clean, efficient, well-maintained, and constantly improving in quality, while public spaces were dirty, overcrowded, and unsafe—and concluded that more resources ought to be moved into the public sector.[14] But today, in the age of individualism, the home is more valued than community structures. We're a "me generation" more empowered as consumers (and home owners) than as citizens. The rise of home life also comes at the expense of community: For example, as more people drink at home in the U.K., about 250 traditional pubs are closed or redeveloped each year; less than half of British villages now have a local one.[15] What was once a vital hub that played a unique role in British history is now an endangered species. Could it be that the importance of the home in modern life comes at the expense of the ideals of a civic society?

Next: The Rise of the Domestic Goddess

The more uncertain the world outside, the more we look to control what we can in our own lives. And so we're getting more passionate about keeping the "perfect" home by diving into domestic duties such as entertaining guests, cooking, and cleaning. These household tasks were once viewed as a mundane hassle, but with less available spare time, they are now seen almost as a luxury. And they are certainly more passions than casual pastimes, at least judging by the number of magazines and TV shows devoted to these subjects. (And Web sites as well. CreativeHomemaking.com, for example, is "dedicated to your homemaking needs: recipes, cleaning tips, home decorating, crafts, organizing, budgeting, and more!")

The type of Martha Stewart-style home artistry that had fallen by the wayside is a means for people who feel stuck in a continuous cycle of pure consumer consumption to derive a sense of satisfaction from producing something tangible, engaging in hands-on activities such as cooking and crafts. This new view of domesticity sees homemaking as fun. There are e-mail groups for "hip domestics" and "domestic goddesses," and books about homemaking that read almost like novels, such as British columnist Rita Konig's *Domestic Bliss: Simple Ways to Add Style to Your Life*.

Cleaning is now almost an obsession. Countless newspaper columns and books advise domestic goddesses on how to keep their homes pristine. And who would have thought that a successful TV show would be based on scrubbing sinks? *How Clean Is Your House?* features grime-busters Kim and Aggie revealing the filth in a hapless volunteer's home; it was such a hit in the U.K., Lifetime TV imported it to the United States, where the two stars "tidy up America one filthy house at a time."

Cleanliness represents the boundary between order and chaos. Having a clean house means you are on top of things. Most people like order after all, but many people have a hard time creating it. Cleanliness equals happiness, but it's always fleeting. As Sherri Mandell writes in *The Forward*: "On those rare days when I do clean and the house is, for a moment, perched on the edge of order, it's like I'm on a ship sailing the tranquil Caribbean seas. Then, as my kids and I and my husband go about our ordinary routine, it's as if I'm watching the sky darken, hearing the first murmuring of thunder. When the inevitable storm of crumbs and dirt and chaos begins to descend, I feel the terror and disappointment of a pilot watching her ship smash onto an unforgiving shore."[16]

"I think there is definitely a big association between how clean your house is and house pride. Your house is an expression of yourself and, I guess, how 'together' your life is."
—Mary, a 30-year-old Londoner

Next: The Kitchen As Favored Space

The kitchen is once again at the heart of the home, but it's not just for cooking and eating—it's a place for entertaining, working, doing homework, and watching TV. In many homes, walls have been demolished to turn the kitchen into a bigger family/leisure space. "The kitchen is not really a kitchen anymore," kitchen designer Johnny Grey tells Katrina Burroughs of *The Sunday Times* in London. "Cooking is only one function. Often, the only time two partners spend together awake is in the kitchen."[17]

As the kitchen's importance rises and family behavior changes, the formal dining room is disappearing. In the U.K., for instance, sales of dining room furniture have declined by 8 percent over the last five years. "Today, dining rooms have become almost defunct as a place where a family enjoys an everyday meal together around the table," says David Bird, senior market analyst at market research firm Mintel. "For those who have a dining room, it is usually kept only for formal occasions or has changed its function completely. . . . Some consumers are now more likely to be found working on their laptop than eating at the dining room table."[18] And with the rise of home schooling, particularly in the United States, some dining rooms are being turned into classrooms.

The kitchen's new role as an entertainment hub means we are spending more on it, from high-end countertops and hardware to restaurant-style ranges. We want sleek lines and streamlined cupboards to hide things away, but we also want areas where we can display recipe books or favorite ceramic and glassware items—Americans in particular are full of pride for the things they have accumulated. It is also important to make an impact with carefully chosen materials and finishes, lighting and countertops. And we're fetishizing gadgets, so retro 1950s-style Dualit toasters and food mixers are must-haves, along with refrigerators equipped with built-in flat-screen TVs or Internet connections.

Meals used to be just about feeding, but now there's enjoyment in the process of cooking—and kitchens are reflecting that. Top-notch appliances intended for serious cooks are common, with home owners shelling out for brands like Viking, Gaggenau, Bosch, and Wolf, spending as much as $8,500 for a Thermador range. Strikingly, a swanky kitchen isn't a sure signal that an avid chef is in the house. Among the wealthy in Britain, "a beautiful kitchen is a must even for those who rarely lift an oven glove," writes Burroughs.[19] A young doctor whose home renovation includes fitting a kitchen with blue slate counters and Viking appliances tells *The New York Times*, "I'm going to have to hire somebody. I don't do any of this. But I look at it."[20] And, surely, his guests will look and admire as well.

Men are increasingly interested in cooking, however, spurred by über-cool or macho celebrity chefs like British stars Jamie Oliver and Gordon Ramsey. These days the kitchen is no longer a woman's domain. But men are less interested in the daily grind of producing family meals than in performing for friends. And like many male hobbies, gadgets play a big part, from $1,600-plus knife sets from Wusthof to professional saucepans. Kitchen designer Poggenpohl is tapping into this trend by joining forces with Porsche to create a kitchen targeted at men. And Pininfarina, which designs Ferraris, also crafts kitchens, with "gleaming, curvy aluminum ensembles that are every bit as sexy as a 328 GTS," notes the *Sunday Times*.[21]

Cooking clubs for men are becoming popular in the United States, with *Back to Basics* on the Fine Living channel and *Easy Entertaining with Michael Chiarello* on the Food Network both spotlighting such clubs. The men meet up regularly to prepare gourmet meals at each other's homes. "Don't miss this classic he-man, meat and potato meal as Michael hosts a monthly get together of men who love to cook," says the Food Network site. "While the men flex their culinary muscles, the women sit back and enjoy the show!"

Next: Bedroom or Boudoir?

We have talked in the media that "sleep is the new sex": Sleep has become the ultimate luxury, a fantasy and a secret indulgence. Human beings can survive longer without food than without sleep, but in our frenetic 24/7 lives, most of us are surviving on less sleep than we need. And when we want to sleep, we can't: More than half of us have trouble sleeping at least one night a week, and Americans sleep on average 6.9 hours a night instead of the recommended 8.5.[22] We'll try anything that might help: herbal teas and remedies, scented candles, soothing white-noise machines, and high-end beds.

British bedding company Ammique claims its beds are specially engineered to send you off to the land of nod; the only drawback is that they cost tens of thousands of dollars. Slightly lower down the scale, Swedish company Tempur-Pedic produces a mattress that molds to your shape; tens of thousands of them sell worldwide at an average price of more than $2,000.

As sleep becomes a treat, so the bedroom becomes a boudoir: an opulent retreat from the hassle of our daily lives, filled with cushions, candles, throws, and subtle lighting. Designer bed linens are big, with names such as Ralph Lauren and Lulu Guinness getting into the market. Indeed, some consumers are so keen on such luxury items that a term has been coined to describe them: "luxorexics." Writing in the *Sunday Times*, Simon Mills observes, "Bed linen is luxorexic pornography. They will talk of thread counts, Egyptian cottons, pillow mountains and the varying water qualities of different American states, and how this can affect the laundering of their treasured duvets and pillowcases."[23]

Next: Teen Bedrooms as Command Central

If adults crave sleep, teens don't. Their bedrooms have become command central, where they communicate with their friends—from both the real and the virtual worlds—around the clock, talking on the phone as they send text messages, e-mail, and instant messages. A quarter of teens fall asleep at school at least once a week, according to research carried out at the Sleep Center at the Children's Hospital of Philadelphia. The reason, says the Sleep Center, is largely the distractions provided by the gadgets in their rooms: computers, cell phones, TVs, and gaming devices, as well as the tendency for teens to call each other for a middle-of-the-night chat. "Those with four or more electronic devices in their bedroom were twice as likely to fall asleep in school," says Jodi A. Mindell, one of the study's authors.[24]

> A third of British kids has high-tech gadgets and equipment worth up to £2,000 in their bedrooms, Lloyds TSB Insurance found, and one in ten kids has up to £5,000 worth. Phil Loney, managing director of Lloyds TSB, says these kids "are, quite literally, sleeping on a gold mine."[25]

With technology providing so much in-home entertainment, teens—like their parents—are finding less need to go out. Parents don't really know what their children are up to in their rooms, but they prefer the kids safely indoors than out in a dangerous world. "I have no idea what the crowd of girls in my 15-year-old daughter's bedroom is doing," says Susan, a 45-year-old Londoner. "But I would rather they were here, where I can keep some kind of control. We've installed a mini fridge in her bedroom that she can have a bottle of wine in if friends come over—but it's one bottle of wine between eight of them. It's better than her going off to pubs, where I can't control it."

The teenage bedroom—a messy, private world where teens can sulk, plot, and dream—is most often a parental no-go zone, but interior design retailers from Ikea to boho-chic Monsoon are barging in. In the United States, Teenage Research Unlimited reports, the 13-to-18 age group has created a staggering $17 billion market for furnishings.[26]

Builders in the U.K. are now designing teen bedrooms around the command-center concept. (Creating rooms that kids love can make or break a deal, since teens can hold significant influence over their parents.) Some showhomes place the teenager's bedroom as far as possible from the rest of the family and display a plasma TV screen, a sofa, a bar, and a pool table, so that the bedroom is advertised as a place for sleeping, entertaining, chilling out, and studying.

Next: Where We Will Live—In and Out of the Neighborhoods

As our homes become more important to us, so does location. There's a migratory cross-flow of people moving in and out of cities, suburbs, and even the exurbs—those spaces far from the urban centers and well past the suburban subdivisions. In the 1940s and 1950s, the postwar boom sent America scurrying out to the sanitized suburbs, and these have remained a cultural mainstay. While aesthetics have evolved from variants of split-levels to McMansions, the picket fences, manicured lawns, and circuitous commutes have long been middle-class norms. What's next is the emergence of new patterns of people flocking both to and from urban settings and rural areas.

Europeans of all ages have always lived right in the heart of many cities such as Barcelona and Amsterdam, and now Americans, too, are rethinking the benefits of urban living. A 2005 report on real estate trends published by the Urban Land Institute (ULI) in Washington, D.C., and PricewaterhouseCoopers notes that, "Mounting traffic congestion and a lack of mass transportation in many built-out suburbs focus attention on infill and mixed-use town center projects with pedestrian-friendly design." The report cites a developer in the Northwest who says, "A lot of multifamily development is taking on the urban-village concept. With fewer fields to plow down, abominable traffic, and the land-density issue, people want to live closer to work or transit. This will lead to more expensive, complex and dense development."[27]

With the boomer generation coming of age in empty nests and with gas prices skyrocketing, there's a strong desire to be downtown with access to mass transit and more social options for diverse age sets. But boomers aren't the only ones leaving behind the cul-de-sacs and tree-lined comforts of suburban life. Some of the "echo boomers"—the 132 million combined Gen Xers and Gen Yers who today range in age from 16 to 43—are also seeking the benefits of 24/7 cities, say ULI and PricewaterhouseCoopers.[28] Waiting longer to have children or opting for none at all, these echo boomers are less concerned about school districts and sidewalks. And both boomers and echo boomers are burned out by traffic congestion and long commutes, and they're willing to trade in fresh air and back yards to be closer to their offices. Watch for a middle-class migration back to cities and a corresponding increase in high-end real estate that offers culture with convenience.

It's not just an American trend. In the U.K., many city centers are being regenerated as old industrial and office spaces are turned into homes. In Manchester, the center has been revitalized with an influx of young people who are choosing to live where they work—two-thirds are single and under 35. In a bid to buck the trend, architects and developers are hoping to attract thousands of families with three- and four-bedroom homes, along with more schools, playgrounds, and other amenities. In addition to families, city centers will have to be geared to the needs of older singles, says the Institute for Public Policy Research, predicting that some U.K. city areas such as Liverpool's Docklands are potential "grey zones."[29]

Still, while cities offer more culture and shorter commutes, there are disadvantages pushing people out. Some urban dwellers are fleeing the soaring cost of living, poor schools, and congestion, hoping to find a better quality of life. And while there's little evidence to suggest that fear of terrorist attacks is persuading Londoners to leave the city, many big-city residents now have a heightened sense of danger (think epidemics as well as terrorism). *The Washington Post* reports, "It is clear that American inner-city residents reacted far more strongly to 9/11 than people in suburbs and smaller towns. Polls taken months after the terrorist attacks on New York and Washington showed that twice as many big-city residents as suburbanites, and four times as many as rural residents, felt 'great concern' about future attacks."[30]

Next: Rural Living Styles

To some, the suburbs seem as bland as ever, so rural areas are starting to look appealing. The U.K. Office for National Statistics reports that the rural population is now growing eight times faster than that of inner cities.[31] (Although Richard Craze, author of *Out of Your Townie Mind*, says that up to 40 percent of those who quit British cities for the countryside end up returning.)[32]

There's a new exodus to the exurbs. Karl Rove, President Bush's senior adviser, describes an exurb as being "like a new suburb" that has sprung up "past the old, established suburbs."[33] As Rick Lyman writes in *The New York Times*, the exurbs "begin as embryonic subdivisions of a few hundred homes at the far edge of beyond, surrounded by scrub. Then, they grow—first gradually but soon with explosive force—attracting stores, creating jobs and struggling to keep pace with the need for more schools, more roads, more everything. And eventually, when no more land is available and home prices have skyrocketed, the whole cycle starts again, another 15 minutes down the turnpike."[34]

These neighborhoods sit far from everywhere but offer more square footage for less, decent schools and more security for the family, and the cleanliness and convenience of newness. The downside is the never-ending commute. Living far-ther means driving longer, and there's a strain on time, but that's the tradeoff for getting the newer and safer. It's a revised take on the old American classic, that driving pursuit of the American Dream out there, way out there.

Next: Smaller, Greener, More Efficient Homes

Out with the McMansion and the sprawl of square footage and in with the effi-cient home that maximizes space and resources. With the fast-growing cost of heating and cooling homes, people are sacrificing size for sound, sustainable structures. Sarah Susanka, architect, author, and proponent of the "not so big" philosophy of residential architecture, encourages home owners to "build better, not bigger." In her series of popular books, including *The Not So Big House*, she espouses the rising trend: "Builders and consumers are realizing that by reducing a home's footprint through better design, they can put the savings into details that are high-quality, energy-efficient and environmentally sound."[35]

Urban life is increasingly about downsizing and maximizing. With home ownership out of reach for many workers and a growing number of people living alone or in smaller family units, ultra-compact homes may prove appealing (at least, if you're not too tall or large). The Micro Compact Home, developed by Professor Richard Horden of Munich Technical University, is a cube 2.6 meters square into which are crammed a kitchen, bedroom, dining area, shower, toilet, work space, and entertainment zone (take a look at microcompacthome.com). Also from Germany is the "Loftcube," now available in the United States (see loftcube.net). Designed by Studio Aisslinger in Berlin, Loftcubes are small, trans-portable living spaces that "suit people of a nomadic lifestyle, living for short periods of time in large cities and dense urban areas." They're a modern twist on the ancient yurt or a newer twist on the modern trailer. Loftcubes could even be set up on the roofs of buildings, which the company considers an "undiscovered treasure of sunlit property." It's all about maximizing space while minimizing impact.

Meanwhile, more banks are offering energy-efficient mortgages (EEM), which give borrowers special benefits when they buy or build homes that are energy efficient. These "green" mortgages are based on the idea that more sustainable homes mean lower utility bills, leaving more funds for costly features— a win-win for bank and for borrower. The National Association of Realtors says it's a good deal, since energy-efficient homes can cut energy costs by a third or even a half.

> Beginning in January 2006, U.S. consumers who buy and install energy-efficient windows, insulation, doors, roofs, and heating and cooling equipment for the home can claim a tax credit of up to $500, according to the Energy Policy Act of 2005. The act also allows a tax credit of up to $3,400 for people who buy or lease a hybrid car, depending on the vehicle's fuel economy and weight.[36]

What's Next? Personal Sustainability

Or, as the BBC says, "Power from the people."[37] It's a movement known as "microgeneration," in which individuals generate their own low-carbon heat and power. In England, a study by the Energy Saving Trust calculates that by 2050 up to 40 percent of the nation's heating requirements and 6 percent of energy requirements could be generated by individuals.[38] A Climate Change and Sustainable Energy Bill proposes to reward people who create their own electricity and power, the BBC notes, observing that, "Solar panels and miniature wind turbines could soon become an officially promoted part of the urban landscape."[39] The sustainability movement in the U.K. is also evident in the new popularity of growing one's own produce. There are long waiting lists for plots of land, or allotments, where you can tend to fruits and vegetables, and there is such an interest in so-called urban farming that apartments being built in the Edinburgh city center come complete with mini-allotments for residents.

What's Next? Fewer and Fewer McMansions

"Release the zoning hounds: The McMansion backlash has begun," declares Christopher Solomon of MSN Real Estate.[40] Around the United States, local governments are coming down on what some call "starter castles," houses that are between about 4,000 and 10,000 square feet. Stricter building limits are being imposed across the map, from Austin, Texas, to New Canaan, Connecticut. New York city councilman Tony Avella, who led a rezoning effort in his Bayside, Queens, district in 2005, explains to CNN/*Money* writer Les Christie, "Overdevelopment is the No. 1 issue in my district. It comes up more than education or police protection."[41] Besides traffic and overcrowding, what gets to local residents is how out-of-scale these homes look in modest neighborhoods. A character in the 2006 film *Friends with Money* who is adding a second story onto her home abruptly halts construction when she sees the bulky structure from out of her neighbor's window. For some big-house buffs, it seems this sort of restraint may no longer be voluntary.

Next: Smaller Homes, Smaller Cars

Along with smaller homes, we'll have smaller cars parked in the driveway—if there's a driveway at all. The benefits are the same: They're more efficient, benefiting both the owner and the environment. Europeans have always been fond of small, snappy cars made for navigating narrow city streets rather than six-lane interstate freeways. The Mini and the Smart Car are stylish as well as economical, and Americans are taking notice: In an age of fluctuating gas prices, there's something obscene about the likes of a shiny new Hummer tanking down the street. As more consumers feel the proverbial pain at the pump from their insatiable supersized SUVs, we'll see smaller electric vehicles gradually taking over.

The market is still very small, but car makers are seeing substantial interest in hybrid vehicles, which run on both gas and electricity. In 2005, the two dominant manufacturers, Toyota and Honda, both reported record results. Sales of Toyota's Prius were up more than 90 percent from a year earlier, and Honda reported that sales of its three signature hybrids—the Civic, the Accord, and the Insight—jumped more than 180 percent.[42]

These numbers are pushing Detroit's Big Three—Ford, Chrysler, and General Motors—to integrate hybrids into their lineups. Bill Ford, executive chairman of Ford Motor, Co., has pledged to increase hybrid production more than tenfold by 2010: "We'll have the capacity to produce at least a quarter-million hybrids a year," he says, "and the ability to scale up as the market demands."[43] A report by J. D. Power and Associates projects that hybrids, which accounted for just half of 1 percent of the U.S. market in 2004, will grow to a 3.5 percent market share by 2012.[44]

Car buyers will need to be courted as much by comfort and convenience, however, as by the promise of cost-savings. J. D. Power reported in its 2005 automotive survey that drive, handling, and performance were the top factors considered by 70 percent of drivers looking for a new car. By contrast, fuel economy ranked 9th out of 15 options.[45] Car manufacturers have their work cut out for them—balancing price and performance isn't easy. A hybrid costs as much as $3,000 to $4,000 more than a comparable option, and starting in 2007, competing technologies such as more fuel-efficient gasoline and diesel options will be on the market.

If it's going to cost more, it better look good—and offer top-notch technology and performance. Consider Toyota's Lexus GS 450h, released in spring 2006: It's the first full hybrid with a front engine and rear-wheel drive, and it's more about its image than anything else. As Hybridcars.com notes, "Buyers of the GS 450h probably won't be motivated by saving the earth, saving gas, or saving money at the pumps. The only saving that might motivate this segment of the market is saving time."[46] (Since drivers need to fill the tank less frequently.) Many buyers will be drawn to hybrids not because they're earth friendly but when they're earth shattering.

Next: Owning Versus Renting

Many people around the world aspire to home ownership. The percentage of home owners in any country depends on various factors: income levels, government incentives, and the availability of cheap mortgages and/or financial help provided by the extended family. Also important are timing of marriage and childbirth, birth cohort, and whether a household has a second income. And parental home ownership increases the probability of ownership across social class (and especially for lower-income households).

In communities with a high proportion of home ownership, statistics show that crime rates are low, standards of living are higher, and families feel more secure and confident about their future. In the United States, home equity constitutes the bulk of wealth held by most low- to middle-income families, one reason why the government makes a concerted effort to raise home-ownership levels through tax breaks and other incentives. The aspiration to home ownership by low-income immigrants and ethnic minorities has also helped support a strong U.S. real-estate market.

In the United States, 68 percent of all households own their own homes, on par with the U.K. (69 percent) and Canada (66 percent), the *Boston Globe* reports.[47] Russia has a particularly high home-ownership rate (71.5 percent), because the government offered Russians their state-owned apartments at minimal prices after the breakup of the Soviet Union in 1991. And for generations, Australians have demanded the right to buy (or even be given) land and to develop it for the highest possible economic return. In some European countries, however, ownership stands at less than half of households—Germany has one of the lowest rates among industrialized countries, at 42 percent. The *Globe* notes that this is due in part to the large down payments required (often 20–30 percent of the purchase price) and laws limiting rent hikes.[48]

Next: New Modes of Owning

The rising cost of real estate has put home ownership beyond the means of many aspiring buyers. The average price of a London home has surpassed a quarter-million pounds (more than half a million dollars), and in Sydney it's nearing the half-million mark in Australian dollars (about $350,000). And since more of us are living alone (in the U.K., Social Trends estimates that by 2020, as many as 40 percent of households will consist of one person),[49] getting into the real estate market with one income is increasingly out of reach. (That said, more single women today are jumping into the real estate market, buying property without waiting until they're in a committed relationship.)

Young singles hoping to buy are turning to their parents for financial help: Research by the Joseph Rowntree Foundation in the U.K. indicates that British parents expect on average to contribute £17,000 so their adult children can buy their first homes, and 22 percent are prepared to borrow money to help out children hoping to buy.[50] As Melanie, 31, from London explains: "My parents loaned me the money to buy this flat. Most of my friends' parents have also helped them get on the property ladder. It's almost impossible to do it on your own." Some buyers are also teaming up with friends or siblings to buy a property.

Another trend is flipping homes: looking not only for a home for the family, but for one that can pay the family bills. It has become common practice for people to buy a house, move in, fix it up—and then sell it at a profit as the market continues to rise. This is a style of living for many; gone are the days when one bought a home for life, or even for a decade.

Next: Ways to Rent

The latest trend in the rental sector is to test-drive a new area before buying there. Couples in their 30s and 40s with young children like to try out a neighborhood for a year or two before deciding whether to settle there. In some countries, some parents rent homes in a desirable school district to guarantee a place for their child; once they're in, they can buy wherever they choose. Others are renting for the sheer ease of life without ties—and endless projects around the house. Renting can buy a more glamorous lifestyle, allowing the buyer to live in areas where home prices are out of reach; there's also less maintenance and more flexibility to travel. Renting also gives young people the ability to move with their jobs, as well as the convenience of living next to public transport and other amenities.

A primary reason to rent, of course, is that buying a home has become a dream that's beyond the financial grasp of most young people. It's also beyond the grasp of many middle-income earners: "When you are 42 and you still can't buy a home, or even get close to buying one, then you are in great trouble," a British nurse tells the BBC, noting that one senior nurse is thinking about becoming a plumber in order to afford a home.[51] While soaring property values are bringing profits to home owners (on paper, at least), others are lagging far behind. The British government's 2004–2005 housing survey shows that more under-30s are renting than buying, and that the average age of the first-time buyer has risen from 32 to 34 in the past ten years.

Next: One Home Is Not Enough

Ownership of second homes abroad is a real growth area, particularly among the British; some French villages are now more English than French. More than half a million British households owned a second home in 2005, an increase of 10 percent over the previous year; 180,000 of those are on foreign soil.[54] The majority are in Spain and France, which are served by budget airlines, but the British are also buying second homes in long-haul destinations such as the United States, Australia, Canada, the Caribbean, and South Africa. Buyers are motivated by better weather, along with prices that are relatively low compared with real estate costs in the U.K. And because baby boomers distrust pension companies and the government to look after them in their old age, a second property is viewed as an alternative pension.

> In Montpellier, France, and Seville, Spain, home prices have more than doubled since 2001, largely because they're serviced by budget airlines that bring in British buyers seeking a place in the sun.[55]

In the United States, Knight Ridder reports that 1 million Americans have retired to Mexico, Costa Rica, and emerging markets in Eastern Europe because the cost of living is so much lower.[56] Largely, however, Americans are buying second homes domestically, and they're buying them more than ever: About 40 percent of homes sold in 2005 (3.3 million) were non-primary residences, compared with 36 percent in 2004 and 33 percent in 2003, according to the National Association of Realtors.[57] Looking just at vacation homes, the association reports a 17 percent rise in 2005, accounting for more than 1 million homes.

Critics of second homes say they restrict the supply of available housing to locals, forcing prices to rise. Second-home owners typically use local services such as libraries, post offices, and schools far less than locals, which undermines their viability. This puts a squeeze on those looking for jobs and homes (mainly the young), forcing them to leave the area and look elsewhere, which exacerbates the problem. (One response to the problem: Michael Eavis, founder of the Glastonbury Festival in the U.K., is helping to fund cheap local homes built on his land that are available only to locals.)

And Therefore Next

If there is any single element that looks like an overarching driver to many of the trends we're looking at here, it's energy cost. Its implications for home building (size, materials, location) are significant, but its influence may go well beyond that in the immediate future and (with no real alternate sources) is likely to be felt for some time to come.

chapter twelve

big next: the pace and place of work

In the original *Next*, we prefaced a chapter titled "You Call This Work?" as follows:

> As we usher in an era of global markets, automated production, and virtuality, we're
> not just seeing changes in the workplace, we're also seeing changes in the worker. The
> fact is, our transition from a nation-based Industrial Age to a global Digital Age will
> require new job parameters, new skills, and new approaches to how we conduct our
> day-to-day business—and plan our careers.[1]

Indeed, it's been a busy decade in the business of work. We've experienced a bipo-
lar rise and fall of the dot-coms (and by some recent indications, another rise—
although this one is likely to be felt much more strongly in India than in the
West). We've seen greed on a grand scale, with corporate crime by the likes of
Enron and WorldCom. We've rallied for workers' rights and fair wages from Wal-
Mart and others. And we've seen such fervent youth labor unrest in the streets
and academic institutions of France that the government announced a total
reversal on labor policy. It's been a time of shakeups and layoffs.

Perhaps it's no surprise we're retreating, thinking more about the balance of
life and work. Maybe we welcome the advance of mobile technology so much
because we can get some distance, some refuge in the sanctity of a family home
or in the cozy familiarity of a cafe. It's little wonder we want to be known as

remote, distance, and distributed workers. It seems a little less risky, a little safer to straddle the line between being here or there. We've learned from the past. Now we're more about control, making decisions that are just as good for us as they are for the company. We're feeling more independent, free to set out our own terms—take a chance, become a free agent.

Businesses certainly feel the tension. Gone is "My way or the highway," and here is the yoga-ization of the office and progressive plans for work spaces with expensive lighting and air systems to promote health and productivity, "green" building materials, and an impressively cool aura. There's a cost benefit to alternative ways of working that hasn't gone unnoticed either. When people feel better, they perform better and, in the case of the virtual worker, they cost less than the average cube dweller. But as our spaces get smarter, we will also need to conserve space for the sake of money and the environment; we'll have more technology to work with but less space to work in.

Telecommuting can be a win-win for everybody—workers save on the costs of commutes with less gas consumption and fewer expenses for meals and clothes. We're now free from the structure and limits of space, but the primacy of place is now more important to us than ever. We're looking at our physical space with greater sophistication and higher standards. Beyond today's communal coffee-shop office, we're seeing the evolution of central hubs that ground and connect remote workers in a single social and professional space. With entire cities building wireless infrastructures (as Philadelphia and San Francisco are doing in the United States), the new hotspots will really be hotspots. But as technology becomes more pervasive at home and work, how will we balance our lives with our work?

Next: Technology Lets Us Work Anywhere, at Any Time

Technology will be key to the juggling act of work and life. All it takes now is a laptop and a cell phone to transform into the portable and mobile worker—business is possible at any time, anywhere. About 12 percent of U.S. workers are considered distributed, or untethered from the office, according to *Business Week*.[2] Whether in an office or not, we're able to have around-the-clock, around-the-globe conference meetings and calls from home or the office at all hours of the day. We can be remote but connected. It's fast, cheap, and easy for Boston to be on the phone to Bangalore with emerging technologies like VoIP (Voice over Internet Protocol), also known as the digital phone.

According to Frost & Sullivan market research, 5 billion calling minutes on IP telephony were logged in 2000; in 2006, that volume is expected to reach 243 billion minutes.[3]

While being wired used to be the height of modernity, now it's old-fashioned. Parts of the world that have lots of wires (telephone, Internet, etc.) are busy getting wireless connections to untether themselves. And those parts of the world with few installed wires are going straight to wireless. Wi-Fi access points—all those hotspots—are expanding from the confines of airports, libraries, and coffee shops to encompass whole cities. Working in the park on your laptop is now a real possibility. Watch as Better Business Bureaus start boasting of wireless capacities in city brochures and Web sites, touting travel destinations for work and pleasure.

In just one year, from January 2005 to January 2006, the number of worldwide wireless hotspots almost doubled, from 53,779 in 93 countries to 100,355 hotspots in 115 countries.[4]

The top three Wi-Fi cities in January 2005: London, New York, and Paris; in 2006: Seoul, Tokyo, and London.[5]

Technology is the new bag of tricks for a mobile workforce. Ferris Research, a San Francisco research firm, offers ideas for "the ideal collaboration toolset for distributed workers."[6] What do people need in their kits? Ferris cites lots more technological abilities, including remote-control access to other people's computer screens; one-to-one telephones and on-demand conference calls, the more integrated the better; instant messaging; an easy-to-use database; a wiki, or Web site that allows people to easily add content; threaded discussion groups; group scheduling; video pictures, notably of faces to help build team spirit; and group polling. It's a lot of stuff, but look for even more products and services that allow us to feel freer, yet also more linked to others, and help us shape both our physical and digital environments.

"We will see a revolution where things will become very much Web-enabled. You will be able to access all your software from anywhere in the world on any device with a couple of biometric swipes—from the whole of my e-mail archive to all of the software I'm licensed to use. I believe you will either pay through subscriptions or have the service funded by advertisements."
—Richard Holway, of technology consultants
Ovum Holway, in the *Financial Times*[7]

The increasing consumerization of technology will also mean better synchronicity, so that personal and work life will be unified through hardware and software that's smarter and more precise. And we'll depend even more on technology to underpin life-over-work time-shifting. As Cynthia Crossley, a Microsoft director, says, "There are three basic things people will always want to do: stay in touch with each other, get more done and have more fun. Technology keeps making these things easier, to the point where it becomes seamless to an individual."[8]

But while technology has in many ways made our lives easier and often vastly more efficient, the time and resources it takes to stay current can cause us great "techno-stress," a phrase coined by clinical psychologist Craig Brod in the 1980s and further explored by Larry Rosen and Michelle Weil in 1997's *TechnoStress: Coping with Technology at Work, Home and Play.* Technology moves ahead on all fronts, and we struggle to keep pace. Our biggest struggle with all this technology, however, will be how to stay connected all the time without feeling connected all the time. Technology has made work ubiquitous.

Next: Work Bleeds into Life

We're struck by the difference in the expectation versus the reality of "connectivity technology"—the Holy Grail of time-saving has turned into an "always on" lifestyle for many of us. Crackberry, anyone?

Work increasingly fits around other aspects of life, and we're really struggling to construct a framework to manage all our activities. As technology makes jobs more portable, it's also obliterating the line between work and personal life.

Consider, for example, the new work lives of junior lawyers. Technology has changed the nature of their jobs for better and for worse. "Fixing an error in a company filing takes minutes on the computer instead of hours at the printer," Amy Kolz writes in *American Lawyer.* "Researching case filings now takes two hours on Westlaw versus three weeks of digging through law books."[9] But tools like cell phones and high-speed connections have lawyers working everywhere and all the time. While some partners may wonder why offices are empty at night, their underlings are actually busy around the clock, Kolz reports: "Associates are no longer shackled to their desks, but they now sleep with their cell phones close at hand." One associate from Shearman & Sterling tells the magazine, "Technology makes it possible for [partners] to encroach on all of your time, whether you're awake, asleep, or on vacation."

Nearly half of Americans planned to work through Labor Day 2005, the day designed to honor workers, according to a survey by Pittsburgh human resources consulting firm Development Dimensions International. Of the 1,100 people surveyed, 42 percent said they would go into the office or spend time checking e-mail and voicemail or doing other job-related tasks.[10]

There's no question that we've accelerated our pace. We're doing more in less time, but we're still putting in more time. The result? Overwork. A 2004 study by the Families and Work Institute, a nonprofit center for research, confirms this: One in three employees reported being in contact with work outside of normal hours at least once a week.[11] In fact, the study classified one-third of all U.S. employees as chronically overworked, which translates to a lot of worker mistakes, resentment toward employers, and poor health. What's next for the overworked? It's all about attitude. The study found that people who perceived themselves as family-centric or dual-centric (same amount of emphasis on family and work) were less likely to be overworked. We may be toting around more technology, but we can control it—we can turn it off.

With more overwork comes overtime outrage. The *Seattle Times* reports that the tech workers whose endless hours and boundless ambition propelled the dot-com era are backing off, putting in fewer hours than they were five years ago, according to the U.S. Bureau of Labor Statistics.[12] Software workers specifically are logging six fewer hours per week. More telling, the newspaper reports, a growing percentage of people believe there's no price tag on our personal lives. In a survey of 4,600 people in 2005, Salary.com found that given the choice, 39 percent of respondents would choose more time off over a $5,000 raise, a 20 percent increase from just three years before. While the majority of employees still opt for more money, there's a growing desire to put family and self before business.

There's a rising movement against the round-the-clock race and the always-on mobile world. With more people working across times zones, it takes more hours to straddle everyone's waking periods. It's something we learned back in 1997, when we were based in Europe, handing off activity to our U.S. colleagues, materially increasing our productivity. People will increasingly want to time-shift tasks that let them "switch off" and just relax.

What's Next? Unplug to Think

Look for more of us to unwire, but also look for more of us to unplug. People are slowing down. If you call designer Philippe Starck's Paris office before 1 p.m., you're told that this is their "thinking time," during which they don't take calls or respond to e-mails. The U.K.'s leading cellular carrier, Orange, recently launched ads that say it's OK to turn your phone off; the slogan: "Sometimes things need to switch off, for people to switch on." Not putting your cell phone on the table during lunch will be a real statement of giving your undivided attention.

What's Next? Homework at Work

If work now travels home with us, home travels with us to work as well— employees will continue to do their home banking, book vacations, instant-message with friends, and help research their kids' homework at the office. Few organizations have been able to prevent the use of freely available software such as Google Desktop, America Online, and Skype, because users see it as a valuable tool in their daily work.

Next: The New Face of Business—the Free Agent

Free agents are about independence and individuality. They're about the freedom to move from job to job, project to project, anytime and anywhere. They have greater say about how they want to work and what best suits them. They're the creative class, doing what they love. They're the "me lancers" who call the shots about what projects to take on. They're remote workers like those taking advantage of the iWork program at Sun Microsystems, mixing and matching the when, where, and how of work.

What's most striking about free agents? They're productive and happy. (After 30 years on the job, Ira took the plunge into free agency at the beginning of 2006, and he's happy to report both prosperity and job satisfaction—something about liking his boss.)

"Our people working these remote schedules are the happiest employees we have, and they have the lowest attrition rates," says Bill MacGowan, Sun's senior VP for human resources, in *Business Week*.[13] They are also 15 percent more productive, he says. Meanwhile, Sun's policy, which gives nearly half of workers the option to work remotely, helps save the company about $300 million in real estate costs, says *Business Week*, and gives Sun a much wider pool from which to hire. As MacGowan puts it, "Would I rather settle on someone mediocre in the Bay Area or get the best person in the country who is willing to work remotely?"

Free agents have all kinds of options now. eBay alone has inspired a new class of entrepreneur who has ditched a day job to make a living at home. And people are doing it everywhere. In Britain, it's estimated that 70,000 people make at least a quarter of their income off the site, and about 8,500 professional eBay sellers in Australia derive a primary or secondary source of income from the site.[14] eBay provides the ultimate virtual job. It can be done from anywhere with no overhead—the ultimate equalizer in the global marketplace, a free-agent paradise.

In Australia alone, the research shows that nearly 12,500 stay-at-home moms and dads and almost 7,000 single parents sell on eBay to supplement their family income; about 5,500 retirees use the site to make some extra money.[15]

Next: The In-Between Space

The coffee bar has become the de facto office for many virtual workers and an ad hoc venue for meetings. But distributed workers have a desperate need for places to blend virtual and physical work spaces. In 2007, 20 million people worldwide will use third places, in-between environments—neither traditional office nor home—and spend 25–35 percent of their work time there.[16]

Forty percent of the workforce will be considered distributed by 2012.[17]

As "work clubs" of sorts, third places serve as local community destinations in a borderless world. Many will develop in rural and suburban locales to help connect talent to nearby metropolitan areas.

It's clear too that as we become more autonomous in our work lives, more remote from co-workers and clients, we'll have a strong need for actual connection in a physical space. Third places will be our touchstones, places to converge. We already have the virtual equivalent in online collaborative work spaces like MayeticVillage and Backpack, and we share calendar space on Yahoo, but we need something more. It will be truer than ever that people need to be around people. And it seems the possibilities for that are expanding.

More official hubs are emerging for mobile workers. Various members of the Internet Home Alliance (IHA)—including Cisco Systems, Cushcraft, Hewlett-Packard, IBM, Microsoft, Panasonic, and Taubman Centers—collaborated to test a center for distributed workers in a 2,400-square-foot space in a high-end shopping center in Plano, Texas. Conforming to Grantham and Ware's notion of the third place, "Connection Court" was on the edge of a major city in a spot that draws many mobile workers (Plano, a Dallas suburb, is home to several Fortune 500 companies). The center was free and open to the public from April to October 2004.

Did people use it? It was considered a popular destination, with an average of more than 1,400 sessions per month, the IHA reports.[18] People liked it, too, saying it was comfortable and conducive to individual and collaborative work; about 80 percent who tried it said they would recommend the center to someone they know. And the IHA says users preferred working in Connection Court over coffee shops, airports, and copy centers because of its professional look and feel, and conducive environment. Watch as permanent spaces like this spring up from city to suburb.

Variations on this idea are appearing around the globe, contributing to a new mode of working. One style setter is The Hub in London, a pay-as-you-go space for freelancers who work in progressive and ethical businesses or organizations. It bills itself as "3,174 square feet of derelict warehouse transformed into an incubator for progressive ideas. A place for getting things done. All the tools and trimmings needed to cultivate an idea, launch a project, host an event and operate a business."[19] What's striking is the emphasis on physical space as a draw: the specifics of square footage, the feel of the surroundings. It's a real antidote to autonomous virtual living. As the Web site says, it's "about what happens somewhere between the photocopier and the wood-burning stove. About the impact of chance encounters on endgame results."

Space has become the missing link for the mobile worker, and filling the gap will be the next big thing. It's a long way from private clubs like Soho House in London and New York, or the club that hosts Amsterdam's freelance creative community—or, for that matter, the 7-Eleven parking lots across the United States that are becoming staging areas for recruiting day laborers.

In his book *Bowling Alone: The Collapse and Revival of the American Community*, Harvard professor Robert D. Putnam purports that social bonds are the most powerful predictor of life satisfaction—attending a club meeting regularly, for example, is equivalent to doubling your income.[20] At the turn of the last century, Putnam says, America's social capital stock was reduced by urbanization, industrialization, and vast immigration, uprooting people from friends, social institutions, and families. America corrected its course within a few decades as a range of organizations appeared, from the Red Cross and Boy Scouts to the YWCA and the Urban League. This points to the importance of the next wave of social networks as a vital antidote to new ways of working.

The third place also involves new ways of living. As part of their research, Charles Grantham and David Ware, of the Work Design Collaborative, have initiated the Live/Work Project, a prototype of a residence-cum-work space. With 2,180 square feet of living space and 980 square feet of work space, the building in Prescott, Arizona, is a "living laboratory" for businesses to discover how integrating work and life might look like in terms of technology and interior design. Its goal: "a facility that enables you to actually experience the workplace of the future."[21]

Already, however, there are entire communities designed around the idea of the distributed work force. Mesa del Sol, on the perimeter of Albuquerque, was designed by New Urbanist Peter Calthorpe. It's a combination of Connection Court—with top-notch meeting rooms, videoconferencing hookups to China and India, and support staff available for a fee—and an escape from big-city headaches where the mobile worker can really enjoy life. It's envisioned, says *Business Week* writer Michelle Conlin, as "a place where you can hit the slopes in the morning, tee off after lunch, then jam in some collaboration with co-workers in India before David Letterman. In other words, a desert idyll for those who want to go off the grid but remain connected, and keep their New Economy-size paychecks while living a New Mexico-priced lifestyle."[22]

Conlin notes that Mesa del Sol is specifically targeted at the "creative class," as described by Richard Florida in his book *The Rise of the Creative Class*. Florida asserts that creativity is being increasingly valued at home and at work, giving rise to a new class of worker. And it doesn't matter where these creative minds live (and work), as long as they can get connected. It's what he calls a "no-collar" workplace.[23]

> "Creativity has come to be the most highly prized commodity in our economy— and yet it is not a 'commodity.' Creativity comes from people. And while people can be hired and fired, their creative capacity cannot be bought and sold, or turned on and off at will."
>
> —Richard Florida[24]

While some people may commit to living in communities of likeminded mobile workers and others join hubs or connection centers, the significance of space will be a defining discussion for the distributed set.

Next: The Office: A Far Cry from Cubicles

There's a push to cater to the needs of office workers and put them at ease in the corporate environment. There's more natural light, more open, breathable space, more of the natural world. The dehumanized workplace is being reinvented.

Yoga is just one approach to improving hard results by pursuing soft techniques. Corporations are checking out how yoga and meditation can help relieve stress and tension—and increase productivity. And entrepreneurial yogis are putting together workplace packages to meet the demand. Om Yoga in New York counts Accenture and the Association of Legal Administrators on its client roster.

Businesses are working hard to make offices more welcoming. Companies are designing spaces that bring people together in new ways, in buildings that are more environmentally conscious. But as more workers crowd together in smaller spaces, personal space will be at a premium.

To facilitate social interaction and face time—a key advantage of the business office over the home office—open floor plans have replaced cubicle culture. Many young businesspeople can't even remember what those cubes look like. The idea is not just for workers to be out in the open but for designs that actually integrate the needs of people from all rungs of the ladder and facilitate business processes and flow. There's a lot of expectation on our work spaces now: They will need to be open but private, and full of form but fully functional.

One noteworthy example is the new BMW hybrid space in Leipzig, Germany, which incorporates both its plant and its corporate offices. Designed by architect Zaha Hadid, the building is intended to fulfill BMW's desire for a "loosely coupled organic network" of people and processes from all areas of the company under a single space—a first in the history of automakers.[25] Hadid describes the project to *Wallpaper* magazine as "a formidable opportunity to translate motion into design." The result? Cascading floors on three levels that integrate open office areas with overhead conveyer belts that move car bodies in different stages of development. Space is divided and becomes multilayered and multifunctional, uniting office workers and plant workers in a single production area.

As *Wallpaper* puts it, "The new building melds the worlds of white-collar and blue-collar workers—exactly as BMW intended. This is a democratic space, one where Post-it Notes and spot welders are never too far from each other." It's workspace that breaks down class and social divides. And it's design that mixes social and business forces. As *Wallpaper* describes it, above the foyer is a conveyer belt that moves the morning's production run into the storage area—a constant reminder of the production process. On-time and downtime merge for everyone from the top dog to the little guy.[26]

Influx Insights reports that more than 20,000 businesses in the U.K. use communal seating arrangements.[27]

London-based architects Buschow Henley, who designed such an office for communications-strategy agency Michaelides & Bednash, explain how a simple and cheap idea gave the office a unique energy: "The seemingly singular response of a table around which this young organization meets provides an iconic place to work, grow, and develop media strategies. The design used a modest furniture budget to create a radical working environment."[28]

There is also a trend to integrate organic elements into the office, to bring the outside world in and create a more natural working environment—think earth tones and more waterfalls. (At Chiat/Day, we had the good fortune to work in Frank Gehry-designed spaces that featured design elements influenced by his native Canada—water, timber, and fish were prominent.) There's also a push for more natural light and ventilation. Sunlight is key to avoiding seasonal affective disorder (SAD), which can cause depression, suicidal thoughts, even alcoholism. A few offices are using special SAD lamps to help combat the effects of artificial lighting.

In 2005, Microsoft started offering SAD sufferers a high-intensity, full-spectrum bulb that costs $1,000. About 200 of its 30,000 Seattle-based employees took advantage of the benefit in its first year.[29]

Another way to attract young workers is to infuse the office with all the trappings of hip, à la cool hotels. As *Wallpaper* says about "the Gherkin," the skyline-changing London headquarters of Swiss Re, "We are particularly enamoured of the extraordinary view from the rooftop restaurant and bar. Staff canteen by day—it adds a dash of glamour to even the most solitary sandwich—at night, the space is available to hire only if you pass the most stringent vetting. A room with a view but only for a few: nothing beats a bit of sky-high elitism."[30] More people will be looking to their work space as not just a physical destination but a symbol of their attitudes, their personalities, and their aspirations—and that office environment should not only represent who they are, it should awe and impress others.

"Green" buildings are good to work in and good to brag about. These are environmentally sensitive buildings like Goldman Sachs' new headquarters in lower Manhattan, which features low-flow plumbing and carpets with fewer chemical levels, and the Hearst Tower, which uses glass with a coating that lets in sunlight but keeps out solar radiation, interior walls with low-vapor paints, and formaldehyde-free furniture.

These offices project a company's environmental consciousness and also attract clients and employees who want to work in a building that makes them feel and look good. While green buildings cost more up front, they save money in the long run—and help burnish a business's corporate image and messaging.

In 2000, the U.S. Green Building Council, a construction-industry group with an environmental mission, developed a way to score a building's environmental performance in terms of energy and water efficiency, air and atmosphere quality, and use of renewable materials and resources. The Leadership in Energy and Environmental Design ratings (LEED) range from certified (26 points) to platinum (52 points). The process is lengthy, but certification helps a business prove its environmental commitment. According to *The New York Times*, about 3,400 projects nationwide had registered for certification as of February 2006, and 400 had been granted LEEDs ratings.[31]

With the conspicuous openness of new office designs comes a greater need for privacy. More offices will incorporate havens where employees can engage in private phone calls or meetings; in the BMW offices they're called "think tanks." Our office space will become more important to us as we try to stake out our own identity and territory in open plans and, often, smaller spots.

Order will help with control. As we juggle the real and the virtual and with space at a premium, workers will want to exert more power over place. Like the guy in *Office Space* who's obsessed with his stapler, we'll be hyper-territorial. Look for more sticky notes and signs that indicate "Jane's scissors" and "Don't touch." And with fears of bird flu, worldwide epidemics, and super strains, people will be more aware of others' germs and hygiene habits. It makes the idea of telecommuting all the more appealing.

> A survey by ServiceMaster Clean, a janitorial services company, found that three-quarters of workers believe their office is not as clean as it should be. Workers also see an increase in germ-spreading: 54 percent said they saw fellow employees leaving the restroom without washing their hands, versus 45 percent in 2004.[32]

What's Next? Storage Systems As Status Symbols.

As clutter gets more conspicuous without the confines of the cubicle, organization will become a key office skill. It's the old "a cluttered desk is a cluttered mind" thinking at work, but more magnified. The new office darling will be someone who's got order in the bag and who's mastered the nuances of clear nomenclature and taxonomy. Our ship-shape storage will be a metaphor for our success in streamlining our lives.

What's Next? Gas Prices Squeeze "Extreme Commuters"

Supercommuters—those who spend more than a month of every year driving to work—are now spending not only oppressive amounts of time getting to work, but huge sums of money as well. Drawn to the far outskirts of cities by more affordable housing and good schools, these commuters have swelled in number, rising by about 75 percent since 1990, according to the U.S. Census Bureau.[33] As gas prices go higher and higher, however, the long-distance workers might soon start to rethink the daily pilgrimage.

Working from home means far less gas consumption—and, too, less strain on the environment and the infrastructure. After gas prices skyrocketed in the wake of Hurricane Katrina, there was a nationwide cry from state leaders on up to President Bush to conserve fuel, forcing policy considerations as significant as year-round adherence to daylight saving time. There's rising pressure also on businesses to provide more progressive work policies. And an organization called the Telework Exchange, a for-profit alliance of tech companies with bumper-sticker slogans like "Honk if you'd rather be teleworking" and "My other car is a PC," is calling for the government to start instituting telecommuting policies.

The group is urging adoption of federal telework requirements, noting that government white-collar workers spend $19 million a day and use 31 million gallons of gas each week to commute.[34] If the average federal employee works at home two days a week, each year the worker would save $4,372, get 98 hours of life back, and spare the environment 3.6 tons of pollutants, according to the Telework Exchange. Telecommuting will be a big cause of championing by workers and environmentalists alike in the coming years.

What's Next? Shortages of Workers for Old-Style Businesses

Businesses are going to have to adapt to woo the free-flying free agent. And yet there's a disconnect between modern workers and employers' old attitudes. "We still have employers thinking they're going to manage their employees' careers and determine what's most important for their professional lives, whereas most employees don't think that way anymore," says Richard Lamond of staffing and recruiting firm Spherion. "There are significant differences in the viewpoints of the worker and the employer about what motivates and drives retention." Even as the talent gap gains momentum, fewer than one in five employers is well-positioned to attract and retain top employees, according to 2005 polls by Harris Interactive for Spherion.[35]

Next: Value-Added Employment

While freelance contractors are on the rise in some countries and specific industries—including our business, marketing communications—permanent jobs are still prevalent. We may have jumped the gun on forecasting a free-agent nation because influencers in elite, opinion-making jobs are much more likely to be freelance, and they extrapolate from their own life experiences. But the organization has not been replaced by the independent contractor, contrary to many of the prior predictions about the demise of the workplace.

There are, however, meaningful changes under way in the content and context of permanent jobs. We're living in an hourglass economy, and the jobs landscape is a snapshot of a growing class divide. The number of high-paying jobs is rising faster than lower-paying ones, while middle-income jobs are drying up. Tomorrow's employer will seek techno-savvy personnel who possess state-of-the-art skills and, especially, the ability to keep reinventing themselves.

Employment gurus like William Bridges, a consultant and author of *Jobshift: How to Prosper in a Workplace without Jobs*, argues that the qualitative nature of jobs has changed, and that this is more significant than whether the total number of jobs has declined. He told the *Financial Times*, "This idea that everyone has to show they are adding value in their work is really very far reaching."[36] Tomorrow's best talent will find their competitive advantage in "intelligent flexibility," in an ability to learn how to learn so that they command a place in the talent pool, which has become an organization's greatest asset. By 2010, it will be the management of one's relationships—an ability to make contacts, to network, and to be a team player—that will be most rewarded.

We'll end up with a yin—the right people will spend more time working for the employers that they suit, and vice versa (a shift away from the dot-com tendency to jump every time a better offer was had)—and a yang—people setting up microbusinesses, becoming self-employed, and opting for temporary and/or portfolio work, with no binding ties beyond a work-for-hire arrangement.

While the numbers show that non-agricultural self-employment in the United States has declined since the 1990s and has almost halved since the 1940s, many experts caution that official statistics don't paint accurate pictures of the labor market. Journalist Daniel Pink, author of *Free Agent Nation*, observes that categorizations of work have not caught up with the way people are actually working. For example, how should we count a part-time employee who is also proprietor of his own business? And what about the free agent who has incorporated herself as a business and is therefore reported as an employee? (In some countries, the tax system has made it easier and less costly for people to effectively incorporate themselves.)[37]

Workers are now moving in and out of various categories, segueing from one to another as their lives change. "People increasingly make their own patterns of work, and are more prone to vary their pattern at different periods of the lifecycle," says Valerie Bayliss, author of an expansive report on modern working patterns for the U.K.'s Royal Society for the Encouragement of Arts, Manufactures & Commerce.[38]

Meanwhile, job growth in the United States and the U.K. has been slower in recent years than after previous economic recoveries. And unemployment rates are likely quite a bit higher than the numbers show: Jeremy Rifkin, author of the 1995 classic *The End of Work*, argues that we need to factor in temp and part-time workers seeking full-time jobs, those who have given up the job search and so fall out of the statistics, and the 2 percent of the potential workforce in prison. Rifkin had forecasted machines replacing laborers in developed countries, and today he believes that prediction was conservative. His current focus is on the rise of structural unemployment—Rifkin believes that today's "boutique industries" will never employ the same numbers as the "Fordist-style" manufacturing economy of decades past. Bayliss argues, however, that "in the end, technology breeds more jobs."[39]

Insecurity is pushing people to become more competitive, even to "brand" themselves in the same way that products, services, and corporations use branding to differentiate themselves from the competition. Previously, when people had stable jobs in stable organizations, they could rely on their co-workers to know who they were and what they were capable of. But with corporate downsizing and more people jumping (or being forced) into free agency, more workers are competing for attention and assignments.

What's Next? Unlocking the Innovator Within

Business-as-usual and job-for-life are history, and life-long learning is a must. Since businesses must either embrace innovation or risk stagnation, innovators are the new heroes, and there are hundreds of MBA courses in innovation to help them.

Next: Sex, Power & Relationships—The New Politics of Business

New power dynamics and struggles will emerge as we negotiate the physical and the virtual worlds of work. And as this culture evolves, questions arise about how we'll negotiate relationships across gender lines and office levels of hierarchy. For example, in some corporate cultures, late nights are prized as the mark of hard work and ambition, but for mobile workers there are no visible indicators of time and effort (beyond, perhaps, a 3 a.m. time stamp on an e-mail). Watch as new office politics emerge over Wi-Fi connections and videoconferences. With communal tables and online meetings, there is no literal head of the tables, but power plays will form in new ways. Consider how the passive aggressive micro-manager can exert influence and power over the distributed worker just by scheduling calls and online meetings at unsocial times. The next big thing will be virtual office politics.

As the talent shortages rise and competition stiffens, watch as women eke out an edge in the job marketplace. In big cities in the Western world, white, middle-class men over 40 generally rule business's upper echelons; they certainly rule the board. But female self-employment and women-owned businesses are on the rise. Women aren't stepping aside—they're stepping out and they're doing it on their own.

Women-owned businesses without employees are growing at twice the rate of all U.S. firms without employees—18 percent between 1997 and 2004—according to a 2006 report released by the Center for Women's Business Research.[40] Most striking? The highest growth rate for these firms was in industries historically dominated by men: agricultural services, construction, and transportation. And these businesses account for a lot of money, about $167 billion, nearly a third of the revenue of all firms with no employees.

As the United States continues to prosper, traditionally male work such as manual labor is shrinking; growth sectors such as information technology are going to require even more educated workers. Women will continue to fill this gap, because in nations where both genders have educational opportunities, women are less likely to drop out of school. (Ireland is typical of the trend: Female employment rose steadily in the years 1970–1990, while male employment declined. Studies show that women did not take jobs from men; rather, "male" jobs dried up, and many "female" jobs were created.) Globally, economists say, an expected shortfall in skilled employees will give women's prospects a boost over the next ten years.

What will be lacking for women now will be support groups with established mentoring programs to help them in the difficult start-up phase. Watch as more women-based networking groups and mentoring centers emerge.

As for what will become of men in the workplace, they are changing priorities. Men are carving out more balance between work and life to spend time with their families. Gen X dads are more active caregivers for their kids and displaying greater emotional intelligence than their fathers, who were always at work. Men are also trending toward work that has traditionally been deemed as women's work, taking on jobs as nannies, secretaries, and even housemaids. In the United States, the human resources director of the Visiting Nurse Service of New York has tried to fill nursing vacancies by recruiting active and retired firefighters and police officers. It's also increasingly common for men to be employed by their wives. The National Association of Home Based Businesses estimates that the number of husbands working for their wives or becoming partners in businesses already established by their wives increased 50 percent between 1995 and 2000.[41]

How are the sexes mixing at work? With more singletons in the workplace, the role of the office as social center has taken primary focus. "Adult Americans are telling us that they do mix business with pleasure, and that that's not necessarily a bad thing," says Genia Spencer, a managing director at Randstad USA, an international staffing agency. "With Americans spending more and more time at their jobs, the workplace is increasingly becoming a source of social activity and a venue for romantic interaction."[42] In a 2006 Randstad survey of 1,478 employed adults, 30 percent said they have dated a co-worker and 24 percent said they feel comfortable discussing their romantic relationships with their work colleagues.

Social networks will be at the heart of the new business culture and a key to success. At a time when jobs are less secure and employees less loyal, social capital is more important than ever. Our professional networks will overlap more with our social networks. Technology will help us nurture relationships by keeping us in touch across virtual and physical space, time zones, and cultural divides. And as we connect as mobile workers, we'll form online relationships with people we know only virtually; common values and interests will overcome the lack of shared history.

A Glance at the Developed and Developing Marketplace

The crucial factor in jobs now is not whether they're in manufacturing or service, but how much wealth they're creating. Manufacturing once delivered the highest value, and high-tech industries, such as drugs and aerospace, still do. Writing a computer program creates more value than producing a computer disc.

Developing countries are doing more manufacturing, and developed countries are doing less—which is nothing new. Still, in 1970 around a quarter of American workers were in manufacturing; now it's under 10 percent. (Most other developed economies show similar numbers: In the U.K., such jobs dropped from 35 percent of the workforce in 1970 to 14 percent now.) That's a lot fewer jobs, but much higher productivity—America remains the world's biggest manufacturer. Japan is in second place, with China a distant third, producing $700 billion worth of manufactured goods, half of America's total. Most people today work in services: In the United States, as many as 80 percent.

For developed nations, the challenge is to encourage innovation fast enough to create an offsetting number of new jobs—and to have a flexible labor force that can shift to new sectors as needed. (After all, many of the jobs that now employ millions of people didn't exist or weren't even imagined a generation ago. Back in 1990 very few of today's router makers, server manufacturers, Web designers, and e-commerce specialists had any idea of what lay ahead.)

In any economy around the globe, unemployment is enemy No. 1, a triple negative for civic stability. People who are out of work don't contribute output or income tax and are less likely to spend. Unemployment benefits are a net drain on the economy, and where there's widespread unemployment, there's likely to be deprivation and disorder. Almost by definition, developing countries have massive problems of under- and unemployment. Given that most have high birthrates, too, this means they have to create new jobs fast just to absorb the growing workforce. The Arab world alone needs 80 million new jobs by 2020 just to maintain unemployment at the current high levels.[43]

Who's had success in creating or luring jobs? India has been a pioneer, offering high skills and low costs. A few plans announced by U.S. firms in 2005

include: J.P. Morgan Chase said it would double, to about 9,000, its staff there
to settle complex structured-finance and derivative deals; Microsoft said that
over the next four years it would invest $1.7 billion in India, about half of which
would go toward its existing R&D and technical-support operations; Intel
unveiled plans to invest more than $1 billion over five years, largely to expand its
R&D center in Bangalore; Cisco Systems said it would invest $1.1 billion. But
India's not dependent on foreign investment alone: The three biggest Indian IT-
services firms—Tata Consultancy Services, Infosys, and Wipro—are each
recruiting more than 1,000 people a month. India's draw will only get bigger as
it continues to deliver on its intellectual might.

Some developing nations plan to boost employment by opening new sectors to
investment, such as mining in Vietnam, agribusiness in the Philippines, and outsourcing services in South Asia and Eastern Europe. Others are trying to reduce the
legal and regulatory burdens that restrict investment. Egypt's government
announced late in 2005 that it would tackle the country's 20 percent unemployment rate through low-cost business loans, land reclamation, and the construction
of several hundred desert townships; the goal is 4.5 million new jobs by 2011.

Many developing countries have neither the cash nor the expertise or the
structures to pursue an effective pump-priming path to job creation. The
recourse? Foreign direct investment (FDI). Recent World Bank research indicates FDI creates positive "spillover" effects, including job creation, technology
transfer, enhancement of technical and managerial skills, productivity gains, and
backward and forward linkages to local firms.[44] Almost all developing countries
have undertaken at least some liberalizing policy reforms in recent years with a
view to attracting FDI. Moreover, policy trends that assist local private-sector
investment in poverty alleviation—such as the creation of industrial clusters—
should also benefit foreign firms.

Richard Freeman of Harvard argues that a turning point in economic history
is the global workforce's doubling in size since China, India, and the former
Soviet Union embraced market capitalism—he says that in 2000, those countries
contributed 1.47 billion workers to the global labor pool.[45] The new entrants to
the global economy brought little capital with them, substantially lowering the
global capital/labor ratio. This puts great pressure on labor in both developing
and developed nations.

Globalization means jobs emigrate to workers or workers immigrate to jobs.
But that's tough for governments. They may understand the potential economic
benefits of labor mobility, but they also have security concerns and perceive
immigrants as economic threats. In developed countries, local workers often disdain more menial tasks, but the unskilled immigrants who are drawn into such
jobs tend not to get immigration rights, so there's widespread employment of

"illegals." At the other end of the scale, there's global competition for highly educated and skilled knowledge workers.

Freeman argues that while the World Bank and the International Monetary Fund have tended to "protect capital," they now need to change course and help countries develop policies that minimize the costs of adjustment to workers during what is likely to be a long transition.[46] To avoid backlashes and instability in this new global economy, Freeman warns the global community that gains must be spread widely. And that without new approaches to globalization, workers around the world are sure to get the short end of the stick.

And Therefore Next

Technology, "always on" connectivity, has achieved its full impact—but probably not exactly as we'd foreseen. It hasn't made us so much more efficient so as to enjoy a better balance of work and leisure. How many people do you know who are working fewer hours than they did a decade ago?

With today's technology—access to information, the ability to connect (and stay connected) to a multiplicity of colleagues anywhere in the world, and the ability to move information and even goods around—anyone can play. Certainly, there are more home office workers and more "free agents" (some by choice and more still, we suspect, by circumstances of the job market), all enabled by technology, which has helped level the playing field for independent workers. To do many of the tasks demanded by today's economy, place is truly irrelevant (and businesses certainly understand that place is a cost—a significant one). Has there ever been a merger more sensible than FedEx and Kinko's? Hell, throw Starbucks into the mix, and we'll have an entire sub-economy predicated on the non-office worker.

To us, who still feel a bit like the pioneers of virtuality, this decade has been largely about watching it become mainstream—in terms of possibility more so than reality. In principle, virtuality is the gift of the information economy, versus the industrial economy that preceded it. So why has the concept not taken off?

For workers, there is some element of identity (and that concept is under siege as well) associated with work space: "Where's your office?" "How big is your office?" "Inside or window?" "Steelcase or Eames?" These distinctions all seem to be kind of primal. And no matter how well we can do it (from wherever), we seem to maintain an overarching concern that we need to be present to assert our worth, really stay in the game, or even watch our own back. Virtuality takes real confidence. At the same time, for the employer, there seems to be a fundamental unwillingness to accept the notion that work, even the work of ideas, can be conducted from anywhere other than the office (or, at least, work at full capacity).

chapter thirteen

big next: it's a shopper's planet

"In order to gain and to hold the esteem of men, it is not sufficient merely to possess wealth or power. The wealth or power must be put in evidence, for esteem is awarded only on evidence," wrote Thorstein Veblen, the Norwegian-American economist who coined the phrase "conspicuous consumption" at the turn of the 20th century.[1] In the 21st century, luxury has become a byword for accomplishment; if you can't drive your Porsche into the boardroom, you can still distinguish yourself with your $150,000 Porsche watch. Luxury has also become a way to reward ourselves for surviving another day in a tumultuous world.

The "new normal," the post-9/11 state of mind, means we live for today, so why wait for reward? Products have become more tied to perceptions of who we are, and what we stand for, than ever before. We're placing more and more emphasis on knowledge, on having the smarts to know the cost of everything (or, at any rate, on having Froogle and Shopping.com keep us informed), even at a time when we seem to know the value of nothing. There's a carelessness about cost or its implications. It's as if spending money is a means to an end for many of us, a way to let off some steam.

Today there is luxury in award granting, in letting oneself enjoy a congratulations for having endured the moment or moved over a hurdle, even if the next one lies just ahead. There is little disciplined waiting, even if there's no real cash on hand—the simple explanation for why we have the highest credit card debt in history. People feel entitled to spend on luxuries that make them feel good when they've worked hard to achieve a certain level of financial and worldly success; think of these as earned indulgences.

But that's by no means the only reason we treat ourselves. Concerns about the environment, about terrorism, about the prospect of a less dynamic global or local economy generate a sense of needing protection, and a strong desire to live more fully in the moment. And then luxury items, are (re)positioned in the mind's eye, and our collective psyche, as a way to escape. People no longer want to deny themselves anything.

Another dimension of the New Normal is that luxury, and one's rights to it, cuts across all demographics. Luxury and style have become confused, as have luxury and taste, and luxury and wealth—that is, you no longer need to be wealthy to have luxury.

Thriving in parallel to the lust for luxury is a seemingly contradictory mind-set that questions the value of material goods. People in this camp are the "No-Nos," says Pierre-Francois Le Louet, director general of Paris-based fashion forecasters Nelly Rodi, while the other group is the "Excesses."[2] If there is no need of material things in the hereafter, why do we place such importance on them today? The events of 9/11 prompted many people to reconsider what they truly valued in their lives. While the dot-com bust had already encouraged such contemplation, the terrifyingly sudden loss of life brought the issue home.

> The poster child for what Le Louet terms the "Excesses" is Paris Hilton: She "exemplifies this woman, who is sexy, completely obsessed by brands, consumption and is a show-off," he tells the *Australian Financial Review*.[3]

Instead of accumulating things, this second group of consumers wants to focus on living more purposeful and meaningful lives. Personal fulfillment is the new priority. Brands are slowly becoming less powerful as a means of constructing and expressing individual identity; over-the-top branding—Burberry, Tommy Hilfiger, or even Donna Karan from head to toe, for example—is falling out of fashion, at least in the West. (In emerging economies, however, conspicuous consumption is on the rise.) Flash is being replaced by a more individualistic mixed-and-matched look, with traces of "retro" and "comfortable" inserted into a fashion repertoire.

People are increasingly disenchanted with acquisitive lifestyles. It's no accident that in 2005, donations were among the most popular Christmas presents in the U.K.: Consumers eschewed the annual spending fest, instead giving the cost of a gift to charities such as Oxfam, which then gave a suitable present to needy people around the world. Oxfam says 85,000 people bought school dinners for children in Africa, spending about half a million pounds; donors also paid for 4,000 lavatories and 70,000 assorted livestock.[4]

As a counter-manifestation of an outward display of wealth, more complex status systems are emerging for what's known as "inconspicuous consumption." People shop at Target or Wal-Mart and then spend tens of thousands on dues at private clubs—it's all about high-low living. Displays of wealth are moving away from logos that scream "Look, I'm rich" to discreet branding identifiable only by those in the know. (Ira once worked with Ralph Lauren on a line of Polo shirts that moved the well-known logo off the chest and down to the bottom front shirt fly, allowing it to remain discreetly out of view if the wearer chose to tuck in the shirt.)

> One incentive behind spending by the rich is connoisseurship, according to a Ledbury Research report cited in *The Economist:* "Connoisseurs are people whom their friends respect for their deep knowledge of, say, fine wine or handmade Swiss watches." Another motive is being an early adopter of new technology. "Both are arguably consumption that is conspicuous only to those you really want to impress," notes the magazine.[5]

Conspicuous consumption, after all, isn't so impressive when luxury is mass-marketed and more accessible to the masses. Cheap look-alikes for brands like Burberry and Chanel are available to anyone, along with fake designer handbags or watches; runway fashions seem less exclusive when stores like H&M or the U.K.'s Top Shop sell budget copies.[6] H&M has gone one important step further, commissioning original designs from fashion icons Karl Lagerfeld and Stella McCartney and selling them within the chain's price parameters. In both cases, customers stormed the stores, and the collections sold out nearly instantly. As an article in *The New York Times* notes, "Cruise ships, years ago a symbol of the high life, have become the ocean-going equivalent of the Jersey Shore. BMW produces a cheaper model with the same insignia. Martha Stewart sells chenille jacquard drapery and scallop-embossed ceramic dinnerware at Kmart."[7]

At the same time, there seems to be less joy in shopping. "After nine go-go years, a lot of people are just shopped out," Tim Denison, a consumer psychologist with the U.K. consultants SPSL, tells the *Sunday Times.*[8] "There isn't a lot they want to buy anymore. Retail bargains are not as compelling as they were."

This decline in "acquisition joy" is a yin; the yang is the energy of shoppers who camp out overnight to acquire Tom Ford for Estée Lauder or Stella

McCartney for H&M, or who participate in the annual bridal-clearance frenzy at Filene's department store. For some people there is still excitement in the "new" and in beating the system by scoring great prices, a phenomenon associated with eBay, too. Like so many trends, the countertrend is real.

Next: Continued Tyranny of the Middle

High/low is the new aesthetic: Today's woman wears Zara with her Chanel, or Chanel with her Zara, and diamonds and pearls mixed and matched with costume jewelry from flea markets or artisans, or chain stores like Claire's Accessories (all over the United States and now in much of Europe as well) and Urban Outfitters (which is expanding from the United States into the U.K.). Blissful bargains are being snapped up at one end of the continuum—meaning "ca . . . ching, ca . . . ching" for mass retailers—and at the opposite end, think bling. Correction: "Bling, bling," as in lots of it.

Status, these days, sits at the top and at the bottom of the market—and the in-between brands, products, and services have become white elephants. "White elephant" is a phrase often associated with the myriad department store chains that carry a "stuck in the middle with you" product mix, draining shoppers' energy as they drag themselves from floor to floor.

Mass-market discounters like H&M, Kohl's, Target, and Wal-Mart are driving the retail market—the emphasis is on affordable brands. It's all about "mass-tige," relatively cheap fare that carries a touch of prestige.

> "The term 'bling bling,' used to describe diamonds, jewelry and all forms of showy style, was coined by New Orleans rap family Cash Money Millionaires back in the late '90s and started gaining national awareness with a song titled 'Bling Bling,' by Cash Money artist BG. The rapper . . . told MTV, 'I'm so surprised that that word has spread like it has. But I knew it was serious when I saw that the NBA championship ring for the Los Angeles Lakers had the word "bling bling" written in diamonds on it.' "
>
> —MTV News[9]

Neither of us was surprised by the divergent fates of Marshall Field's and Target, a history that tells the story of the new retail landscape. Back in 1990, the Dayton Hudson Corporation, Target's parent company, acquired Marshall Field's. It was Target, founded in 1962 in Roseville, Minnesota, that became the power player over the next 14 years; by 2004 the holding company was known as Target Corporation and Marshall Field's had been sold to May Department Stores, then one of America's largest department store conglomerates.

What changed in those 14 years? Big-box stores (Old Navy, Barnes & Noble, Pier 1 Imports) taught us about the power of the supersized, super specialist. Department store chains, now middle-aged and misunderstood, are relics of another time. May is now part of the Federated Department Stores family, where all the old-line stores have been migrated into either the Bloomingdale's or the Macy's brands. As of 2006, Marshall Field's is part of Macy's.

We are struck by the degree to which everything in the middle has fallen on hard times, whether it's the middle class, the middle-aged, or businesses wedged into the center—the proverbial middle market. It seems the extremes are where the action is. So, while Marshall Field's was once an engine—allowing its management to expand and explore and, especially, make its Target—today it's yet another stable asset, struggling to maintain scale and relevance. When Federated subsumed Marshall Field's and, as part of a broader corporate reorganization, began renaming the stores as Macy's, it was just following the trend to merge, consolidate, streamline, optimize. Big gets smarter, and stealth gets even faster.

Today Target is independent and thriving, and Federated is re-energized, leaning into its size, and its two power brands, to ensure that it sustains massive sales. One is taken by the numbers associated with both companies: Target has more than 1,300 stores in 47 states (along with target.com), while Federated owns 922 department stores and 735 bridal and formalwear stores. Along with Macy's and Bloomingdale's, the Federated brands include classic (and mostly disappearing) names like Famous-Barr, Lord & Taylor, Foley's, Hecht's, Kaufmann's, and Strawbridge's.

And about those white elephants, the department stores? They're in the process of another makeover. Faith Hope Consolo, the Manhattan real estate maven, told the *New York Daily News* that the city's department store retailers are in the throes of re-imaging themselves, like aging Hollywood stars. "Borrowing from fancy retailers like Harvey Nichols in London and Holt Renfrew in Toronto, department stores are becoming big stores that run themselves like a series of boutiques," she says.[10] Big is learning from, even mimicking, small. The *Daily News* also quotes Paco Underhill, author of *Call of the Mall*, on his prognosis: "The department store isn't dead but the huge old grande-dame store is a bit of a white elephant."

Next: Buying Experiences

"Experiences add more to our happiness than possessions." It's not Thoreau, but a quote from global equity strategist James Montier of investment bank Dresdner Kleinwort Wasserstein, who reviewed international studies on the link between money and happiness. He argues that a satisfying experience—be it a safari, a concert, a day spent scuba-diving—is more fulfilling than a new car or fancy watch.[11]

Consumers are increasingly subscribing to this point of view. Luxury is being seen in terms of activities that deepen one's appreciation of life: a weekend away, a cooking class or a long massage. Instead of showing off baubles and gadgets, more of us will flaunt our exclusive personal experiences. Average affluent (or luxury) household spending on luxury experiences in the United States nearly doubled in 2005, to $22,746, according to Unity Marketing, which included spending on travel, dining, entertainment, spa and beauty services, and home services.[12]

One of the most expensive restaurants in the United States is Masa, chef Masa Takayama's hot spot in New York City's Time Warner Center. It seats just 26 diners, who spend $300–$500 each for a three-hour sushi indulgence.

Boomers, heading into their golden years with unprecedented vim and vigor, are driving this "luxury as experience" market. Unity notes that they're looking less for the material goods and trappings of luxury and more for a chance to do things in style in a way they couldn't afford when hampered by kids (the average boomer is now in the mid-fifties).

"The amount that people spend on retail goods as a proportion of consumer spending has gone down in the past 10 years," says Nick Gladding of Verdict Research, which tracks trends in the U.K. retail sector, in the London *Times*. "That money has migrated to restaurants, leisure and budget travel, as well as mobile phone calls."[13]

Travel, notably, will be come to be viewed "not just as a vacation but as a way of culturally differentiating yourself," says Ken Esterow, president and CEO of Cendant Travel Distribution Services.[14] In a travel-industry forecast for 2020, Cendant says the number of consumers flying will double and that they will choose more varied locations and novel activities to showcase their individuality. Travelers will seek controlled danger, unusual environments and cultures, and physical or emotional development. (Cendant is an interesting model for how to "surround" the notion of travel as experience, as its "travel distribution brands"—including Orbitz and Cheap Tickets—dovetail with its "travel content brands," including the Wyndham, Days Inn and Ramada resorts, as well as the Avis and Budget car rental companies.)

Consumers are also more willing to pay for wellness—not just healthy foods and supplements but yoga classes and other activities that promote internal luxury (i.e., health) versus external luxury. When people do spend on deluxe items, it's often to heighten life's experiences, so we buy gourmet coffee and decadent bed linens.

Marketers are taking note of the primacy of meaningful experiences. Sony named its super-premium line of electronics products Qualia, a word it defines as "phenomena of the heart and mind that cannot quite be described in words." For instance, says Sony Corp. CEO Nobuyuki Idei on the company's Web site, "I remember the time I went to the Grand Canyon and rode a mule down to the Colorado River. . . . When we finally reached the river, I saw a sky full of stars. . . . Even now, when I look at starry skies, I remember the qualia of that time." And as the site says, "From now on, people will be willing to pay more for qualia experiences"—make that $2,600 for high-end headphones.[15]

Next: Enhancing the Shopping Experience

If buying itself is an experience, it's less likely to feel like an empty pursuit. A special experience also takes us away from the mass-market feel of shopping centers and strip malls, which provide shoppers with convenience but not much fun. (Similarly, searching on Amazon can make life easier, but it's not as rewarding as picking up new finds in a book shop.)

"There is a lot of sameness in the high street," says Andrew Newman, a consumer psychologist at the Manchester Business School in the U.K. "Many stores are offering the same sort of proposition, and that means we feel less excited by it. The way they are laid out is very similar. There's nothing new about them."[16]

So shoppers are looking for alternatives to today's Main Street USA, packed with fast-food chains, a Starbucks or two, the same handful of fashion outlets, and perhaps a Barnes & Noble where a small bookstore once stood. And, living wired lives, we crave compensatory human contact and sensual experiences.

That's the appeal of shopping in boutiques or vintage stores. The most popular brands are those getting smaller and truer—people like the idea of returning to a small shop or patronizing a chic bakery like Poilane in Paris and London. A loaf of bread may cost a small fortune, but buying it is more fun, less stressful, and an experience in itself. Toronto's World's Biggest Bookstore, a beloved but somewhat long-in-the-tooth megastore, met the arrival of Barnes & Noble and Borders by leaning into its time-worn image, advertising "Great prices, great books, so-so environment." The store actually saw an increase in incremental sales during the year the competition opened in its University of Toronto neighborhood.

People also value a simplified shopping experience as an alternative to wandering through endless store aisles: Vino 100 is a chain of wine shops across America that sells exactly what's promised: 100 wines, nothing more or less.

Next: Pampering

Special services are one way to amp up the shopping experience. The ultimate example is Daslu in São Paulo, Brazil, an exclusive store that sells designer brands along with fine wines, fast cars, and yachts. Champagne is freely available, the staff know customers' first names and sizes, a helipad caters to customers who can't face the traffic, and golf carts ferry guests to the in-house bar, restaurants, vast gardens, library, and spa. Lounging is encouraged. Customers pay top dollar not for the goods themselves but for the rarefied experience.[17]

Expect to see more of this pampering from elite shops and brands. Some merchants will deliver purchases anywhere in the world by hand to please their customers, for example. High-end retailer Jeffrey in Manhattan tells the story of a customer in Atlanta who need not shop at all: He simply ships a selection of every new season's highlights, and she keeps what she wants, returning the rest. Some brands are taking the privileged first-to-board, cordoned-off cachet of first-class flying into new realms. Part of the pleasure is just the exclusivity, being seen by those who aren't included. Munich fashion boutique Eggeringhaus invites its best clients to movie screenings, where they can meet and greet other members of the in crowd. Brands are also offering clients special access to cultural activities or even—for Lexus owners in Florida—privileged parking spaces at sporting events.

And many consider the American Express concierge program the ultimate in pampering, since it provides access to tickets for cultural events in advance of general sale.

> Sales associates at Polo Ralph Lauren stores bring customers snacks or refreshments, walk their dogs as they shop, or provide concierge services, making restaurant or salon reservations as needed.

Pampering can also mean small treats for the more average consumer. On Australia's Gold Coast, those waiting to have their cars serviced at Sunshine Ford are offered espresso, freshly baked cookies, newspapers, and magazines in a congenial and spotless environment.[18] Customers at Umpqua Bank in Oregon can use a computer café, watch flat-screen TVs showing financial news, and enjoy the bank's own branded coffee and chocolate, served on a tray after each transaction.

Next: Keep Customers Entertained

Its marquee lit up by rows of bulbs, Hershey's Chocolate World on Michigan Avenue in Chicago, which opened in mid-2005, is an entertainment destination. "The new candy-pushing emporium [is] not so much a retail store as an interactive theater where the theme is easy to grasp and the sweet point of the show never changes," reports the *Chicago Tribune*.[19] The newspaper points out that it's a textbook example of the retail theory proposed by Joe Pine and James H. Gilmore in their 1999 book *The Experience Economy:* That because consumers are looking for "meaningful interactions far more than mere stuff," companies must learn to "script and stage compelling experiences" to get shoppers' attention.

Lego has redesigned its stores and taken the product out of the packaging so consumers can play with it. At a Whole Foods that opened in Austin, Texas, in 2005, shoppers dipped strawberries in a chocolate fountain, selected from the 800 beers in the walk-in beer cooler, or bought a hot doughnut from a guy hawking them. It makes the tedious experience of food-shopping fun—as *USA Today* described it, the store is "the grocery equivalent of Disney World for food junkies."[20]

One of the pioneers of this practice is outdoor sporting goods company REI, which calls its flagship store in Seattle "among the Emerald City's top sightseeing attractions." Customers can curl up by a big stone fireplace or try out mountain bikes and other gear on trails, a climbing wall or a waterfall—all within the store's compound. Boston-area chain Jordan's Furniture offers an Imax theater at one location, a trapeze school at another, and a Motion Odyssey movie ride at a third.

Next: Guided by Experts

Shopping is also appealing when it's a learning experience, whether it's an in-store training session on using your new Apple computer or a tutorial on giving yourself a proper shave, as Kiehl's did for a limited time. Indeed, The Art of Shaving, a retail chain, offers shaves—service as well as state-of-the-art products—from Las Vegas to San Antonio to New York City. As more elements of life become de-skilled and more choices proliferate, consumers want to buy from people and brands that know more than they do. Home Depot gets straight to the point with its advertising slogan: "You can do it. We can help." Ikea offers its customers help selecting all the items they'll need to redo a room, even if shoppers then go off and buy some pieces elsewhere.

There are hurdles to offering this help: Training staff is time-consuming and expensive. Home Depot minimizes the problem by recruiting electricians and plumbers, and others with relevant know-how. Outdoor-equipment stores like EMS and REI likewise look to hire enthusiastic campers and hikers. Perhaps one day computer terminals in stores will serve the same role as knowledgeable sales assistants.

Some stores work around the issue by emphasizing the experts behind the scenes. The Origins beauty-products chain has come out with a line created with alternative-health guru Andrew Weil; life-size photos of the white-bearded doctor convey that his knowledge is present, if not the man himself. In the U.K., apothecary Neal's Yard Remedies focuses on communicating how much it knows about the natural remedies in its products.

"The skin-care industry is experiencing an interesting shift. Whereas the best-known products used to be based on the personalities of beauty mavens such as

Estée Lauder and Helena Rubenstein, today's brand stars come with more serious credentials: a medical degree."

—*South China Morning Post*[21]

Next: Customizing Commodities

Nike has made buying shoes more interesting by turning the process into a creative endeavor: Online shoppers can now design their own models, choosing everything from the color of the swoosh to a personalized message that appears on the tongue. And at Earnest Cut & Sew in New York, customers choose detailing (studs and buttons), pocket styles, and denim texture for their made-to-fit jeans, sewn on-site in the store's basement.

For the very elite consumer, the perfume house Creed is now offering its clients the chance to design and name their own perfumes. The recipes will be kept on file and refills dispatched as required. Christofle lets customers submit drawings, photographs or simply ideas that the company will then translate into custom pieces of flatware. And some high-end retailers let shoppers create their own chocolate, with various quantities of cacao roasted to different degrees.

More accessible to the masses: Custom-blended makeup, such as that offered by Three Custom Color Specialists, or the ice cream with customer-picked mix-ins served at the growing Cold Stone Creamery chain. People will increasingly expect to be able to customize their goods, to feel more involved in their consumer choices.

Customization has now become high-tech, too, so clothing can be perfectly tailored to both your body and your tastes. A system called Bodymetrics can calculate your precise measurements using a state-of-the-art body-mapping system. A line of denim by British designer Tristan Webber uses Bodymetics to tailor-make jeans to an individual's shape; the buyer's name is then imprinted on the size label. With the help of TiVo and other digital recording devices, we're even customizing our TV schedules.

Customization is "a democratic desire," says Sharon Lee, co-founder of research and trend consultants Look-Look, Inc. "Every person wants to say this is much more me and I'm not part of this kind of mass culture."[22]

What's Next? More and More Custom

Whether we'll get one-of-a-kind earrings crafted by a silversmith of our choosing or commission dress shoes, we'll be ever more interested in unique items that speak to our connoisseurship. Such products also serve as a counterpoint to "masstige" and our tireless search for low prices. Also look to Web sites like Novica.com, where people can buy items from local artisans around the world, which serve as custom gifts and novelties to showcase.

What's Next? Beyond Zero

Consumers' expectations outstrip what can be achieved or delivered, even when what they get is actually great. Previous generations would call it being spoiled. In psychological language, it's the hedonic zero point—a kind of pleasure threshold. Anything that scores above that zero point feels good, and anything that registers below it feels like a letdown. Most shoppers have a rising pleasure threshold: They become accustomed to the comfort and convenience and power of the shopping experience, so it takes even more comfort and convenience and power to wow them next time. And when everything around is brighter and better, nothing stands out. Where is satisfaction for today's spoiled shoppers? It turns out that the most satisfying things or experiences may be those with no expectations attached—spontaneous, unplanned, and serendipitous.

Next: Buying a Lifestyle

Consumers are increasingly interested in buying into a mind-set rather than just merchandise. They're drawn to the shop that offers a point of view, where they can go as much for the vibe and the experience as for the goods on sale.

These stores present a highly "edited" selection organized more around mood or emotional attributes than product categories. Colette in Paris is the ultimate example, offering its take on what's ultra-cool now, from avant-garde magazines to the niftiest cell phone to an esoteric brand of soap. Every Sunday it's dismantled and restocked, with some products taken out of rotation and others shown in a new way.

Colette and likeminded stores such as 10 Corso Como in Milan and Jeffrey in Manhattan present "an odd shopping experience—kind of like an insider's conspiracy," says *The Scotsman*.[23] These shops are tastemakers—and so while their customers want to stand apart from the crowd, they're too time-starved to make those choices themselves.

The experience is echoed for the less moneyed crowd in stores like Pottery Barn or Habitat in London, where home goods are grouped with a designer's sensibility. Even Whole Foods is getting in on the trend, with some stores now selling organic clothing, bedding, and towels at premium prices, steps away from the cheeses and olives, and the natural beauty products. The goods are all linked by a common mind-set. And if you buy into it, then visit the chain's first "lifestyle" store in L.A., built with environmentally friendly materials and selling every-thing from world music to nontoxic paint.

Some consumers, however, are turned off by curated consumption, dismiss-ing certain retailers for becoming too homogenized around a particular style or taste. The goods have been too highly edited for them, or the whole ensemble too perfect. The urge to recapture the experience of discovering things for yourself is prompting a return to second-hand shopping: finding treasures in vintage or antique shops, or even in the trash.

In turn, some retailers are picking up on this, mixing older pieces in with new lines. In New York, boutiques like Find attract fashionistas with a mix of gently worn designer items from previous seasons and relatively inexpensive pieces from local designers.

What's Next? What's Its Source?

As the world becomes more connected, and brands become more accessible, where those brands come may become increasingly important. A growing num-ber people want their money to stay local to support neighborhood stores and create and protect local jobs; it's also a personal response to globalization. Local markets also allow consumers to feel the passion of the people behind the prod-uct and to find out more about it.

There's also growing interest in brands that reflect national traits. Spanish shoemaker Camper emphasizes the local and rural over the global and urban, and has built a position around slowness: "Walk, don't run." "We are part of globalization, but we get our values from the Mallorcan countryside," says Miguel Fluxa, son of Camper's founder.[24]

Designer Paul Smith wants his quirky designs to evoke British individuality and eccentricity, while Tommy Hilfiger's ad campaigns clearly champion America with fresh-faced, athletic models sporting red-white-and-blue fashions. The American Apparel chain touts its domestic status not only in its name but in its signage, which explains that the T-shirts are made in an L.A. facility. Smaller brands like American Spoonbread and Maple Grove Farms of Vermont use their names and packaging to recall gentler times when ladies made jams and pancakes from scratch.

BuyAmerican.com, established in 1999, is for people "passionate about America and purchasing quality American-made products." The site represents more than 600 American manufacturers selling thousands of products made in the USA.

Expect to see the rise of more national brands as part of a made-in-China backlash. While consumers want to buy ultra-cheap goods, they also fear Chinese manufacturing and production power. And some have started boycotting brands because of their manufacturing policies. Clothing tags in Australia that read "Designed in Australia, Made in China" try to have it both ways, but some shoppers question why products can't be both designed and produced there to keep the money in the country.

Next: The Rise of Ethical Consumers

Choosing national brands is one way to express your ethics as a consumer. And, having altogether shed any leftover hippie connotations, shopping with a conscience is now cool. Rock stars like U2's Bono and Chris Martin of Coldplay promote fair trade, and actors including Cameron Diaz and Leonardo DiCaprio extol the joys of driving the environmentally friendly Toyota Prius. Brands such as People Tree, beloved by celebrities such as Sienna Miller, and Edun, the brainchild of Bono and his wife, Ali, sell fashion with a conscience.

Growing numbers of people want to think about the impact our consumption has on the planet. As more ethically motivated products appear in stores, choosing organic or fair trade is becoming a little less inner-directed—motivated by health concerns—and more outer-directed—motivated by issues of sustainability.

In Britain, for example, the market for ethical clothes has grown by 30 percent since 2003, to £43 million, according to the Co-operative Bank's 2005 Ethical Consumerism Report.[25] That's partly because consumers have more to choose from: In the U.K. the number of products certified by the Fairtrade Foundation increased from just 150 in 2003 to more than 1,500 three years later.[26]

> U.K. supermarket chain Sainsbury estimates it will sell £45–50 million worth of Fairtrade products in 2006, a 50 percent increase year on year over the previous two years.

Marks & Spencer was the first major U.K. retailer to begin selling clothing made from 100 percent Fairtrade cotton, and it also banned a range of chemicals that could harm the environment, factory workers, and customers from use in the manufacture of its clothes. The "Look Behind the Label" campaign tells customers how its products are sourced and made. Hot on its heels was the U.K. fast-fashion chain Top Shop, which has appointed its first buyer to source ethically made clothing.

And witness the American Apparel chain, which pays what the company claims are the highest wages in the industry—it is prominently touted. To further please the conscious consumer, there's the Sustainable Edition line, made with certified organic cotton. And finally, the merchandise is logo-free, for consumers who spurn the "false tribalism of the brand scheme," in the lingo of CEO Dov Charney.[27] The formula seems to be working: The chain opened its first store in 2003 and now has upward of 100 outlets worldwide.

Growing awareness of ethical issues is now having a notable impact on consumer choices. Market research firm Datamonitor expects that loyal consumers of natural food, drinks, and personal-care products in Europe and the United States will almost double from 89 million in 2004 to 173 million by 2009. The proportion of loyal users in the United States is projected to rise from 12 percent in 2004 to 24 percent by 2009; figures for Europe are marginally higher.[28]

There are differences in national attitudes. U.K. consumers are more focused on fair trade than those in southern Europe, where shoppers tend be concerned about not buying from certain companies, reports *Brand Strategy*. Dutch and French consumers are the most willing to pay a premium for ethical products. In the United States, organic sales are growing dramatically, and fair trade is gaining a foothold.[29]

Ethical consumption isn't just about buying fair-trade goods or organic items—companies are giving people more ways to participate. American Express has launched Red, donating 1 percent of Red card users' spending to fight HIV/AIDS in Africa. The phone company Working Assets donates a portion of its fees to advance global causes; it entices customers with the promise of free ice cream from Ben & Jerry's, the Vermont brand that champions small farmers and protests biotechnology.

Along with the rise of ethical consumption comes great interest in corporate social responsibility, but despite companies' efforts to demonstrate ethical behavior, consumers don't trust them. According to *Marketing Week* in the U.K., research commissioned by design consultants Fitch in the U.K. found that 68 percent don't believe brands are interested in improving consumers' lives, although 40 percent believe they can collectively change corporate attitudes, behavior, and communications.[30]

Next: The Online Option

Ten years ago we found ourselves watching a true commercial revolution: the emergence of e-commerce. We cited a U.S. Department of Commerce forecast that Internet retailing would reach $7 billion by 2000 and added, "If mail-order sales can be used to determine the potential for Web retail sales, as some suggest, that figure could reach US$115 billion in five to eight years."[31]

As it turned out, we've blown right past that lofty number. According to comScore, online spending for 2005, including travel-related spending, totaled

$143 billion, representing a 22 percent increase over 2004.[32] And there is simply no end in sight.

During the 2005 holiday season, about a third of American consumers bought something online, about 10 percent more than the year before, and they spent quite a bit more: Nielsen/NetRatings, which includes spending at auction sites such as eBay, put the increase for November-December 2005 at 30 percent (for a total of $30.1 billion in spending).[33]

While online shopping still represents less than 6 percent of all American retail sales, it's certainly become a mainstream behavior. What's the driving force? Convenience, for one, but it's bargains we're largely after, as well as a greater sense of control in our interactions.

On Black Friday (the day after Thanksgiving, traditionally the start of the holiday shopping season) in 2005, Amazon and eBay were the two biggest shopping sites in the United States, followed by Wal-Mart. And while people generally go to these sites seeking discounted prices, they end up giving in to the temptations of high-end goods. *The New York Times* notes that Walmart.com sold $100 cashmere scarves and $250 chocolate gift baskets exclusively online over the 2005 Christmas season.[34] The blending of high-low tastes has contributed to this phenomenon.

Online stores also cater to a sense of personal connection and control. A survey by Vivaldi Partners and *Forbes* shows that the fastest-growing brands are Internet names like Google, Amazon, Yahoo!, and eBay.[35] Why? Online, users feel like they're in charge, seeking out the brand when and how they like. Some established offline brands are now seeing a bulk of sales from their Web sites. During the 2005 holiday season, L.L. Bean and luxury retailer Neiman-Marcus both said online sales surpassed in-store and catalog sales for the first time.

> More than 627 million people, about 10 percent of the global population, have shopped online at least once, according to an AC Nielsen study.[36]

When the online relationship between consumer and company is threatened or changed, things get heated. When eBay announced fee increases in 2005 for the fifth time in five years, the move ignited fury from its members, who called for boycotts and protests against "Feebay" and "Greedbay." Still, eBay's brand is so strong, it wasn't worried: In a *New York Times* article, William C. Cobb, head of North American operations, noted that, "This is like when fans of a team call in to a talk radio station. For the most part, while they're screaming at us, they're also wearing that jersey for us on Sunday and rooting for us, with paint on their face."[37]

What's Next? On-Demand 24/7/365 Deliveries

Sure, we can buy our groceries online now, but who wants to wait until tomorrow for that double-chocolate-chip ice cream when we have a craving right now? Watch for the next wave of cybershopping to include local dimensions that promise delivery within a relatively immediate time frame so that the accommodation of urgency is part of the shopper's pleasure.

What's Next? Wiki Shopping Fever

The concept of the wiki, which we already touched on, has come to the world of shopping. Two such concepts, allowing users to contribute, remove, or edit content, officially premiered in April 2006. ShopWiki.com is from two founders of DoubleClick, the online advertising pioneer, and features a database of tens of millions of products from more than 120,000 online stores that it checks regularly. After specifying what type of item you're looking for, you get a long list of product options; unlike most wikis, here a ShopWiki staffer writes the initial entry. As for user contributions, "these should be written from the point of view of a really great salesperson," Kevin P. Ryan, ShopWiki's chief executive, told *The New York Times*.[38] "It should be totally objective, like, 'Tell me in three minutes what I should be thinking about when it comes to buying refrigerators.'" There's also the Amazon version, ProductWikis, which are components of product pages (just below customer reviews). "Customers really seem to like it, and are becoming more and more involved in refining the wikis," spokesman Andrew Herdener told the *Times*.

Next: The Impact of Word of Mouth

An important effect of the Internet on consumers is the ability to share product information and shopping experiences like never before. We've always told our friends about great stores or lousy service, but now we can tell the whole world on sites like ripoffreport.com. Or we can learn from other everyday folks: Instead of using a travel agent, we can plan our own trips with recommendations from the travelers who post their recommendations and experiences on sites like tripadvisor.com. It's all part of our desire for authenticity and transparency, and plays into the need to "see through" marketing hype.

Word of mouth has always been strong, but technology has multiplied and broadened its effects. Amazon's ability to recommend titles based on the buying habits of others is an example of the Internet supercharging word-of-mouth marketing. Many other sites, in retail and beyond, make it easy for visitors to "tell a friend"—about anything from products and recipes to music and downloads. (Since the friend's address may then become part of the marketing database, this can have ill effects, unleashing a torrent of spam and vows never to return to the site.) And today it seems like virtually any destination, any class of trade, has a dedicated blog, as well as a customer-feedback back channel—search "consumer opinion" on Google and you'll get upward of 1.4 million hits, leading with epinions.com and its peer-to-peer reviews on virtually anything.

Since people consider their peers the best sources of information about brands, companies are increasingly moving away from their reliance on top-down messages and fostering more dialogue between consumers and employees.

Next: Disposable Goods

Bargains are so easily found these days that some consumers are scooping up goods in bulk. When handbags in the hottest styles are just $20 at Forever 21 or H&M, shoppers buy a few, then toss them when the look is passé. In the U.K., the Office for National Statistics says the price of women's clothing fell by a third in the past 10 years; vacuum cleaners dropped by 45 percent, and personal computers by 93 percent.[39]

There is no stigma in cheap fashions anymore, with everyone from students to fashion editors picking up bargain T-shirts and trendy pieces from stores like Target. It's high-low again: Shoppers who get a bargain are savvy, but they're seen as equally smart to spend top dollar on high-quality designer items.

The effect of this throw-away culture is that people are running out of room to store all their finds. While Americans stuff their closets, attics, and basements, Europeans living in smaller homes are resorting to self-storage—a concept unheard of in the U.K. ten years ago but now an industry that's growing by 10 percent a year.

> "For the most part, the cheap-chic consumer is someone who wants a top or outfit to wear two or three times. Durability is not an important topic."
> —Harry Bernard of fashion-marketing and consulting firm Colton Bernard, Inc., in the *San Francisco Chronicle*[40]

eBay too has contributed to the notion of short-term ownership—use something for a while, then sell it when you're ready for the new model. Consumers are also digging through their basements and garages for profit. The days of personal curating are over: Where once people may have kept their belongings for their children and grandchildren, now their stuff is sold to the highest bidder.

Getting the short end of the stick are charities. Those with stores that sell used goods are seeing a drop in the quality and quantity of donated items as people put designer clothes and other higher-end products on eBay instead. Plus, revenue is minimal from garments that originally cost the donor perhaps less than $10. Some charities are launching their own online shops to compensate for the losses.

Next: New Distribution Channels

For some brands, the future will lie with unexpected distribution outlets. The German brewer Karlsberg, for example, is looking to secure distribution for a test product through pharmacies, of all places: Karla is a mixed drink consisting of 70 percent beer fortified with vitamins, folic acids, and the like.

Tabooboo is a U.K.-based sex toy company that created the first-ever sex toy vending machines so that its well-made and -packaged products would be sold in cool environments like clubs, bars, gyms, and even hair salons rather than porn stores. Its bright-pink machines are concentrated in London but can be seen in Japan, Italy, and the United States as well.

In the future, distribution will follow consumer expectations—they expect access to products they want wherever they happen to be, even if the stuff isn't what they came in for. Video stores clued in quickly, stocking popcorn, candy, and ice cream by the checkout counters.

Next: New Forms of Transaction

Forget your credit card, cash or even Paypal; more people are turning to alternative currencies, bartering their skills, goods and time. This meshes with a craving for a more traditional "village-style" life with all its personal interactions. In the town of Ithaca, New York, more than 900 people and businesses accept Ithaca Hours as a form of payment. The concept, started in 1991 by social activist Paul Glover, reflects the notion that an hour of labor should always have the same value, no matter whether it's spent babysitting or running a company.

There are now at least 30 imitators in the United States alone and various similar organizations such as Time Banks in operation across Europe. The weeklong Burning Man Festival, which presents itself as an experiment in community and self-reliance, operates on a gift economy and doesn't allow any cash commerce.

SwapAGift.com is for people who want to buy, sell, and swap merchant gift cards. Users list their cards, how much they will sell them for, and which cards they would swap for.

The idea of swapping is also growing. Swapstyle.com is a fashion site where you can swap, sell or buy with others around the world with no fees.

Freecycle.org, started in Tucson to reduce waste, is divided into local groups worldwide, moderated by a volunteer, where people advertise things they want to give away. Craigslist and similar sites like Gumtree include categories for free or swapped merchandise in their classifieds.

Next: Membership over Ownership

Consumers are now prepared to pay for getting goods when they want them and how they want them, and then having them gone as soon as those goods are no longer useful. Borrowing and sharing products is not only for the cost-conscious consumer. Maintaining a yacht, a fancy car, jewelry or art takes time and money, so various elite clubs allow you to use the luxe item anytime without any of the hassle. The NetJets concept of fractional jet ownership has been a big success in the United States and Europe. High-flyers who can't stand the inconvenience of commercial air travel can buy a share of a plane in exchange for a certain number of flying hours, or they can make a one-off payment for 25 hours of flying time.

If a yacht is more your thing, then you can buy a partial ownership and take to the seas with a group of your closest friends via Fraser Yachts Worldwide. The Classic Car Club in the U.K. is an exclusive club that lends members dozens of classic, sports, and luxury cars for an annual subscription—the only other thing they pay for is gas. There's also P1 International, where £2,500 to join and £13,750 for an annual membership buys 50–70 driving days in a Range Rover, a Bentley, or a Ferrari.[41]

Membership schemes aren't confined to the most luxurious goods. If you get bored of your bags easily, then Bagborroworsteal.com allows you to use a different must-have designer bag of the season for a fixed fee every month. In Switzerland, you can even "lease" a cow and receive Swiss cheese made from its milk through the Kuhleasing company. You get to meet your cow too: Customers are expected to work at least one day in Kuhleasing's alpine meadows before collecting their cheese in the autumn.

> "Exclusive Resorts, a vacation ownership club, has 2,000 members, with three tiers of memberships ranging from $195,000 to $395,000 and annual dues from $9,500 to $25,000. Membership includes 15 to 45 days in any home belonging to the club, whether it's in Los Cabos, Mexico, Italy's Tuscany region, New York, or London."
> —*Wausau Daily Herald* (Wisconsin)[42]

Next: Strictly Private

Membership in exclusive clubs is now one of the greatest luxuries one can claim. One of the greatest status symbols in cities like New York and London is having a child in one of the right private schools (and sometimes any private school). In New York, where demand far outstrips open seats, getting in is a competitive sport, with parents hiring consultants to advise them on the best tactics. The parents write application essays and attend lengthy interviews for the privilege of paying as much as $10,000 a year—and that's for three-year-olds. In London it's even more, about £10,000 ($17,000). Attending one of these schools then helps students gain entry into the next tier of exclusivity: elite colleges.

At least one private school in New York City (Riverdale Country Day, in the Bronx) charges more in annual tuition fees, $29,500, than Harvard.

Ultra-exclusive private clubs are becoming a feature of many leading cities. It's a luxury just to qualify for an invitation: The Core Club in New York, for example, is said to thoroughly research the background of everyone it invites in. Members pay $65,000 to join and an annual fee of $12,000.[43] For London's Soho House, exclusivity means that members over 27 are being actively discouraged. The club, which has a branch in New York and plans another in Miami, is trying to regain some "edge."[44]

Next: New Plutocrats Flaunt Their Wealth

While "old" money is taking a more discreet approach to luxury, the new plutocrats from Russia, China, and India are keen to display their recently acquired wealth. For them, it's bling all the way, decadence to the Nth degree.

London, a three-hour flight from Moscow, has been dubbed Londonski as wealthy Russians flock to the city. The most high profile is billionaire Roman Abramovich, who now owns the premier Chelsea football team and has settled into a $50-million home in the exclusive Belgravia area. Up-market boutiques, jewelry dealers, real estate agents, and luxury car showrooms are employing Russian speakers to cater to their money-happy new customers. A spokeswoman for Asprey's, the London jeweler, tells *The Wall Street Journal Europe* that Russians are the best customers, readily laying out $10,000 for an alligator bag or $180,000 for a diamond ring.[45] Vertu, a British subsidiary of Nokia, has opened a store in Moscow, with another planned for St Petersburg. What does it sell? Gold and platinum phones studded with diamonds.

The phenomenon may be limited to the first generation of wealth: Research by U.K. branding specialist Added Value and the Walpole Group, which represents luxury-goods companies, found that while the initial wave of Russian oligarchs loves to display their wealth, their children are likely to be more low-key.[46]

The most ostentatious spenders of all are the Chinese, the report says. There are more than 300,000 Chinese worth over $1 million, according to Merrill Lynch & Co. research cited by *Business Week*, and they're embracing luxury goods with open arms.[47] Goldman Sachs says that five years ago, China accounted for just 1 percent of luxury-goods sales. Now the Chinese are the third biggest luxury spenders in the world, and they will reach the top spot in the next ten years, ahead of Japan and the United States.[48]

Notably, the Chinese are beginning to spend on art—but unlike the Japanese, for whom the height of luxury is a French impressionist painting to hang in one's home, they are regularly outbidding American and European collectors for Chinese paintings and porcelain. They're rediscovering their heritage and buying back their culture. As Henry Howard-Sneyd of Sotheby's tells *The Sunday Times*, "Fifteen to 20 years ago, no Chinese would touch the stuff. It all left the country. Now they are beginning to try to buy it back."[49] Russians, too, are investing heavily in their nation's art and antiques. It's a growing market that's worth an estimated $1.5 billion a year.[50]

In April 2006, a Chinese entrepreneur paid the highest-ever price for a cultural relic in China, according to a state television report. The art collector spent $20 million at auction for an 8th-century porcelain vase.

In India, there are now about 1.6 million households earning around $100,000 a year, and they're developing an appetite for luxury goods including clothes, jewelry, handbags, watches, and gourmet food and wine, according to research by Indian firm The Knowledge Company. Their spending is limited only by a lack of luxury retailers, The Knowledge Company notes, opening up opportunities for luxury-themed malls and for Indian companies to compete in the space alongside Western brands.

Even in Vietnam, where more than a third of the population lives below the poverty line, there is a thriving luxury-goods market. BMW sold around 50 cars when it entered the country in 1994; last year it sold 600—40 percent of which were the top-end 325 series at $75,000 a piece.[51]

And Therefore Next

The global truth about shopping is that both buying and selling is pleasurable—from eBay's virtual participants to shoppers and shopkeepers exchanging local currency for a mass-manufactured and -marketed item. There's an undeniable thirst for the next discovery, the newest and greatest thing, be it fashion or function; and we want the best and most fair pricing for a trusted brand that's part of the household routine. Shopping has become a passion, a sport. The notion that we're seeing a period of "extreme shopping" is not a surprise—it's enabled by sophisticated search engines that can find and source the most obscure and can aggregate comparative pricing from willing vendors around the world. The true meaning of extreme shopping in this context really relates to the divergence of shoppers at opposite ends of the spectrum—with the Wal-Marts and hypermarkets of the world occupying one extreme and the highest-value specialists at the other. We see both accelerating at the specific expense of the middle.

chapter fourteen

big next: the art of eating well

If 20th-century science fiction had come to pass, our meals today would consist of highly nutritious little pills. No troublesome cooking, no dishes to wash, no worries about unbalanced diets. And while robots did all our work, we'd be dedicating ourselves to leisure pursuits.

Science fiction did come true in some ways. Millions of us pop daily vitamin supplements, which sometimes serve as substitutes for real meals. But eating has a primal potency—our relationship with food is rooted in our emotions, our consumption driven by compulsive urges. And the fact is, although technology is advancing at breakneck speed, we're making do with bodies that evolved in response to ancient conditions. In effect, people in developed places are living digital lives in prehistoric bodies.

Science, though, has enabled us to understand which prehistoric conditions we need to maintain in order to stay healthy—regular intake of fruit, vegetables, and fiber, for example. Food production is certainly a lot more high-tech than it was 50 years ago, with its satellite-guided harvesters and fully automated milking operations. And food itself and how we eat—ready-made gourmet ethnic meals heated in the microwave and consumed in front of a wide-screen TV—would probably surprise yesterday's speculators. But food remains one of the most fundamental, inescapable features of life.

As such, it can bring great enjoyment—to the extent that we're now seeing the advent of "gastroporn"—and great stress. For one thing, eating now has a moral overlay: If you are what you eat and you eat bad food, are you a bad person? If you don't heed the nutritional information on food packaging, are you to blame for your health problems and even for those of your children? Very high percentages of people are now routinely torn between food as a source of pleasure and comfort, and food as a source of anxiety, guilt, and confusion. With ever more nutritional information available, more experts are issuing advice that contradicts previous thinking and, often, the opinion of other experts. And while we're almost totally dependent on whatever food is commercially available, the message from the media and from health authorities is that corporations can't be trusted to put our health before their need to maximize profits.

As America (and much of the West) becomes progressively fatter, we are also facing a public health and economic issue—who is responsible for the "spread," and who will pay for the cost of its consequences? (As a practical example, should weight be considered as much of a criterion for pricing life insurance as smoking?) Unlike cigarettes or alcohol, we can't choose to give up eating altogether.

What we're eating now paints a clear reality of 21st-century living. Take Tropicana's recently introduced Essentials line, amped-up orange juice in such varieties as Light 'N Healthy Calcium, Pure Premium Orange Juice with Fiber, Healthy Heart, and Immunity Defense (which, according to Tropicana, is an "excellent source of essential antioxidants and selenium to help protect against free radicals"). Clearly, significant numbers of consumers are obsessed with health and the particulars of their diet, a trend reflected in our growing interest in organic and local food. Or note the fact that dinners made at home from scratch now account for only about a third of evening meals, according to the Institute of Food Technology.[1] We're too busy to cook, beset by the demands on our time, so we're choosing takeout or prepared foods. At the same time, we're hooked on TV cooking shows. Our attitudes toward food today are complicated, and revealing.

Interestingly, eating did not earn a chapter of its own in the original *Next*, even though a broad range of food topics managed to find their way into the work, including observations on organics, functional foods, and the food headline of the day: BSE (mad cow disease). We suspect it has earned a place of its own right in this book because food has become a much more important part of our leisure and entertainment culture. Consider, for example, the level of media devoted to food compared with its real import (as is the case with home). We love food, and we fear it too, as its "abuse" becomes a health issue of increasing magnitude. "Globesity" is already far more pervasive—and more troubling—than it was a decade ago.

Next: We Are What We Eat

"Tell me what you eat, and I will tell you what you are," the French epicure Jean Anthelme Brillat-Savarin, author of *The Physiology of Taste*, declared to post-revolutionary Americans in 1825. The essence of that thought has surfaced in various forms over the centuries. "You are what you eat" became particularly fashionable with the macrobiotic movement in the 1960s and has become wide-spread since then, spawning movies, TV shows, books, and endless articles and papers.

However the thought is served up—plain and unadorned or garnished with wit—it's proving true on many levels. On the most superficial level, people have always identified other nationalities with distinctive foods. In popular slang, the British refer to the French as Frogs because they eat frogs' legs, while the French refer to the British as Les Rosbifs ("the roast beefs") and to the Italians as Les Spaghettis. Americans sometimes call the British Limeys because of the sailors who used to drink lime juice to ward off scurvy, and the Germans Krauts because they eat sauerkraut. The Japanese refer to Westerners, and things considered distastefully Western, as Bata-kusai ("stinks of butter") because they smell of butter.

On a deeper level, cultures are often strongly influenced by their predominant food. Many Asian societies grow wet rice or "paddy rice," which permeates their cultures because it requires sophisticated irrigation and intense social cooperation. Rice accounts for a third of Asia's caloric intake, and people make religious offerings of rice—rice embodies the spirit of the culture. The lives of many nomadic peoples are shaped by the needs of their herds, which also serve as food. This would include the reindeer of the Saami (Lapps) in the Arctic regions, the cattle of such African peoples as the Samburu and the Maasai, and the horses of the Mongols.

We now understand that "you are what you eat" at a cellular level as well. Our bodies are constantly reconstructing themselves, and the raw material for renewing our cells comes from the proteins, vitamins, and trace elements in our food. Now, health authorities around the world are trying to get people to grasp this notion as they attempt to head off a crisis of obesity.

Mindful eaters—the types who buy organic food and who take an interest in how food is produced and processed—really take "you are what you eat" to heart. And these days eating preferences are no longer just statements of custom but also of principle. As growing numbers of people eschew meat, for example, statements like "I'm a vegetarian" or "I'm vegan" aren't solely about eating habits—they are declarations of identity.

"Organic," for one, has become a badge that carries with it all sorts of socioeconomic and political notions about its consumer. The pantry "overflowing with every type of juice box, soy milk, rice milk, organic pretzel, organic granola bar, and organic raisin the consulted nutritionist could think up" says volumes about the ultra-yuppy Manhattan parents in *The Nanny Diaries.*[2] Likewise, one can hardly pick up a motherhood-themed chick-lit novel in the U.K. without running across references to organic baby food. No self-respecting Hampstead mom would serve her offspring anything but, even if she's not quite sure why she's buying into this fad that became a trend and is now a parenting mandate.

> "'It's like all that bloody organic stuff,' Maeve continues, now on a roll. 'We never had organic food, did we? And what harm has it done us? None. I can't see what on earth is the point in spending three times as much on organic food.'
>
> 'Oh God,' groans Sam. 'You know what? I bloody agree with you, but look,' and she opens her fridge door and beckons Maeve over to have a look. Organic milk. Organic cheese. Organic bread. Organic vegetables. 'Isn't that ridiculous? I think exactly the same thing, but I've done it because everyone else does it.'"
> —Jane Green, *Babyville* (Broadway Books, 2004)[3]

Next: The Mainstreaming of Organics

The casual references to organics in trendy fiction highlight the degree to which this movement now pervades everyday life, at least among the affluent, educated, and socially aware. The U.S. organic market has been growing at a compound annual rate of 21.4 percent between 2002 and 2007, according to Datamonitor estimates, set to reach a value of $30.7 billion by 2007. The European organics market is expanding at a similar rate.

The reasons for buying are complex: A 2004 survey by Whole Foods found that a majority of respondents believed organic foods are better for the environment, better for their health, and help support small and local farmers. Almost one in three respondents said organic products taste better, and 42 percent said they offer better quality. The survey revealed that more than half of Americans (54 percent) have tried organic foods and drinks, and nearly one in ten consumes organic products several times a week.[4]

> According to market research firm Mintel, the proportion of Americans who actively shop for organics as a deliberate policy rose to 10 percent in 2004, up from 7 percent in 2002; the proportion of occasional buyers rose to 34 percent from 30 percent.[5]

Once the preserve of Birkenstock-wearing devotees of unorthodox lifestyles, found only in health-food shops, "organic" has now proved its case well enough to be factored into the everyday decision-making of a substantial number of consumers. As part of a broad cluster of what some term "ethical principles" (fair trade, pollution reduction, and so on), "organic" is becoming a proposition that pragmatic, mainstream consumers can embrace both rationally and emotionally. It's appealing not only because the food is grown under strictly monitored conditions but also because of the mind-set that goes with it: respect for the environment and an awareness of and concern for the bigger picture.

People have kicked against the advances of modernity by idealizing nature ever since industrialization started pulling large numbers of people off the land and into towns. From such philosophers as Jean-Jacques Rousseau ("The Noble Savage") through creative visionaries like William Blake ("dark Satanic mills") up to the "Mother Earth" idealism of the hippie movement, modern man has had a love-hate relationship with the implications of science and technology.

Paradoxically, the advances of science have given the idealists' emotional mistrust of modernity very logical underpinnings. Thanks to increasingly sophisticated techniques, scientists have been able to reveal just how deeply the products of today's society affect all living organisms, including humans. While "organic" is by no means a panacea for modern ills, it certainly offers clear and well-documented benefits. So in the early 21st century, the desire for "natural" products that are produced with respect for the wider environment is no longer solely the preoccupation of a marginal group of wide-eyed idealists—McDonald's, for instance, now sells organic milk in its British restaurants.

Organic food production is on the increase around the globe, with almost 23 million hectares of farmland managed organically, according to Organic Monitor. Much of the increase is in developing countries in response to opportunities for export.[6]

In most of the developed world there are now well-established organic food brands that are gradually becoming as familiar as their non-organic counterparts. Major food retailers in all developed markets now stock organic versions of dairy products, meat, fruit, vegetables, cereals, beer, and wine. In the United States, chains such as Safeway include organic products in their store-brand lines, priced higher than nonorganic equivalents but lower than the name brand organic products. The retailers are, in effect, priming the pump—making organic products more accessible to a wider market.

This practice is especially prevalent in Europe. In the Netherlands, giant retailer Albert Heijn (part of the Ahold group) stocks an extensive range of its own organic products under the AH Biologisch label. The range guarantees "no use of artificial fertilizers, no use of chemical pesticides, no chemical or synthetic additives," with the boasts that its standards are even higher than those of SKAL, a nonprofit organization that grants qualifying products its own EKO seal of approval. *Biologique*, "organic" in French, has a special resonance in the home of gastronomy and the doughty defender of Appellation Contrôlée (the certification of origin). Carrefour, the international food retailing giant, claims it has supported organic agriculture since 1992; it's developing organic product lines in four major European markets—France, Spain, Belgium, Italy—as well as in Thailand, China, Argentina, and Brazil. Its original organic product, the *boule bio* (a round bread loaf), is now the No. 2 seller in its bread line, beaten only by the classic baguette.

> Understanding the nomenclature: We made the point in *Next* that terms like "organic" and "natural" were constantly misused and abused, as they had no standard reference, nor regulation on their meaning. In October 2002, the U.S. Department of Agriculture established national standards governing use of the term "organic": To qualify, food must be produced without conventional pesticides, hormones, bioengineering, ionizing radiation, or fertilizers made with prohibited synthetic ingredients or sewage sludge.

In the early days of organic production, the products couldn't match the glossy, cookie-cutter visual appeal of competitors made using more industrial processes. Joni Mitchell may have pleaded, "Give me spots on my apples, but leave me the birds and the bees please" in "Big Yellow Taxi," but many consumers were put off by blemishes and irregularities. Now, organics producers have sharpened their marketing and presentation and improved pricing; at the same time, the average consumer has gained a broader tolerance of organics' aesthetic shortcomings. And as food shows and cookbooks teach us to really focus on taste, some people are finding organic produce to be more flavorful than its conventional counterparts.

Next: More Functional Foods and Products

Organic or not, the allure of any food that can make or keep you well is on the rise. But these days, talk goes beyond oat bran and flax seed oil; think more technical chatter about lactose-free products, low glycemic indexes, antioxidants, added vitamins, and transgenic ingredients. A new breed of "functional foods," or "nutraceuticals," has emerged to help people self-medicate. And as we become hyperaware of the connection between diet and disease, the new healthy identity will be all about being fortified, supplemented, and turbocharged by food products.

Consider the rise of foods supplemented with the important omega-3 fatty acids found in fish; gluten-free products for the gluten intolerant; and antioxidant-rich products like pomegranate juice, marketed as "The antioxidant superpower" by the Pom brand. Watch as more brands promote their health benefits more loudly.

American scientists have even found a way to make bacon healthier, genetically engineering a pig packed with omega-3s. Might baby-back ribs be the new broccoli?, asks Robert Smith on NPR's blog.[7]

"The global market for functional, fortified and better-for-you foods is growing rapidly as more affluent consumers put health and wellness at the top of their agenda," reports private equity company 3i.[8] Indeed, health and wellness is replacing convenience as the major influence in food choice decision-making, notes Australian publication *Food and Pack*.[9]

The United States, the EU, and Japan are the biggest markets for functional foods, says *Food and Pack*, with 2003 retail sales tallying $18.5 billion in the United States, $15 billion in the EU, and $9 billion in Japan.[10] A Euromonitor report forecasts the Western European market for fortified foods growing by 28 percent to 19.7 billion euros by 2009, following a 23 percent jump between 2002 and 2004.[11] As the three dominant markets mature, brands can capitalize on a new interest in wellness in developing markets such as Russia, China, and Mexico. Wal-Mart is the largest retailer to go on an organic offensive, putting America's organic farmers on edge because of the prevailing assumption that it will drive down prices. Within a narrow time frame, Wal-Mart intends to double its organics offer, with extended choices in produce, dairy, and dry goods. Short-term beneficiaries may include Dean Foods (soy milk), Cascadian Farms (owned by General Mills), and Kraft, through its ownership of Boca Burgers.

What's Next? The Demise of One-Note Diets

We're seeing a backlash against Atkins as people re-embrace healthy carbs and start to query any diet that suggests butter, cream, and unlimited red meat are the smart way to eat. Beyond that, there's a growing belief that there's no such thing as a diet that's right for everyone. Personalization—whether based on lifestyle, ethnicity, blood type, or something else—will become an important component of diet programs.

Next: Organic Grazing

The days of sitting at a table and lingering over three square meals are long gone for most people in all developed and many developing countries. Modern lifestyles mean fragmented schedules with meals eaten on the run. In response, the snacking and grazing culture has grown. Of course, on-the-go snacks have always been a part of life, but traditionally they were local specialties freshly pre-pared by street vendors, such as noodles in the Far East, corn on the cob in the Americas, and candied nuts in southern Europe. In the developed world snacks are now largely of the type on display at any service station—even those that haven't turned into mini supermarkets offer a vast array of sweet and savory junk food for hurried motorists. It's not surprising, either, when you think that these mini-marts make more profit on their foodstuffs than on the gasoline they sell.

Not surprisingly, rampant snacking has been fingered as one of the factors behind ballooning obesity rates. And consuming these empty calories is coming under increasing scrutiny as a health risk. The U.S. government has been chewing over the idea of a snack tax for more than a decade, and the U.K. is making threat-ening noises about further restricting the advertising of unhealthful foods to children.

No wonder snackers are getting more health-conscious and looking to organic foods to fill them up. Organic snack-food sales increased 30 percent in 2003, mak-ing snacks the second-fastest-growing organic segment after meat and poultry, according to a survey for the Organic Trade Association.[12] And in a *USA Today* online survey, 37 percent of respondents said they would buy an organic version of their favorite snack if it provided nutritional benefits.[13] "Organic" is now proving a stronger driver than "natural," sales of which have been flat for the past two years.

The healthier-snacking movement has been a boon to nuts and dried fruits. Brazil nuts in particular may have the best claim to being the original natural and organic snack. Harvested from trees in the Amazon rain forests, they contain protein, fiber, various vitamins and minerals, and antioxidant compounds. Fresh fruit is also getting packaged in snack-friendly forms—witness the success of presliced-apple packs, with consumers paying a premium for the convenience of bite-size pieces out of the bag (about $3 for a pound). According to *The New York Times Magazine*, Nielsen research showed the presliced-apple market zooming up by 300 percent in 2005.[14]

Next: A New Emphasis on Local and Fresh

"Organic" has been the focus of some of the most nutritionally aware for the last two or three decades, but now it's moving into the mainstream. Today's leading-edge nutrition consumers are turning their attention to local sourcing. Buying products locally is increasingly seen as one of the best ways to ensure that one's food is truly fresh—picked not long before consumption.

We want a closer connection between farm and table. The practice plays into ethical concerns about supporting local communities and businesses, and minimizing pollution from long-haul distribution. Consumers are worried about factory farming, pesticides, produce flown thousands of miles to satisfy out-of-season demand, and the ethics of big corporations. The idea is to "Eat organic, buy local," the motto of the U.K.'s Soil Association, an organic-production standards and benchmarking body.

"If fresh food is necessary to health in man and beast, then that food must be provided not only from our own soil but as near as possible to the sources of consumption."
—Lady Eve Balfour, founder of the U.K.'s Soil Association[15]

Consumers are craving both communal and cultural interaction when shopping—the sort of experience they imagine that their grandparents enjoyed. Farmers markets and small specialist shops are becoming the hub of communities in the United States, U.K., Australia, and New Zealand as they provide specialized products and the opportunity to build personal relationships with the people who supply your food. Farmers market shoppers are sophisticated buyers who want to know where and how their food was produced—and they are prepared to pay a premium if need be.

The local-food trend is more advanced in the U.K. than the United States, perhaps in part because the distances are shorter. As part of an Organic Action Plan launched in 2002, the British government's goal is for 70 percent of in-season organic food to be domestically sourced by 2010, and some supermarkets are already exceeding this target for some products. The Waitrose supermarket chain runs a Locally Produced program highlighting British regions that are home to small producers making specialty products; a locally produced "stamp" is given to products made within a 30-mile radius of the branch where they are sold.

In the United States, consumers interested in local produce can use LocalHarvest.org to link to small growers that sell direct; buyers can choose listings within specified distances from their zip codes. High-profile proponents of the concept include chef Danny Meyer, who brought his Manhattan restaurant the Union Square Cafe to national prominence by championing produce from the farmers market a block away. And Alice Waters of Chez Panisse in Berkeley has long emphasized using only the freshest regional ingredients. Even large catering concerns are getting in on the act: the Palo Alto-based food service provider, Bon Appetit Management Co., sponsors an annual Eat Local Challenge at the 190 restaurants it runs. The task is to create menus made up of ingredients that originate within 150 miles of the particular chef's kitchen.

Related to the focus on local foods is the rise of the slow food movement, which began in Italy in 1986 as a response to the opening of a McDonald's by the Spanish Steps in Rome. An international organization with 83,000 members, it opposes "the standardization of taste," promotes gastronomic traditions and generally argues against the homogenization of fast food.

If you really want to know where your food comes from, grow it yourself. In the U.K., allotments—plots where the elderly and keen gardeners have traditionally grown their own produce—are in huge demand. And rather than the traditional retirees, the long waiting lists are filled with high-flying professionals who, if time is short, hire professional gardeners. Apartments being built in Edinburgh's city center come complete with mini-allotments for residents. The suburban British are even taking to hen-keeping, reports the BBC, with courses filling up weeks in advance and, at one time, a three-month wait list to buy the Eglu, a designer must-have coop.[16]

Of course, those who don't grow their own or live near production areas are limited to a supermarkets selection of produce, which may come from hundreds or even thousands of miles away. "Fresh" is an enduring buzz word in food marketing whose appeal is immediate and whose connotations seem clear, but the closer one looks at the word, the harder it is to define. After all, "fresh" conjures the image of produce piled alluringly in green markets or at the fruit or vegetable counter; it conjures the image of "straight from the farm." When that's not the case, however, fresh isn't necessarily better. Produce in the freezer section is picked at the perfect moment of ripeness and quickly frozen so that in some instances it's more flavorful and nutritious than "fresh" produce that's been freighted long distances. "Americans are starting to realize that 'fresh' and 'raw' aren't always the same thing," says Alton Brown, host of the Food Network's *Good Eats*, who relies heavily on top-quality organic frozen vegetables.[17]

Next: The Chef as Celebrity

With increasing outlets—from the Food Network to Web sites like epicurious.com—to flaunt their flavors, recipes, and talent, chefs have become familiar, almost comforting household brands. True to our need to tie emotion to food, we've placed great import on the role of chefs, elevating the role of the cook to superstar status. Ruth Reichl, editor of *Gourmet* magazine, suggests that diners are in search of a personal connection as much as a tasty experience: "The more people can identify with these chefs, the more they want to go to their places, buy their books, have some kind of contact with them."[18]

The high-profile chef also caters to a culinary cultural shift. As the tradition of passing family recipes from mother to daughter fades, these chefs can bridge the generational gaps by offering easy, accessible options that women and men can try even at the end of a long work day (or, at least, envision themselves trying).

In a post-Thanksgiving *Wall Street Journal* article, Pia Catton writes, "For thousands of would-be cooks from the famous Generation X (or Y and maybe Z), [the holiday] might well have been a disaster without the help of a nearby gourmet market, ready to deliver a 'home cooked' Thanksgiving meal (assuming that Mom didn't save the day). Yes, these young women can make sense of elaborate spread sheets, quote Shakespeare and tone discrete muscle groups—all at the same multitasking moment. But put poultry in front of them and panic sets in."[19]

Celebrity chefs not only make it looks so easy, nowadays they're also attractive, tantalizing figures seducing audience with the promises of succulent, even sexy dishes. With their appeal to a range of sensual experiences, it's not surprising these cooks have become their own brand of scintillating celebrity.

Consider the likes of the Food Network's Giada DeLaurentis and Rachael Ray, both attractive and inviting and certainly appealing to a male audience. Not at all surprising, then, that a key Food Network demographic is the 18-to-35-year-old male.[20] As journalist Frederick Kaufman noted on the NPR program *On the Media*, "You're seeing men in bars watching Giada; they're watching Rachael next to the football game. And it's almost this kind of strange surreal experience of having somebody cook for you while you're sitting there drinking beer alone in a bar, crunching a potato chip. It's this kind of outrageous sense of happiness and perfection given to you in this completely virtual manner."[21]

That may go a long way toward explaining why, as Kaufman points out in *Harper's*, the Food Network reaches 87.5 million households, and why its share of the cable market has been growing more than twice as fast as MTV's and almost triple that of CNN.[22] He notes that producers envision ten new channels in the next ten years, among them Food Network Italian, The Gourmet Food Channel, The California Food Channel, The Food and Wine Channel. Next, we may just find too many celebrity cooks in the kitchen.

Next: Gastroporn

It's one of the ironies of modern life that cooking shows and books are so hugely popular when much of the time we eat on the move or settle down in front of the TV with a microwaved frozen dinner. The preparing, cooking, tasting, and eating of food have become voyeuristic pleasures separated from physical reality and carried out by experts who go through the moves with practiced ease. Not unlike pornography.

Food and sex are two basics of human life. While essential for the survival of the species, we take pleasure in them for their own sake, and increasingly we take pleasure in reading about and watching them. In fact, much of the aesthetics and dynamics of pornography have carried over into representations of food—with the advantage that people aren't embarrassed to consume food pornography, or "gastroporn."

As with pornographic images, so gastroporn delights in extreme close-ups, focusing in tightly on detail to give a vivid sense of texture and to arouse the senses. Pornography simulates the sensual excitement of sex without the complications of dealing with a real person, while gastroporn enables the onlooker to savor an impossibly perfect-looking dish without having to do anything—and without the fattening calories. Both pornography and gastroporn play on the fact that the mind is the most important erogenous zone and the body's seat of sensual pleasure.

The vocabulary of celebrity chefs has certainly become highly sensualized: Food is routinely described as succulent, moist, mouth-watering, tantalizing, tender, juicy, melt-in-your-mouth. This sexualization of food and cooking is personified by voluptuous chef Nigella Lawson, who tells readers in the preface to *How to Eat* that her "slavering passion" for food is the book's starting point.[23] On Salon.com, Charles Taylor asks of Lawson's TV show: "Has television ever given us anything more pornographic? It is, without apology, the most consistently lubricious show on the air."[24]

Gastroporn is whimsically celebrated in the Web site FoodPorn.com, which is playfully divided into sections that mimic typical porn sites: Asian, Barely Legal, Hardcore, Self-Pleasuring. A movie category links to such sensual food films as *Eat Drink Man Woman* and *Chocolat*. The site warns in its mock disclaimer: "If you are under legal eating age, are offended by food, or if it is illegal to view or consume food in your community, please leave now. This site is not acting in any way to send you food; you are choosing to receive it. Continuing means that you understand and accept responsibility for your own actions, thus releasing the creators of this Web site from all liability, including drooling and weight gain."

Indeed, as our plastic surgery-obsessed culture pursues physical perfection on the one hand and frets about health issues and the obesity epidemic on the other, eating for pleasure has become naughtier than ever. Food and sex have been linked since Roman times at least, but what's new now is the heated moral arguments that surround food and the whiff of sinful decadence and moral laxity that accompanies overeating. In this environment, gastroporn is a way for anybody and everybody to partake in such indulgences with a minimum of guilt.

Next: What We Don't Eat

The human species has sustained itself by eating anything nontoxic, including both meat and vegetables. But in societies where food is plentiful and the culture sophisticated, people become pickier about their food. They can afford to avoid or even ban certain foods—for example, observant Jews and Muslims don't eat pork or shellfish, and Hindus don't eat beef. (One exception is China, one of the oldest and most sophisticated civilizations, where the old adage is "We'll eat anything with less than six legs and its back to the sun.") In developed markets, where eating is about pleasure and, increasingly, enhancing health and longevity, people are increasingly selective about what they eat.

For example, within little more than a generation, offal (the internal organs of a butchered animal) has gradually gone from mainstream fare to something modern kids would shudder at the prospect of eating (although ironically their chicken nuggets and other "fun" foods often contains just that). Tongue, heart, liver, kidney, sweetbreads (thymus glands or pancreas), and brain now rarely appear in food retail or restaurants, except as gourmet delicacies turned out by high-end chefs.

Food avoidance isn't just a matter of distaste for certain types of food. It also means buying into the notion that certain foods affect health. Worries about cholesterol and mad cow disease have increased the number of people who avoid red meat. And general concern about modern methods of rearing animals has made many people inclined to eat less meat of any color, even if they don't become completely vegetarian. The "foods to avoid" issue is further complicated by the penetration of GMOs (genetically modified organisms) into foodstuffs. However, after some outcry against GMOs in the 1990s and early 2000s, especially in Europe, they have not become a high priority for most consumers.

From nuts to dairy, various products are now being cut from diets as food intolerances and allergies are blamed for a whole range of ailments (reflecting the widespread mind-set that there's an explanation for everything and that everything can be fixed). Nut allergies are now so prevalent that food manufacturers and retailers put warning labels on products if there's any possibility they contain even trace amounts. And whole categories of typical Western food are out of bounds to people suffering from lactose intolerance or wheat-gluten intolerance.

A recent report on marketresearch.com estimates that around 8 percent of infants and children are afflicted with food allergies, and the number with severe peanut allergies is soaring; about 11 million Americans overall suffer from allergies and far more from food intolerances.[25] In Europe, 1–7 percent of people in the EU have food allergies, according to estimates from the European Federation of Allergy and Airways Diseases Patients' Associations.[26] But the British Nutrition Foundation puts the figure for British people classifying themselves as food intolerant at as much as one-fifth of the population.[27] Testing for food intolerances is now a booming business, as is supplying suitable foods.

It may well be that there's a certain "group think" element to the food allergy and intolerance phenomenon, especially since a lot of intolerance is self-diagnosed. In America, the number of children claiming to have peanut allergies doubled between 1997 and 2002.[28] In the U.K., the dairy council claims that as many as 45 percent of Britons believe they're lactose intolerant. But European Community estimates show that real food intolerance and allergies affect just 3–7 percent of the population.[29]

Next: The War for Young Palates

We see the new breed of celebrity chef influencing millions of people: A single ingredient featured on a TV show is almost certain to be in high demand in stores over the following days. There's no doubt they carry a lot of clout when it comes to selling ideas, so it's particularly significant that "The Naked Chef" of British cuisine, Jamie Oliver, decided to tackle a subject that's been worrying governments and parents in many countries: the dietary habits of children. Oliver took his "Feed Me Better" campaign to improve the quality of school food into a south London school, an effort he showcased through a four-part TV show.

The program prompted the British government to pledge an extra £280 million ($400 million) to raise the quality of food served to children. As in the United States, school systems had responded to budget cuts by bringing in low-cost outside caterers and branded vending machines. According to the BBC, one London borough had been spending as little at 37 pence (50 cents) per pupil on ingredients.[30] In the United States, where one in five children is overweight, the food provided to schools by the Department of Agriculture tends to be "at the bottom of the barrel in terms of healthy nutrition," says Dr. Walter Willett of the Harvard School of Public Health.[31]

In France, vending machines were banned from secondary schools in 2005; some 8,000 had to be removed (they were already banned from primary schools). And while France spends between $1.50 and $4 per pupil on its relatively gourmet school lunches, all is not well there either. According to a BBC report, almost a fifth of French children are overweight at a time when only 20 percent of the population eats the traditional balanced French meal.[32] Rather, they are turning to junk food (amazingly for a nation that resists American influence so fiercely, 1 million people eat at McDonald's every day) and developing the same poor consumption habits as Americans. For example, the average French person now consumes 75 pounds of sugar annually, 50 percent more than just five years ago. Kids under 15 consume most of all: about 86 pounds a year.

In virtually every country in which convenience food and sugary snacks and soft drinks are sold—in most developed countries and many developing countries too—the war for young palates is shaping up to be long and hard fought. A British reality show put the issue in stark terms with its title, *Honey, We're*

Killing the Kids. Each week a family's eating and living habits were exposed to the scrutiny of the nation, with experts using technology to show how the children could look at age 40 if the family didn't change its lifestyles.

Children can be picky eaters, but they love food that's sweet, brightly colored, presented in fun formats, and marketed with fun advertising. Plus, they are masters of pester power. In the short term, this means easy feeding for parents and irresistible profits for food companies; in the longer term, it means heavy costs for treating the effects of obesity, such as diabetes. And so the clamor is growing to regulate junk-food marketing aimed at children.

> "In the most damning government assessment yet from the National Academy of Sciences, health-science and nutritional-policy experts sharply criticized the marketing practices of food and beverage companies and called for a congressional crackdown if the industry fails to mend its ways. At issue: the need to shift advertising away from high-calorie, low-nutrient products and instead promote healthier fare."
>
> —*Business Week*[33]

What's Next? Breakfast Foods Against Bulging Bellies

The first meal of the day is the one that sets you up right for the rest of the day, and if you stock up on the right sort of nutrients, you can feel full and energetic enough to avoid the constant snacking that puts on the pounds. Will the multinational food giants respond to this opportunity, given that the best they've been able to do so far is market sugary cereals to a generation of overweight youth? Will we see other nations adopt the U.K. policy of tight restrictions on advertising to kids?

Next: The Rise of Chocolate, Coffee, and Tea As Health Foods

Chocolate, coffee, and tea have been global for so long it's easy to forget they were originally confined to the areas in which they originated: coffee in Ethiopia, chocolate in Central America, and tea in Asia. When they eventually appeared in sophisticated society in Europe and North America, they were credited with bestowing health benefits. By the 20th century, people regarded them as conferring more generic benefits—tea for refreshment, coffee for stimulation, and chocolate for sheer pleasure. Now, nutritional science is revealing some unexpected properties in chocolate, coffee, and tea; it seems they are, in fact, functional foodstuffs.

The chocolate industry cites a number of salutary effects of real chocolate. For starters, it contains cocoa butter, which, like olive oil, reduces cholesterol. It's also high in a number of vitamins and minerals, including fluoride and potassium. The antioxidant flavonol helps to regulate blood pressure—Harvard Medical School research has shown its benefits can be as great as those of aspirin. A 50-gram chocolate bar contains the same concentration of flavonols as two glasses of red wine, four cups of tea, six apples, or seven onions.

Real chocolate does not contain processed sugars and fats; it should also contain no vegetable fats besides those that naturally arise from the cacao. So the key to guilt-free chocoholism is a product with high cocoa content—at least 60 percent. High-end, gourmet brands led the way, and mass-market brands such as Lindt and Nestlé have followed. In the U.K., Green & Black's (green for organic, black for dark chocolate) has grown from a strictly niche player into an increasingly mainstream, widely available brand. It's still small in terms of retail sales (£13.5 million), but is recording year-on-year growth of 63 percent (versus 2.1 percent for the total confectionery market).

Love of chocolate used to be a slightly shame-faced admission, but these days women and even men brazenly admit to being "chocoholics." The Web abounds with sites dedicated to the substance. In fact, there may well be more people around the world who regularly take pleasure in chocolate than in alcohol or even sex. The research group Datamonitor calls chocolate "the new coffee" as chocolate cafes pop up around the United States.[34] More than just chocolate shops, these cafes and lounges will be places for people to indulge and linger over a few treats in a coffeehouse setting.

Suddenly, the question "Would you like some tea?" no longer gets a straight yes-no answer. There are black teas, green teas, red teas, and white teas, along with flavored teas, herbal teas, and herbal infusions. Any self-respecting food retailer, bar, or restaurant now routinely stocks a variety of teas and tea-like beverages, many of which would have been consumed by a marginal few just a decade ago. As with other food and drink products, organic provenance offers an additional layer of appeal. Like Green & Black's in the chocolate category, Colorado-based Celestial Seasonings has grown from a quirky local brand into a global player; it offers some 80 different teas that tout a variety of benefits.

Increased awareness of the health aspects of tea now means half of the adult population in the United States drinks specialty teas. Green, white, and red teas are especially high in antioxidants, plus tea may also improve coronary health. One Harvard study, for example, examined 340 people who had suffered heart attacks, finding that those who drank a cup or more of black tea daily reduced their risk of heart attack by 44 percent compared to a control group.[35]

For the most part, coffee hasn't enjoyed the healthful halo that glows over tea and chocolate, but for many its ability to get the gray matter buzzing is seen as a mental-health benefit. And now reports are beginning to surface that coffee has real health benefits. Recent research shows a clear correlation between coffee consumption and lowered incidences of type 2 diabetes. This was the finding in a study by Dr. Frank Hu of the Harvard School of Public Health, who tracked more than 100,000 people over almost 20 years; his results were similar to those of a Dutch study.[36] The Harvard findings held true even after accounting for risk factors linked to diabetes, including age and weight. Hu's study showed, for example, that four to five cups of coffee per day cut the risk of diabetes in men and women by 30 percent; men who drank six or more cups reduced their risk by more than 50 percent.

Arguing the benefits of a strong cup of espresso, dietitian Chiara Trombetti of the Humanitas Gavazzeni institute in Bergamo, Italy, notes that it contains beneficial tannins and antioxidants; it can relieve headaches; it is good for the liver and can help prevent cirrhosis and gallstones. The caffeine can also reduce the risk of an asthma attack and help improve circulation.[37]

The worldwide spread of Starbucks and similar local variants of "barista" coffee establishments is testament to the reinvention of coffee and its resonance among consumers. The exaltation of coffee is helped by the emphasis on quality, flavor, varieties, authenticity, and brands playing up fair-trade and organic credentials.

Next: Cheers to Wine and Superpremium Spirits

In recent years wine has become a more viable option for the six-pack set. (Note that after accounting for inflation, the beer-drinking market grew only 2 between 2000 and 2005 in the United States.) The low-carb craze has put a damper on beer sales at the same time that wine's health benefits have received greater attention and prices have dropped. And the quirky, eye-catching labels that bear names like Funky Llama, Fat Bastard, and Wrongo Dongo strip the stigma of knowing nothing about vines and vintages and make selecting a bottle more accessible to the masses.

Wine's popularity is really on the rise in the United States, with Americans on their way to becoming the largest consumers of wine in the world, according to Datamonitor. The research firm estimates U.S. consumers will account for a quarter of worldwide wine consumption by 2008—up from 19 percent in 2004—even though Americans tend to pay more for wine than Europeans. (A typical bottle in the United States costs twice as much as one sold in France and more than three times the average in Italy.)

Drinkers are also turning to premium and super-premium spirits. They are showing a more widespread appeal and acceptance, especially among younger people. Even rum, long considered a low-brow liquor, has gained some cachet with luxury labels like LVMH Moet Hennessy Louis Vuitton launching a line called 10 Cane, described as an unrivaled rum-tasting experience. And forget about the rum and Coke of old: Promotional material for the brand advocates mixing it with fresh ingredients in cocktails or with tonic. Industry experts say 10 Cane is just the beginning for super-premium rums.

Vodka's appeal is spreading too, with U.K. company Blavod Extreme Spirits planning expansion into two new markets, Peru and Vietnam. New flavors are keeping consumers intrigued, like the green tea vodka put out by the Charbay Winery and Distillery. Described as the first of its kind in the United States and a sipping vodka of sorts, it's said to contain four varieties of the tea, all of which contribute to a calming and comforting taste. It's a hearty attempt to combine alcohol and healthy-eating trends.

What's Next? Premium Drink Bars

These bars will pop up to promote various brands, serving only one spirit and organized around the experience of that drink and its mixers. They'll be short-lived but have serious talkability while they're on the scene.

Next: Global Gastronomy Meets the Mainstream

As we travel more expansively and watch more food shows that introduce us to international cooking, it's no surprise that our tastes are going global. The proverbial melting pot has given way to a literal stew of new flavors and tastes. Consider that despite Americans' love of the classic hamburger, Chinese restaurants in the United States now outnumber McDonald's, Wendy's, and Burger King outlets combined.[38]

Supermarkets have helped turn the exotic into mainstream commodities, with sushi chefs slicing sashimi next to the Mediterranean olive bar and more international product lines are sharing shelf space with American staples. Ethnic food sales tallied $75 billion in 2004, which translates to $1 of every $7 spent on groceries.[39] Between 2003 and 2004, more than 2,000 ethnic food products were introduced in the United States; growing segments included Chinese, Japanese, and Thai, as well as Caribbean, African, and Mediterranean.

Watch as more prepackaged and frozen ethnic meals mingle with frozen fries and pizza. Foods that can easily substitute for familiar fare are most likely to cross over quickly, says *Food Technology*, the magazine of the Institute of Food

Technologists; examples include Indian street foods such as samosas; warming spices such as curry and cardamom; Middle Eastern and Indian flat breads; Indian dosas (similar to crepes); and spreads like hummus.[40] Top sellers include Indian and vegetarian frozen meals and sauces, such as Sable & Rosenfeld's Coconut Curry and Cashew Chicken, the report says.

A growing Indian population in the United States has sparked interest in Indian cuisine. And not just the old familiars like simple curries, but more specialized dishes from different regions of the country. As *Specialty Food* magazine says, "Professional chefs, home cooks and diners are discovering the culinary splendors of Indian cuisine, recognizing the difference between North and South Indian styles of cooking as well as variations from regions such as Kerala and Chettinad in the south, and Gujarat and Goa on the western coast."[41] Draws include manageable portions and a great diversity of options. And according to *Specialty Food*, Indian snack foods like namkeen—made with various flours, ground lentils, nuts, spices, and dried fruits—are ideal for people on the go.

Spain is also an up-and-coming leader of world flavor. Spanish cookbooks and restaurants are becoming more prevalent, and these have created an appetite for traditional dishes like tapas and paella. The small servings that define tapas provide an alternative to the mega-portions of most American dishes; they also offer the more calorie-conscious eater the option to taste modest amounts of several dishes.

What's Next? New Delicacies

Foods unfamiliar to everyday shoppers, like Greek yogurt, jicama from Mexico, Japanese sushi rice, and Portuguese peri-peri sauces, will be front and center in the gourmet groceries that spring up in newly developed urban areas. Here, trendy shoppers are also likely to visit tasting bars and attend cooking classes. The continent most likely to emerge as hot in such shops? Asia. Watch also for African specialties like injera, the soft Ethiopian bread that also serves as an eating utensil.

And Therefore Next

What we eat is one of those things that changes completely on a regular basis and that also remains very much the same. Kids for 40 years have begged their parents for McDonald's burgers and fries; what's different now than in 1967 is that portions are larger, the toys with the meal are grander, and the availability of fast food around the world has grown dramatically. (McDonald's, which actually started its international expansion in 1967 with outlets in Canada and Puerto Rico, is found in 119 countries today.) Maybe food is the greatest proof positive of today's globalized world: From Argentina to New Zealand to Slovakia to Colombia, McDonald's has brought quick eating to the planet. In many ways, McDonald's is a snapshot of then, now, and next eating as it struggles to balance a new commitment to healthier eating with real people's demands for comfortable food when and where they want it. Its menus now reflect global menus, local favorites, and a few nutritious alternatives. (In *Next* a decade ago, we noted McDonald's role as purveyor of glocalization—the McSandwiches that mix the signature special sauce with the most popular filling in each market, from salmon in the Nordic countries to Indian spiced chicken in the U.K.) While McDonald's is sometimes offered up as an example of Americana at its most obvious, the golden arches are a powerful symbol of how the world eats. On a Web site called bantransfats.com, we found information about proposed changes to the New York City Health Code, including initiatives to partially phase out trans fat from New York City restaurant cuisine and to add caloric content on each and every menu and menu board. This war on trans fat will be the new anti-smoking crusade for sure. And the campaign to make food more healthful is only just beginning.

chapter fifteen

big next: entertainment evolved

Perhaps the biggest difference in our view of entertainment in 1997 versus 2007 is embodied in the title of our chapter on the subject in the original *Next:* We called it "Gimme a Break."[1] Now, the very notion of a hard line between work and play (or most other aspects of our life) is rapidly diminishing. As discussed elsewhere, perhaps this is the truest meaning of convergence. The other difference that's most noticeable is the degree to which our primary focus on entertainment used to be out of home (though we did address the home theater, which was just getting popular ten years ago).

What's new now is the disappearing boundary between passive entertainment and active leisure. Entertainment has always been equated with passivity—we sit in the audience, the responsibility to entertain falling on the object of our attention—while leisure activities are generally considered active, like golfing or pursuing a hobby such as photography. The purpose, by and large, has been the same: to relieve the stress of everyday life.

Technology is changing the nature of entertainment, making it more interactive and more user-directed for less passive consumers. Says *The Economist:* "Ever more people will upload short video clips to new websites such as YouTube.com, go to Netflix.com to rate their DVDs, to Amazon.com to discuss books and their own blogs for online debate." It's all part of the "age of mass participation," as the magazine calls it.[2]

Today we can determine when we want entertainment and in what format. Think of watching downloaded TV shows on a video iPod versus planning your night around favorite programs. Or of downloading selected tracks from an album and inserting them into playlists instead of buying a CD and listening to it in one chunk.

Meanwhile, leisure pursuits, especially sports, are taking on an entertainment component. At the Torino Winter Olympics, half-pipe snowboarder Shaun White rode triumphantly to the gold while the sound system blared AC/DC's "Back in Black." Ballroom dancing and figure skating merged with reality TV in ABC's *Dancing with the Stars* and *Skating with Celebrities* on Fox. Poker has spawned a whole genre of TV shows, with fans choosing from pop versions with celebrity players (Bravo's *Celebrity Poker Showdown* and E!'s *Hollywood Hold 'Em*) and serious pro tournament coverage on the Travel Channel (*World Poker Tour*) and ESPN (*World Series of Poker*).

Seeing entertainment in terms of its role as a stress reliever may also be outdated. Hobbies are considered interests we nurture purely for pleasure, but Web technology is allowing more amateurs to turn personal passions into profits at minimal expense or risk. A foodie's blog on restaurants and recipes can generate enough traffic to attract advertisers; the daily diary of a single woman in the city can lead to a book deal. And in today's highly fast-paced society, hobbies can get competitive, with pressures to be the first to experience something new. Eating out or seeing a movie can be motivated by more than just the pursuit of leisure.

At the same time, activities that used to be largely a chore have been reclassified as entertainment. The lines between commerce and entertainment are blurring, with retailers trying to make the mundane more fun. Customers while away hours checking out new technology at an Apple store or enjoy lattes while banking at one of Abbey National's in-branch cafes in the U.K. With desire, rather than need, the driving force behind many consumer purchases in the West, shopping has become part of the entertainment spectrum, either on its own or packaged with other entertainment activities, like lunching with friends.

Next: Technology Keeps Transforming Entertainment

Ten years ago, we noted a significant tinge of nostalgia coloring leisure. Today we see very little that isn't technology-enabled and forward-thinking. It's the triumph of technology as entertainment.

For young people especially, the two are almost synonymous; the majority of the U.S. teen market uses a computer, goes online, participates in video gaming, and uses a digital camera. Besides providing diversions, new technologies have given us a new notion of what entertainment can be. For one thing, it's there on demand, with the possibility of quality entertainment where, when, and how we want it. And it's made all kinds of interests and hobbies more accessible to more people.

A notable example is how technology has made music such an integral part of our world. It has been absorbed into our daily lives: When we don't have the stereo or car radio on, we listen on our personal MP3 players, through our computers, on our satellite TV stations. This is especially true for teens. And today's technology even makes it easier to record your own music and then share it with friends or strangers. For example, Apple's Garage Band software is a key component of its iLife suite.

Greater access to the Internet, coupled with their ability to adapt new technologies, make tweens the trend leaders as DIY musicians.

Photography has also become ubiquitous: Where taking pictures used to be viewed as a way to record special moments, it's now a running commentary, part of the wallpaper of our lives. The miniaturization of digital devices allows for a maximization of consumption—the digital camera has virtually become a pocket photo album. And its ease of use has made photography a hobby for the masses. With free online services like Flickr and Fotopages, photoblogging lets all would-be artists show their work to the world.

For better or worse, technology has brought gambling to the masses. Where once gambling entailed an outing, sometimes a long trek, millions of Americans now engage in Vegas-style betting via the Internet—to the tune of about $10 billion a year, according to a *60 Minutes* report.[3] On the show, Nigel Payne, who runs an online gambling concern called Sportingbet, estimated that upward of 12.5 million Americans use the Internet to participate in some form of gambling. (Although Internet gambling is illegal in the United States, offshore gaming companies get about 80 percent of their traffic from the United States.[4])

"PartyPoker.com, a leading Web site, is host for about 32 hands of poker play per second, according to a British securities filing by its parent company, PartyGaming. In 2005, that amounted to about $1,454 wagered per second, or $45 billion for the year—and PartyPoker is just one among some 2,400 online poker sites."
—*The New York Times*[5]

One downside of technology as entertainment is that its mesmerizing appeal can be hugely addictive. Health-care specialists estimate that 6–10 percent of the approximately 189 million Internet users in the United States have a dependency that can be as destructive as alcoholism and drug addiction, and a growing niche in addiction recovery caters to onlineaholics.[6]

Online video viewing is now common among Internet users. Almost half (46 percent) watch videos at least once a month, while 24 percent watch it online at least once a week, according to a 2006 study by the Online Publishers Association. The most popular videos are news and humor.[7]

Next: Entertainment Platforms Proliferate

As consumers get used to having entertainment available on demand, they're also expecting greater mobility. Portable products are catering to people on the move, whether they're on two feet (personal video players), driving (car television screens), or flying. Airplanes are now seen as places to gorge on guilt-free entertainment for a couple of hours, with games, podcasts, audio books, and satellite TV now multiplying the choices for in-flight entertainment. There's an ADD syndrome permeating our entertainment culture: We have a need to be entertained whenever we're not working.

This portable media landscape has become second nature to kids and has increased their performance expectations for handheld devices. Following the lead of the consumer electronics industry, the toy industry has been introducing a variety of portable products geared to kids on the move. Hasbro's VideoNow XP and VideoNow, Jr., for example, are durable personal video systems that play specially designed discs. Tweens are especially savvy multitaskers when it comes to media choices, and for them one portable platform is often not enough.

Movies are now available on an instant-gratification basis via Movielink and CinemaNow, two new services that offer films for download as soon as they're available on DVD. Both services let people "rent" (keep the download for 24 hours) or buy. Each service is partnered with a limited number of studios, however, and watching on a TV rather than a computer is complicated.

Major television networks are jumping on the bandwagon, offering downloads of everything from previews to full episodes.

Consumers in general are becoming less dependent on—and less loyal to—any single media type. That's largely because with so many options available for entertainment, people are getting what they need when they need it from whatever media source is most suitable at the moment. They are becoming brand and media "sluts."

The question is whether we will continue to use multiple devices—phones, wireless Internet, e-mail, music players, GPS navigation, game players, etc.—or demand more devices that combine all these technologies. Already more content providers, including ESPN and Disney, are using 3G (Third Generation) wireless technology to deliver content directly to customers' mobile phones. With Sony's PSP and Nintendo's DS handheld players, video game devices can now be used as MP3 players, too, blurring the lines between listening and playing.

In the works: HP is developing DJammer, an MP3 player that allows users not only to manipulate music like a DJ but also to interact with others in virtual jam sessions by sharing multiple music streams. In January 2006, Cingular introduced the first Windows Mobile 5.0-enabled "smartphone" in the United States, a mobile that lets users download content on the fly. (The Treo, classified as a PDA, has the same capabilities.) This vision of future connectivity, along with other technological advances, may leave current industry leaders such as Blackberry far behind.

> "The idea that you'll only watch television by plunking yourself in front of a 60-inch plasma screen is growing quaint. Home networks will put TV on your desktop; a proliferation of wireless technologies, from 3G to WiMax, will let you take it anywhere. And in a few years, when the cable companies finally dump their bandwidth-hogging analog channels and go all-digital, they'll be able to offer broadband at speeds that will put TV-quality video on the Net."
>
> —Wired[8]

People are likely to choose whatever systems are most adaptable: We want to access music and cultural inputs at our leisure, and we want to choose what format to receive that information in. We also want products that are truly of our time. The technology must be totally cutting edge for consumers to respond to it. Consumers have become inured to the rapid speed of change and hardly enjoy the "wow" of the present before demanding "What's next?"

What's Next? Media Grazing

A little bit of this, a little bit of that. Think of tomorrow's media consumption as a meal at a tapas bar: a dozen small servings of magazines, TV, and Internet sources, a jug of sangria, and some play-by-play dialogue with companions.

What's Next? Expanding Music Universe

The proliferation of digital music, as well as MP3 players, is diversifying the music market. iTunes carries 2 million songs and counting, compared with just 40,000 in an average bricks-and-mortar music store. Person-to-person networks such as Kazaa take music to even greater extremes, with as many as 20 million songs available for download. Meanwhile, the number of music stores has plummeted in the United States, due both to the MP3 revolution and the dominance of Wal-Mart, which sells 15–20 percent of all CDs in the United States.

Next: The Engaged User

For daily entertainment, consumers are now strongly responding to those brands that encourage creativity and participation and give them the freedom of inter-communication. As we become editors of incoming information, we're increasingly independent: We no longer live preprogrammed lives with predetermined playlists or editorial opinions. The world is now our remote control. We want to engage, interact, and manipulate it to create our own media environment.

Podcasts are a prime example of this independence. Unlike radio programs, which are listened to as they are broadcast, podcasts are consumed at the listener's convenience; they let us not only determine what's on the schedule but also make up the schedule. It can be done with minimal effort via iTunes, which automatically delivers various podcasts to customers who subscribe to them.

Blogs usually let readers comment on content and interact with the source (and with each other). Users can add or edit content on Wikipedia, the collaborative online encyclopedia, with no need to know anything about HTML. Google Maps has spurred all kinds of user-participant sites. There's even a partially viewer-created cable channel, Current TV: People can submit short videos (or "pods") to the Web site, then user votes determine which get on the air.

GarbageScout.com is a collaborative Google Maps-inspired site for people in search of recycled street treasures in New York, San Francisco, and Philadelphia. Urbanites can send camera-phone pictures of their finds along with location information, and the site automatically generates a map marker for each.

The DIY ethos of online entertainment is being incorporated into our lifestyles, by Western tweens especially. Next, an open-source revolution could reinvent the entertainment industry. Many video game companies, for example, are now encouraging users to post game modifications on their Web sites, and players can also download software patches that modify games to their liking. The interactive nature of the technology only seems to make such games more attractive. "Alterations to id Software's *Doom* resulted in modified versions, or 'mods,' whose popularity extended the life of *Doom* years past the point when the game's excitement would have ordinarily dwindled," notes *The Hollywood Reporter*.[9]

"Modding" refers to "the act of modifying hardware or software to perform a function not intended by someone with legal rights concerning that modification," according to Wikipedia. At the eighth annual Independent Games Festival Awards in 2006, the organization honored modders for the first time, handing out $10,000 in prizes for the best amateur modifications of existing video games.

What's Next? Everyone Is Mouthing Off

People used to air their views face-to-face in bars or across backyard walls. Only an elite few and media owners themselves had access to a broader audience. Today, everyone has the ability to sound off to millions via call-in radio, newsgroups, and blogs.

Next: Sharing as Entertainment

Customized entertainment options may be creating a more individualized market, but the next stage of the self-expression revolution is focused on that which can be shared. Online creative expression, found in blogs, video-sharing sites, photo galleries, and DIY music, is a form of individual entertainment, but the experience is complete only when it's shared with friends and peers. Sharing the details of one's personal life has become a major source of entertainment via reality TV. Social networking sites like MySpace, Friendster, and Facebook make the experience digital. WiFi allows users to network and converge all within their own personal space, without having to leave the couch or backyard.

> "Forget the mall. Forget the movies. Forget school. Forget even AOL. If you're a teen in America today, the place to be is the social networking site MySpace," says *USA Today*.[10] Launched in January 2004, the site had upward of 70 million members just two years later, in April 2006.[11]

Music is shared in all kinds of ways. iTunes allows users to post personal playlists called iMixes. Creating custom CD mixes for friends or lovers, along with personalized artwork, is on the rise; sharing music can be an intimate gesture, almost like giving someone a view into your soul. iPod playlists are now being used as a tool to size up the compatibility of potential mates, and sharing playlists and musical libraries is a new form of flirting.

The sharing phenomenon is getting much bigger with online-video sites like YouTube that allow anyone with a video camera to upload their short films, which range from the sublime to the (way beyond) ridiculous. In April 2006, the *Los Angeles Times* noted that "in the four months since it launched, YouTube has become a full-blown Internet tsunami."[12] Indeed, the site wasn't up when we started writing this book, but now, says the *Times*, "it streams about 35 million videos a day and attracts an audience of more than 9 million people a month, according to Web measurement firm Nielsen/NetRatings."

In the video gaming world, the United States is experiencing a substantial shift away from single-player gaming to massively multiplayer online games, long considered mainstream entertainment in Taiwan and South Korea. The shared consumption of video games will steadily increase.

With gamers convening by linked-up machines and Internet users conversing via discussion forums and over instant messenger, there has been a substantial shift away from in-person contact toward anti-social socializing. Instant messaging is a hub of the online experience for teens and has become one of our most popular forms of communication, allowing instant communication with friends abroad or around the corner.

What's Next? Peer Production of Creative Materials

"The age of personal or participatory media" is upon us, declares *The Economist*, and some experts say it could bring about an explosion in creativity.[13] "We are entering an age of cultural richness and abundant choice that we've never seen before in history. Peer production is the most powerful industrial force of our time," Chris Anderson, editor of *Wired*, tells the magazine. The theory is, as connections get faster, users will start to contribute to the Internet as much as they take from it. Of course, many contributors will be deficient in actual talent, but new-media consultant Jerry Michalski insists that, "There's tons of great stuff from rank amateurs."[14] Talented or not, we all have something to say, and more of us will be tempted to tell it to the world. Sabeer Bhatia, who started Hotmail, has now launched BlogEverywhere.com, which lets people attach a blog to any Web page with one click. His prediction? "Just as everybody has an e-mail account today, everybody will have a blog in five years."[15]

Next: The Dominance of Gaming

Video games, rather than movies, are the cultural reference point for today's youth. (Notice how TV commercials and billboards for video games are beginning to appear as often as movie ads.) The majority of today's Western teens, even those living in low-income households, have access to a computer, and gaming is now an integral part of the fabric of young people's lives. According to a 2005 report by the Henry J. Kaiser Family Foundation, more than 80 percent of young people have a video game console at home, and more than half actually have two or more.[16]

Video games alone log about $10.5 billion in annual sales,[17] and market research firm DFC Intelligence estimates the total gaming/interactive market at $28.5 billion—and reaching $42 billion by 2010.[18]

Music placement in video games is seen as a vital avenue for breaking new artists, taking on a role as important as radio or MTV. Playing up this connection, *Video*

Game Awards Hits Volume 1: Best of Video Game Music, from Spike TV and Artemis Records, is a collection of tracks from some of the most popular games.

Gaming isn't just for kids, though. And some numbers suggest kids spend less time gaming than adults: The Consumer Electronics Association (CEA) says that while a third of adult gamers spend ten hours or more a week with console or PC games, just 11 percent of teens do so.[19] According to an Entertainment Software Association-sponsored survey, more than a third of American parents say they play computer and video games; of those, 80 percent say they play along with their kids, and two-thirds believe this has brought their families closer.[20] American men spend more money on video games then they do on music.[21]

Women of all ages are now making gaming a mass cultural phenomenon. Results of a 2006 survey by the CEA "suggest female gamers outnumber male gamers in the 25–34 age category."[22] Women spend hours chatting online while playing online games: It's an easy way to destress. ClubPogo.com, which focuses on diversions like card games and word games, says that more than three-quarters of its members are women. Meanwhile, the Meredith Corporation has launched a game channel on its three most popular Web sites, *Ladies' Home Journal* (LHJ.com), *Better Homes & Gardens* (BHG.com), and *American Baby* (AmericanBaby.com).

In the case of the competitive multiplayer environments that link gamers around the world, the lure is total immersion and interactivity—in other words, their lack of passivity. A multiplayer game on XBox Live provides participants with all the aspects of a game community: the dynamic qualities and intensity of real game play, complete with trash-talking, with no need for actual proximity.

Gaming can be seen as an extension of traditional storytelling; players learn, socialize, escape, and become part of a broader community while being entertained. Games like *The Sims,* an incredibly popular simulation game, let users create and control the lives of virtual people as they literally design a world. They give younger users power they don't have in the real world and an understanding of how economic and social forces operate.

Connectivity is becoming key to the gaming experience, and newer systems have networking capabilities—the Nintendo DS system allows connection with a local wireless network of up to 16 players. PSP, PlayStation Portable, is *the* next big device on the market, offering wireless connectivity, a wide-screen LCD monitor, and the ability to play games, music, and movies wherever the user desires.

Integrating physical action adds another dimension to the gaming experience, breaking down the traditionally static nature of video games. "Exergaming" was brought to mass attention at the 2005 Consumer Electronics Show with a pavilion showcasing video game technology that doubled as sports and exercise equipment. Probably the most well-known example is the extremely popular *Dance Dance Revolution* machine, which requires agile players to hit four large buttons with their feet in time with the beat, matching arrows displayed on the screen.

As part of a three-year deal between the West Virginia and Konami Digital Entertainment, 765 public schools will add *Dance Dance Revolution* to their physical education or health-related curricula.[23]

There's also sports-themed gaming for a virtual outdoors experience. At Urban Golf in London, six state-of-the-art simulators allow players to experience 50-plus courses worldwide using a real club and ball.

Next: Entertainment Choices Create Unique Identities

Technology has become an invaluable tool in allowing people to express their individuality. For Western tweens especially, technology is a key aspect of their creative expression, as much a part of their identity as their choice in clothes. For many people, you are what's on your playlist.

While we may be somewhat uniform in the way we choose to wind down— watching football, shopping, viewing DVDs, gaming, and so on—those with fringe interests can now find commonality and friendships online with others who share those same passions. Subcultures formed around niche interests are on the rise. For example, people have become obsessed with sneakers as a source of entertainment: the thrill of the hunt for rare models, sharing the latest product news with fellow online-community members. Many people today identify with multiple subcultures, and a high percentage of youth have several e-mail and instant messaging handles to reflect specific interests.

With the rise of this "pick and mix" form of entertainment comes a feeling of greater control over one's identity. People can't be pigeonholed by their enter- tainment choices when those choices are so eclectic. A day in the life of a Generation X woman could include watching a French art house flick, listening to a Britney Spears CD, downloading a Brazilian documentary radio podcast, picking up a fanzine from her local club, submitting some Flash animations to Flashplayer.com, reading some of Dan Brown's *The Da Vinci Code*, attending a poetry slam, and spending hours on a Cymbidium orchid-growing community site. She's beyond being defined by any one or even two of these interests—she's not just an "orchid enthusiast" or a "poetry fan" or a "pop-music lover."

Conversely, when it comes to sports, more people want to define themselves by their affinity and are happy to proclaim, "I am a hiker," "I am a cyclist," "I am a surfer." A sense of pride and identity is attached to the sport; being a participant is a way of being. This intense identification spurs the growth of a sports lifestyle. Formula 1 racing is as much about the lifestyle—international travel, glamour, and women—as the cars. NASCAR similarly constitutes a whole lifestyle, albeit a different one.

> With sports more closely tied to lifestyle, sportswear is increasingly driving fashion. A slew of prominent designers have been collaborating with athletic brands, notably Marc Jacobs with Vans, Alexander McQueen with Puma, Yohji Yamamoto with Adidas, and Stella McCartney with Adidas. Athletic apparel has become as much about style as comfort.

Next: Television's Changing Role

We see mainstream television becoming ever less relevant in light of our myriad entertainment choices: The content is too broad for people who know exactly what they want, however obscure it may be, and just where to find it.

Very few TV shows today have the same following they did in decades past. Obsessing as one nation over plot points such as "Who shot J.R.?" was the hallmark of an era when there were only three national broadcast stations and no Internet to lure us away from the set altogether. The degree to which mass-consumed, socially binding programs exert their influence over viewers will inevitably weaken further. A series may lose its spark when it's no longer a given that most viewers saw the previous episode. Already Web sites are being seen as potent media anchors the way television shows once were. And a strong Web base can make it easier to move into other related media such as magazines, comic books, and licensed products.

When we watch TV, our habits are changing with the influence of TiVo and other digital video recorders. Consulting firm The Carmel Group projects that nearly half of all U.S. households with a television will have a DVR by 2010, reports *The Rocky Mountain News*.[24] So while TV is still a passive activity, more of us are controlling our own programming schedules.

> The landmark "Who Shot J.R.?" *Dallas* episode aired in 1980, just as cable TV was coming into its own. That's the year CNN introduced the concept of a 24-hour news network; ESPN and Nickelodeon had launched a year before, and MTV would make its debut the following year.

Next: "Zoning Out" and "Me Time"
as Entertainment

With leisure time becoming so precious, zoning out has become a desired form of entertainment all its own. Much of today's youth participate in "binge chilling," or going back and forth from doing a lot at once to doing absolutely nothing. Entertainment now has as much to do with being switched off as it has with being switched on.

Women, especially those in their 20s and 30s, consider their "me time" quite sacred, whether that entails exploring a new city, hanging out in a café, or getting inspired at a gallery. The café culture, where customers can just sit and "be" without being bothered, has become a central part of the entertainment jigsaw in big cities, whether at small coffee shops or big chains like Borders and Barnes & Noble. One can usually sit uninterrupted for any length of time and enjoy personal time.

At the same time, we're setting aside less time for socializing, instead trying to fit it in and around other commitments. Where Sunday afternoons were traditionally seen as social time to spend with family and friends, many of us now catch up on our e-mail or work responsibilities instead. We make our social time divisible, which is why to many it doesn't seem as rich and enjoyable as it once was.

Next: New Sports Spring Up

Just as today's consumers are offered a bigger-than-ever smorgasbord of entertainment choices, sporting types can now challenge themselves with all kinds of newfangled activities, some never even heard of five years ago.

> The eXtreme Hotel, an 18-room hotel in the Dominican Republic catering to kiteboarders, surfers, skateboarders, and wakeboarders, is the first in a planned line of hotels for action-sports enthusiasts. Each outpost will serve specific pursuits.

Zorbing involves a person strapping himself into an inflatable sphere and getting hurtled down an incline at high speeds. Black-water rafting is much like whitewater rafting but takes place in underground streams in the dark. In the counterintuitive sport of river surfing, riders position their boards upstream, in a rapid, and coast; it's a small niche, but there's a river-specific surfboard available as well as an instructional DVD. Other niche sports cropping up include: kite surfing; the urban obstacle-course sport of parkour; roller derby, which is experiencing a resurgence; jamskating, a combination of roller skating and break-dancing; and beach tennis, a form of tennis played over a volleyball net.

Crossing outdoor sports with performance art and touches of a *Saturday Night Live* skit, extreme ironing involves taking an ironing board to a remote locale—a mountain slope, a treetop, even underwater—and ironing a few items of clothing. As the Extreme Ironing Bureau's Web site puts it, the activity "combines the thrills of an extreme outdoor activity with the satisfaction of a well-pressed shirt."

Next: Sports, Health, and Well-being

A growing proportion of our entertainment time is now devoted to health-related activities. As baby boomers age, they are increasingly preoccupied with health concerns, a trend that dovetails with a broad-based prioritization of wellness and a growing interest in alternative and non-Western belief systems. The goal of physical activity is moving from simple recreation to physical and mental rejuvenation—sports are becoming a means to self-discipline and to a healthier way of living.

> Between 1987 and 2004, the number of frequent health club attendees ("core" members) in the United States jumped by 228 percent to 17.4 million people, according to the International Health, Racquet & Sportsclub Association. Average attendance rose from 72 to 91 days per year.[25]

Some people seek spirituality through physical activity: Taking care of the body honors your inner self, and challenging yourself physically can be seen as spiritual exploration. As yoga becomes more pervasive, its practitioners are seeing this connection explored via Buddhism.

Managing stress has also become a core goal of physical activity. We have seen an increase in contemplative sports like tai chi as well as mental-fitness games like fencing. People are also leaning toward traditional intergenerational games such as bowling that allow for stress-free family time. Capoeira, a Brazilian sport that transcends the boundaries of dance, music, and martial arts, is becoming more popular—the philosophy is that your opponent is not your enemy but your friend, and the purpose is not to emerge victorious but just to keep the action going.

We're still getting much of our exercise at gyms, and gym culture has been growing steadily in sprawling urban locales, though less so in rural areas. We see them as private retreats or ashrams, places to relax our bodies, minds, and souls. Now the gym is becoming a third space, not just somewhere to exercise but a place to be yourself away from home and work pressures, in the vein of a Starbucks or a bookstore. There is a gym in London actually called the Third

Space, capitalizing on this concept. Gyms are expanding to offer more services, from dry cleaning to fully integrated medical centers, and some are trying to market themselves as social destinations, with DJs on certain nights.

And Therefore Next

Perhaps nowhere has the promise of technology paid off more than in the worlds of entertainment and leisure. "Just what I want, just how I want it, anytime I want it" is a pretty powerful offering, and it's come true in this realm. Today, you can get pretty much any content whenever and wherever you are. Now that's progress.

conclusion

then, now, next

What a difference a decade makes. Around ten years ago, when we set out to write the original *Next*, the world was a very different place. The changes are worth a book in itself, but following are a few standouts.

Then

On the political front, we were watching Russia still feeling its newly post-Communist way under the erratic leadership of Boris Yeltsin; Europe was pulling itself together and shaping up to introduce the euro; Britain seemed intent on a fresh start under newly elected young Prime Minister Tony Blair; the United States had just reelected Bill Clinton, who was relatively popular both at home and abroad. Saddam Hussein was ruling Iraq with an iron hand, and CNN conducted an interview with Osama bin Laden.

On the economic front, the United States was moving toward a balanced budget, and the dot-com boom was gathering pace in the West. Pundits were talking about the coming "Asian century," and China was certainly attracting a lot of interest—although 1997 went down as the year of the Asian economic crisis. Crude oil cost less than $25 a barrel.

In the technology world, we had been raving about the Internet to anyone who would listen, but it was a slow-paced novelty that appealed more to consumers than to big companies, and we were having a hard time persuading corporations to take it seriously. Cellular phones were mostly black and heavy with monochrome screens, VHS cassettes ruled the video market, virtually all cameras used film, and Apple Corporation looked to be on its last legs.

Now

Politically, the world is on high alert for the sort of suicide attacks that followed the big ones of 9/11—which happened just a few blocks away from where we worked at the time, and from where Marian lived. The United States has ousted the Taliban's regime in Afghanistan and invaded Iraq. The alleged threat of Saddam Hussein has been removed, but the occupying allies are now barely containing a bloody civil war. Meanwhile, in neighboring Iran, the fundamentalist Islamic government is shaping up to create the sort of nuclear capability that Iraq was purported to have. President Bush is unpopular at home and reviled abroad, Prime Minister Tony Blair is preparing to bow out, Europe is fumbling vital reforms, and Osama bin Laden now makes high-profile media appearances on Al-Jazeera as he continues to elude capture.

On the economic front, the United States has a huge and growing budget deficit, the world has bounced back from the dot-com bust of the early 2000s and is heading toward dot-com boom 2.0, manufacturing has moved en masse to China, and India has become the remote back office and IT center for major Western corporations. A very troubled General Motors is about to be toppled by Toyota as the world's No. 1 carmaker, and the Internet is dominated by Google, a phrase on no one's lips in 1997. Crude oil can cost as much as $70 a barrel.

As for technology, cellular phones have become small, powerful fashion accessories, media centers capable of not only playing video and music but also taking photos and video; VHS tapes have been replaced by DVDs; and film cameras are all but relics, too. Apple is thriving, with no small thanks to its move into music. (And, as it turns out, with a great sigh of relief from the music business, for 1 billion downloads, acquired legally and fairly paid for.) And as for the Internet, we most certainly aren't going around telling anybody that we told them so—honestly, that's not our style. What's certain is that the Internet is now very fast and getting faster, that plenty of corporations are making big money from it, and that free Internet telephony is now threatening the revenues of the traditional telcoms (even those of the wireless carriers—cell phones equipped with the Windows operating system can also use Skype to call out).

So?

It's tempting to think that the changes we've all lived through over the last decade are unprecedented in their scope and scale—tempting but, perhaps, arrogant. It's a half-blind trend watcher who thinks only of the future without observing patterns of the past. So it's worth applying that ten-year time bracket to previous decades.

Take 1936–46, when the industrialized world went from economic depression through a world war and on to post-war reconstruction. Military technology raced from bombs and biplanes to supersonic jets, ballistic missiles, atomic bombs, and radar. Tens of millions of people lost their lives, millions more were displaced, and the world was split into two hostile camps.

Nevertheless, we believe change is now amplified and accelerated at a rate that bewilders very many people, and not just those over 40. That's because most of the world is now connected in real time through a global and increasingly powerful network.

A product launched in one place can be reverse-engineered, copied, and produced on the other side of the world in a matter of weeks. This hard fact sits at the heart of U.S.-Chinese economic relationships, with the United States complaining that pirated and copied technology is a disincentive to innovation. Huh? If they can build them faster and cheaper, and sell them, they win—look at Lenovo.

Ideas build on ideas—they spread very fast through the Internet, they're quickly picked up by the mainstream media and spread further, which then triggers new ideas. Change builds on change, which both speeds up the pace of change and makes the direction of change very unpredictable.

So we propose to use our last few pages to pause and highlight a few of the things that are top of mind right now.

Trend Spotting

THEN: Trend spotting was the cutting edge.
NOW: Trend spotting is decidedly mainstream, part of business as usual.
NEXT: Businesses' expertise and "creativity" is determined, at least in part, by their trend-spotting talent.

Pretty early on we were dubbed "trend spotters"—which was a compliment or a putdown, depending on who was saying it and when. Regardless, it's a fair cop. Our working lives have been spent observing business and societies from the bird's-eye view, the worm's-eye view, and all points in between. Our inclination has been to see the patterns of behavior and meaning that emerge over time, and our purpose has been to think through how those patterns—or trends—will play out into the future.

In our view, that's the essence of trend spotting, and we are happy to carry on wearing the mantle of trend spotters, especially since we were ahead of that curve. It's not without irony that we point out that trend spotting itself has become a trend, to the extent that it's more or less mainstream now in advertising agencies, in marketing and retail organizations, and even in pop culture (we've noticed a half-dozen novels based on the life and work of trend spotters—also known as cool hunters).

Our interest in trends is by no means purely academic; it's an integral part of our work and the value that we as advertising practitioners bring to our clients. Why do advertising people care about trends? Ira always explains that on a simplistic level, the success of an ad campaign is predicated on whether its message is on trend. Putting it more broadly, for any entrepreneurial activity to succeed, it has to tap into the sustained currents of thinking, feeling, and behaving. This is particularly important in our business, because the currents are running fast and wild in today's media environment.

The print media are searching for a revenue formula that works as the Internet increasingly becomes the default source for text information. In fact, the Web is making an equally significant impact on video media now that Apple's iTunes, the world's seventh-largest music retailer, is offering $1.99-a-pop network show downloads. But the three major U.S. TV networks are still very much here, and a fourth one, Rupert Murdoch's Fox, celebrated its 20th anniversary in 2005. The '06 season finale of its breakout hit *American Idol* will command $1.3 million per commercial occasion—Super Bowl-like numbers.

We make no apology for looking at today's trends in terms of their marketing implications. Not only is it what our clients trust us to do, but it's part of the broader evolution of business, which is what shapes so many of our lives.

Bewilderment

THEN: Great enthusiasm for fluid modern times and new freedoms
NOW: Upheaval and uncertainty—with fundamentalisms on the rise
NEXT: Control or chaos?

Changes are coming so fast, over such a broad front, that people are feeling bewildered. Age-old certainties have crumbled, replaced by uncertainties. The basic markers of life no longer feel so concrete, and what used to be bedrock knowledge has come into question: What's a normal family? Where do babies come from? How old is old? What's a job? What constitutes rude behavior? How much is enough? Whom can I trust?

Indeed, we no longer hold solid, widely agreed-upon responses to any of these questions. No wonder people are confused, stressed, and searching for something to believe in—something consistent, something immutable. All the change and instability stir up anxiety—not to mention the headlines filled with news of terror strikes, supersized natural disasters, and looming epidemics. We're sticking to, turning to, or returning to organized religion for a sense of certainty. And we're channeling our energies (and anxieties) into consumption—shopping may or may not be the new opiate of the masses, but it's certainly one of the world's most popular participation sports.

The sense of bewilderment not only stems from all the technological advances and upheavals in the economy—it's also stirred by shifts in people's sense of identity and what they feel is their place in the world. In the United States, Hispanics have replaced blacks as the largest minority population. Both their distinctiveness (see Little Havana in Miami) and their cultural absorption (remember, "Mexican sauces"—salsa, picante sauce, and taco sauce—hold a larger market share than ketchup) have a great influence on this country.

When we're not sure how to answer, "What's the best condiment for my burger?" we know the world has truly changed. Good thing we still have ask.com (the newly restaged Ask Jeeves).

Boundaries

THEN: New technology-mediated horizons; computers open up the world.
NOW: Technology allows us to erect barriers and manage access on our terms, or not at all.
NEXT: Artificial intelligence, where us humans are less necessary, and on the other end of the spectrum, IT-free spaces that let us reconnect with our humanity.

In some respects our worlds have widened enormously. With interactive technology we can connect with people near and far. Through the Internet and multi-channel TV we can see far-off sites and microscopic marvels that our forebears could hardly imagine. Thanks to cheap flights and more routes, foreign cultures are more accessible than ever.

Yet in other respects our worlds are closing in. We seek out communities of like-minded people and avoid contact with those who feel too uncomfortably different. We want safe spaces and seek them even when we travel. Increasingly our interactions with the wider world happen through screens, mediated by technology.

Boundaries used to be purely physical and—before mass travel—pretty easy to control. Now they are much more permeable and harder to monitor. There are foreigners in your neighborhood, in the street, wherever you are. We routinely entertain extortionists, gangsters, serial killers, and mass murderers in our homes every day—or rather, they entertain us onscreen. On the Internet, we interact with people who may or may not be who they say they are. (As we wrote in the original *Next*, "Computers are no longer about technology. They're about something far more important: community and communicating"—for better or for worse.)

We live physically with clear boundaries and a usually manageable level of security. Mentally and emotionally, we live at least part of our lives in a media space that is full of excitement and danger and risk and enemies.

Our enemies, both real and imaginary, are brought into our homes and magnified by the media we choose to consume. They are pornographers and drug dealers intent on corrupting our children, they are wild-eyed fanatics prepared to blow themselves up in our midst, they are scheming scroungers or manual workers who want to take our benefits and jobs. Whichever we focus on, the urge is to circle the wagons to protect our lifestyles. Watch the immigration controversies in the United States and in Europe—this is a social flashpoint, and we don't see it abating for years to come.

This need to control personal space (no doubt one of the long-term, latent effects of 9/11 and the New Normal) is changing significant elements of our social fabric, with salutary or negative implications for commerce. If you're in the business of homes, including décor and hardware to outfit the home (or connectivity for the home office), you are in the money. Building public spaces for entertainment is less promising. Of course, if you're Hollywood, you might just try for better, more original content that creates a real reason to leave home visit the big screen.

Brands

THEN: Brands were labels for excellent products.
NOW: Everything is branded—unless it's unbranded to save money (and therefore a commodity).
NEXT: Brand sluts take control back from brands.

Brands and commerce have completely blurred into the rest of life, but what we have now is just a foretaste of what's to come. As consumers get more control of their media consumption and increasingly avoid advertising, brands are searching for other ways of showing up on the radar.

We can imagine a world where Harvard University merges with MTV, where Pfizer acquires the Mayo Clinic, where the Dutch royal family purchases South

Africa to accelerate that country's rise into the developed world, where Microsoft and eBay form a joint venture that results in the world's largest cybermall and where their role as "un-realtor" makes them the largest landlords in the world.

If these combinations look unlikely, that's the point. Our world is being shaped by the unlikely, the improbable, and the unexpected. It's only with hindsight that we realize how logical it all was. Virgin Records spawning Virgin Atlantic Airline? For sure. Apple Computer becoming a major music retailer? Of course. Wire and Plastic Products morphing into one of the world's top three marketing communications groups? It did (aka WPP). IBM selling its computer division to Chinese company Lenovo? That's right.

These are the kinds of transitions that set the conventional wisdom on its ear—but then, all the details of life as we know it are being upended. Through all the frenzy of weird mutations and evolutions, we (and corporations) have come to rely on brands as reliable markers. But brands have become very mutable as corporations merge, or demerge, or rebrand themselves. And while brand portfolio owners have tried to simplify their lineups, more brands and sub-brands pour into the market every week.

It's overwhelming for those who carefully seek out the right brand and stick with it. But it's turning into heaven for consumers with a low emotional investment who flit from brand to brand (and from bargain to better bargain).

New World Geography

THEN: The United States of Europe
NOW: Irrational exuberance over the possibilities of Chindia
NEXT: The angst of environmental ruination caused by the Chindia explosion

The "United States of Europe" captured our attention in the original *Next*. And now, at the time of writing, economists and pundits are all fired up about the BRIC countries, Brazil, Russia, India, and China: four physically vast nations with huge populations that are forecast to one day dominate the world. Russia and Brazil are still more in the area of promising than performing, but China and India ("Chindia") are hitting their stride.

We suspect we'll be feeling the Chindia impact deeply and for a long time to come. Not so long ago all the talk was about the economic opportunities of selling huge amounts of American goods to the hundreds of millions of Chinese. As it turns out, it's happening the other way round: The hundreds of millions of Chinese are selling goods to us and the rest of the world, and America is building up a huge trade deficit. For its part, India is serving as a combination back office/high-tech center with costs that Americans can't match nor resist.

This is just the beginning. Remember the discussion Thomas Friedman writes of in *The World Is Flat:* "When I was growing up, my parents told me, 'Finish your dinner. People in China and India are starving.' I tell my daughters, 'Finish your homework. People in India and China are starving for your job.' "[1]

The influx of Indians and Chinese into the world economy ultimately benefits consumers all over the world. But look a little further ahead: With 2 billion people new consumers, the impact will be substantial, to say the least. Today, we're looking at oil costing as much as $70 a barrel. Today, an open China and the newly minted tech middle class in India are just discovering the joys of automobile ownership. By 2031, if cars are as ubiquitous in China as they are in the United States (where we have three cars for every four people), the country would be home to 1.1 billion cars—compare that with the current world total of 795 million.[2] Even if hybrid technology advances a little faster, all those extra motorists will generate an enormous demand for oil and put even more strain on the environment—not that the United States is in any position to lecture other countries about oil consumption or environmental impact.

The 2008 Olympics will put China firmly in the spotlight. For a few weeks at least we'll all have a chance to check out what happens when this secretive superpower-in-waiting opens its doors to the world.

Who's in Charge?

THEN: The closing years of the American Century
NOW: Toughing it out in Iraq and piling up the debts at home
NEXT: America trying to hang on to its waning popularity and power

There's nothing new in "Go home, Yanks," but it's been quite a while since so many people felt such animosity toward the United States. As we watch a Bush administration in freefall, in terms of its approval at home and especially in the rest of the world, we are struck by the degree to which the administration seems to be incapable of, or unwilling to, engage in real productive dialogue with the rest of the world. Maybe it's the logical outgrowth of the arrogant jingoism that has characterized America's worldview for as long as we can remember—certainly since the end of the Cold War, when the absence of an enemy left us oddly bereft of a direction to our world leadership.

After more than a decade as the unchallenged superpower with a wide margin of military superiority, it looks as if the United States has found that its might is not unlimited. Sweeping the Iraqi army and Saddam Hussein out of the way took just a couple of weeks, but handling the occupation of Iraq has proved after three years to be a much tougher challenge—and extremely expensive in money and lives.

Would the U.S. administration, the U.S. electorate, and America's allies so readily embark on such an enterprise again? We don't think so. Everything suggests that the world is no longer the United States's to control by "divine right"/"manifest destiny" or any other preordained hegemony. The new United States of Europe is giving our economy a run for its money, and Chindia looms large as the next big challenge. Americans continue to look for any evidence beyond assertion and chest-beating that we are truly prepared for the challenges of the sheer weight of a newly empowered population whose most natural instincts may not be consistent with Western habits, practices, and preferences. And while millions still want to come to the United States, it's far from clear that the American notion of freedom and democracy is what the rest of the world wants or needs at home.

notes

introduction

1. Virginia Postrel, "Consumer Vertigo," *Reason*, June 2005.
2. "All You Ever Wanted to Know about Relationships—but Were Afraid to Ask," World Economic Forum, session topic. www.weforum.org/site/homepublic.nsf/Content/_S15152.
3. Josh Grossberg, "Bono Sees Red," *E! Online News*, January 26, 2006.
4. Gary Silverman, "Bono Signs Big Names to Fight Aids," *Financial Times*, January 25, 2006.
5. *Time*, December 26, 2005.
6. Marian Salzman and Ira Matathia, "The Impact on Shaken Confidence," *Advertising Age*, September 17, 2001.
7. Lynn Trusse, *Talk to the Hand: The Utter Bloody Rudeness of the World Today, Or, Six Good Reasons to Stay Home and Bolt the Door* (New York: Penguin Group, 2005).
8. From www.headbutler.com/books/optimistic.asp.

I

1. Marian Salzman and Ira Matathia, *Trends Voor de Toekomst* (*Next: Trends for the Near Future*) (Amsterdam: Anthos, 1997).
2. "News Summary," *The New York Times*, February 4, 2006.
3. From www.ready.gov/america/overview.html.
4. From www.pollingreport.com/BushJob.htm.
5. From www.transparency.org/.
6. From www.weforum.org.
7. Alex Johnson, "Bay Area Far From Ready for the Next 'Big One'," msnbc.com, April 17, 2006.
8. Steven N. Ward and Simon Day, "Cumbre Vieja Volcano: Potential Collapse and Tsunami at La Palma, Canary Islands," The American Geophysical Union, June 27, 2001.
9. "High Risk of Alpine Fault Earthquake: Ministry," New Zealand Press Association, September 10, 2002.

10. "World Economic Forum: No Looming Energy Crisis," Environment News Service, January 29, 2006.

11. John Guillebaud, "Population Control: Good Stewardship?" *Triple Helix*, Winter 2000.

12. "Living Planet Report 2002," World Wildlife Fund.

13. From www.cdc.gov/flu/pandemic/qanda.htm.

14. Q. A. Ahmed, Y. M. Arabi, and Z. A. Memish, "Health Risks at the Hajj," *The Lancet*, March 25, 2006.

15. Kevin Friedl, "When on Hajj, Wear a Facemask," *Seed*, April 23, 2006.

16. From nces.ed.gov/pubs2006/homeschool.

17. Michelle Conlin, "Meet My Teachers: Mom and Dad," *Business Week*, February 20, 2006.

18. From nces.ed.gov/pubs2006/homeschool.

19. Ibid.

20. Michelle Conlin, "Meet My Teachers: Mom and Dad."

21. "US National Security Whistleblowers Testify on Retaliation," *Voice of America News*, February 15, 2006.

22. Faith Popcorn, "In 2005, Consumers Will Pursue 'Choice Without Challenge'," Arizona Reporter Newswire, December 2004.

23. From en.wikipedia.org/wiki/Wikipedia:About.

24. Ibid.

25. From www.alexa.com/site/ds/top_sites?ts_mode=global&lang=none.

26. Ken Spencer Brown, "Web 2.0, Wikis, Commercial Open Source All Came of Age," *Investor's Business Daily*, January 3, 2006.

27. John Naughton, "The Networker: Wiki's Wacky, but It Really Does Work," *The Observer* (London), September 12, 2004.

28. Peter Mehlman, "Bullseye: How One Shot Ricocheted Through a Comedy Writer's Week," *The Washington Post*, February 19, 2006.

29. From americandialect.org/index.php/amerdial/categories/C178/.

30. From comedycentral.com/shows/the_daily_show/about_the_show.jhtml.

31. From people-press.org/reports/display.php3?ReportID=200.

32. From mediakit.theonion.com/online_main.html.

33. *Larry King Live*, CNN, January 11, 2006.

34. Claudia H. Deutsch, "G.E. Becomes a General Store for Developing Countries," *The New York Times*, July 16, 2005.

2

1. Richard N. Haass, "This Isn't Called the [Blank] Era for Nothing," *The Washington Post*, January 8, 2006.

2. "Europe's Culture Clash," *The Boston Globe*, July 17, 2005.

3. "The New With the Old," *The Economist*, October 14, 2004.

4. Laura Alfaro, Sebnem Kalemli-Ozcan, and Vadym Volosovych, "Why Doesn't Capital Flow From Rich to Poor Countries? An Empirical Investigation," National Bureau of Economic Research, December 2005.

5. Andrés Oppenheimer, "Latin America's Challenge: Learning How to Compete," *The Miami Herald*, November 13, 2005. Translated excerpt from Oppenheimer, *Cuentos Chinos* (Buenos Ares: Sudamericana, 2005).

6. Ibid.
7. From www.eclac.org.
8. Tim Padgett, "To the Left, March!" *Time*, January 9, 2006.
9. "A Different Latin America," *The New York Times*, December 24, 2005.
10. Basildon Peta, "Zimbabwe under Mugabe," *The Independent* (London), November 26, 2004.
11. "Mbeki Does Deal With Mugabe on Fighter Pilot Training," *All Africa*, December 8, 2005.
12. From www.bbc.co.uk/worldservice/specials/1627_new_africa_ws/index.shtml.
13. From www.unaids.org/epi/2005/doc/docs/PR_EpiUpdate_Nov05_en.pdf.
14. From usinfo.state.gov/af/Archive/2004/Nov/24-527969.html.
15. "Human Resources for Health: Overcoming the Crisis," Joint Learning Initiative, Global Equity Initiative, Harvard University, 2004.
16. Babatunde Osotimehin, "The Other Half," *The New York Times*, August 19, 2005.
17. Sipho Seepe, "Getting Small Things Right First," *All Africa*, October 19, 2005.
18. From www.realizingrights.org.
19. George Wehrfritz, "Free Trade Is Not Enough," *Newsweek* (International Edition), December 26, 2005.
20. From www.weforum.org.
21. "Statistical Profiles of the Least Developed Countries," United Nations Conference on Trade and Development, 2005.
22. "Going, Going, Gone! Climate Change & Global Glacier Decline," World Wildlife Fund.
23. "New Funds Make It Easier to Donate Abroad," *The Wall Street Journal*, July 6, 2004.
24. Sam Perry, "Aspen's Meadows Become a World Stage," *Conferenza Premium Reports*, August 23, 2005. From www.aspeninstitute.org.
25. "Global Transparency: Empowerment and Democracy in the 21st Century," The Brookings Institution, March 15, 2006.
26. Ben MacIntyre, "Mullahs Versus the Bloggers," *The Times* (London), December 23, 2005.
27. "Global Voices: International Bloggers Start Connecting the Dots," Personal Democracy Forum, December 15, 2004.
28. From www.rsf.org/rubrique.php3?id_rubrique=542.
29. From www.sifry.com/alerts/archives/000432.html.
30. The Ecoclub Interview, *International Ecotourism Monthly*, Year 6, Issue 67.
31. Eve Conant, "Having Fun Doing Good," *Newsweek International*, April 11/18, 2005.
32. From www.world-tourism.org/newsroom/Releases/2004/february/jerusalem.htm.
33. Augusto Lopez-Claros and Saadia Zahidi, "Women's Empowerment: Measuring the Global Gender Gap," World Economic Forum, 2005.
34. Ibid.
35. "Views of a Changing World 2003," Pew Global Attitudes Project, June 3, 2003.
36. Lopez-Claros and Zahidi, "Women's Empowerment: Measuring the Global Gender Gap."

3

1. Park Bun-Soon, "The Rise of Chindia: Seize the Opportunity," *The Korea Herald*, November 18, 2005.
2. Marian Salzman and Ira Matathia, *Trends Voor de Toekomst* (*Next: Trends for the Near Future*) (Amsterdam: Anthos, 1997).

3. From www.csfb.com/news/html/2005/12_20_2005.pdf.
4. Pete Engardio, "A New World Economy," *Business Week*, August 22, 2005.
5. Tom Doctoroff, *Billions: Selling to the New Chinese Consumer* (New York: Palgrave Macmillan, 2005).
6. Engardio, "A New World Economy."
7. Ibid.
8. "India Calling: A Resurgent India Is Impacting Global and Regional Strategies," World Economic Forum, November 2005.
9. "Davos Agenda: Asia, Climate, Poor," CNN.com, January 25, 2006.
10. Randeep Ramesh, "Chindia, Where the World's Workshop Meets Its Office," *Guardian* (London), September 30, 2005.
11. "India China Bilateral Trade to Hit $20B by '07 Vs. $15B," Dow Jones International News, March 16, 2006.
12. Engardio, "A New World Economy."
13. Ramesh, "Chindia, Where the World's Workshop Meets Its Office."
14. "India, China at Business Forum's Forefront," Associated Press, January 30, 2006.
15. "Expert Roundtable 6: Chinese and Indian Youth," *Business Week*, August 22, 2005.
16. Tom Nissley, "Where Were You When You Realized the World Is Flat (Or Have You?): Conversation with Thomas L. Friedman," Amazon.com.
17. Gary Gereffi and Vivek Wadhwa, "Framing the Engineering Outsourcing Debate: Placing the United States on a Level Playing Field with China and India," Duke University, Edmund T. Pratt, Jr., School of Engineering, December 2005.
18. Mary Hennock, "China's Global Hunt for Oil," news.bbc.co.uk, March 9, 2005.
19. "China's and India's Rising Demand for Natural Resources," World Economic Forum Annual Meeting 2006, January 27, 2006.
20. Benjamin Morgan, "China's Race for Energy Resources Only Just Heating Up," Agence France Presse, January 10, 2006.
21. "Aiyar Tries to Navigate Great Wall of Energy Cooperation," *Indian Express*, January 11, 2006.
22. Andy Mukherjee, "Speed Wobbles Hit Asian Giants," *The New Zealand Herald*, December 28, 2005.
23. Doctoroff, *Billions*.
24. Engardio, "A New World Economy."
25. Ibid.
26. "The Next Wave," *The Economist*, December 14, 2005.
27. From www.mckinsey.com/mgi/reports/pdfs/emerginggloballabormarket/part2/MGI_supply_fullreport.pdf.
28. "The Next Wave," *The Economist*.
29. Nissley, "Where Were You When You Realized the World Is Flat?"
30. "India and China Dominate Buzz at Davos," Associated Press, January 29, 2006.
31. Marilynn Marter, "Spice Trade Is Booming in Food Markets," *Philadelphia Inquirer*, January 30, 2006.
32. Sandip Roy, "Asian Pop: Bollywood Berkeley Is Not Your Parents' Bharatanatyam," SFGate.com, February 4, 2005.
33. Salzman and Matathia, *Trends Voor de Toekomst*.

34. "America's Most Admired Companies 2006," *Fortune*, March 6, 2006.
35. Salzman and Matathia, *Trends Voor de Toekomst*.

4

1. Marian Salzman and Ira Matathia, *Trends Voor de Toekomst* (*Next: Trends for the Near Future*) (Amsterdam: Anthos, 1997).
2. Thomas Fuller, "Europe Narrows the Job Gap," *International Herald Tribune*, September 29, 2004.
3. Paul Meller, "Europeans Not Entrepreneurial? Yes They Are, eBay's Chief Says," *The New York Times*, February 8, 2006.
4. Ibid.
5. Ibid.
6. "Outsourcing in Eastern Europe: The Rise of Nearshoring," *The Economist*, December 1, 2005.
7. Ibid.
8. Ibid.
9. Matthew Campbell and Tom Pattinson, "Young French Choose Britain for Good Life," *The Sunday Times* (London), August 7, 2005.
10. "Animal Frightfulness: Animal-Rights Extremism," *The Economist*, July 24, 2004.
11. From the-tma.org.
12. "Gross National Product: Obesity in France," *The Economist*, December 20, 2005.
13. "Corruption Perceptions Index 2005," www.transparency.org.
14. Zachary Shore, "Breeding New Bin Ladens: America's New Western Front," *Watch on the West: A Newsletter of Foreign Policy Research Institute's Center for the Study of America and the West*, December 2004.
15. "The Politics of Islam in Europe," *The Economist*, March 4, 2004.
16. Shore, "Breeding New Bin Ladens."
17. Christopher Caldwell, "Politically Correct Intolerance," *Financial Times*, December 9, 2005.
18. "Danish Queen Raps Radical Islam," bbc.co.uk, April 14, 2005.
19. Jason Burke, "Threat to Switch Off City's Red Lights," *The Observer* (London), February 19, 2006.
20. Ibid.
21. David R. Sands, "Europe's 'Baby Bust' Signals Major Change," *The Washington Times*, November 24, 2005.
22. Ibid.
23. "Old Europe: Demographic Change," *The Economist*, October 2, 2004.
24. "Migration in an Interconnected World: New Directions for Action," Global Commission on International Migration, October 2005.

5

1. Marian Salzman and Ira Matathia, *Trends Voor de Toekomst* (*Next: Trends for the Near Future*) (Amsterdam: Anthos, 1997).
2. From people-press.org/reports/display.php3?ReportID=254.
3. Bernard-Henri Levy, *American Vertigo: Traveling America in the Footsteps of Tocqueville* (New York: Random House, 2006).

4. From www.barna.org/FlexPage.aspx?Page=BarnaUpdateNarrow&BarnaUpdateID=232.

5. Frank Newport and Joseph Carroll, "Another Look at Evangelicals in America Today," Gallup Poll News Service, December 2, 2005.

6. Ibid.

7. Ibid.

8. From www.barna.org/FlexPage.aspx?Page=BarnaUpdate&BarnaUpdateID=214.

9. Newport and Joseph Carroll, "Another Look at Evangelicals in America Today."

10. From people-press.org/reports/display.php3?PageID=115.

11. Owen Franken, "What Place for God in Europe?" *Christian Science Monitor*, February 22, 2005.

12. *Larry King Live*, CNN, November 2, 2005.

13. From media.afa.net/newdesign/about.asp.

14. "Onward, Christian shoppers," *The Economist*, December 3, 2005.

15. From www.chickfilapressroom.com/press_kit/CFA%20AM%2005.pdf.

16. From hirr.hartsem.edu/org/megastoday2005summaryreport.pdf.

17. From hirr.hartsem.edu/org/megastoday2005_pressrelease.html.

18. Mike Vogel, "Big Box Worship," *Florida Trend*, December 1, 2005.

19. *Today*, NBC, March 3, 2006.

20. David Usborne, "A Town With Extra God," *The Independent* (London), March 4, 2006.

21. From www.barna.org/FlexPage.aspx?Page=Resource&ResourceID=197.

22. From www.barna.org/FlexPage.aspx?Page=BarnaUpdate&BarnaUpdateID=214.

23. Ibid.

24. *Day to Day*, National Public Radio, July 19, 2004.

25. From www.slate.com/id/2103764/.

26. *Day to Day*, July 19, 2004.

27. Maura Farrelly, "Where Americans Get Their News," Voice of America News, August 8, 2005.

28. Nicholas Lemann, "Fear and Favor: Why Is Everyone Mad at the Mainstream Media?" *The New Yorker*, February 14, 2005.

29. The Pew Internet and American Life Project, "Trends 2005: Internet: The Mainstreaming of Online Life."

30. From www.pewinternet.org/pdfs/Internet_Status_2005.pdf.

31. The Pew Internet and American Life Project, "Trends 2005."

32. From www.moveon.org/about.html.

33. The Pew Internet and American Life Project, "Trends 2005."

34. Alain de Botton, *Status Anxiety* (New York: Pantheon, 2004).

35. Timothy Garton Ash, "To Keep Its Dream Alive, America Must End Its Military Obsession," *Guardian* (London), September 29, 2005.

36. "Handling Debt, Be They Rock Stars or Great-Depression Savers," *US Banker*, February 2006.

37. Charlotte Crane, "Consumers May Be Forced to Simplify, 'Trends Guru' Predicts," *Pensacola News Journal* (Florida), January 15, 2006.

38. From www.oprah.com/money/debtdiet/money_debtdiet_main.jhtml.

39. From www.prcdc.org/summaries/changingnation/changingnation.html.

40. From www.census.gov/Press-Release/www/releases/archives/population/005164.html.

41. Hector Tobar, *Translation Nation* (New York: Riverhead, 2005).

42. Elizabeth DiNovella, "Latin Republic of the USA," *The Progressive*, January 1, 2006.

43. Sonya Tafoya, "Shades of Belonging," Pew Hispanic Center, December 2004.

44. "Bush: U.S. Must Break Oil 'Addiction,' " cbsnews.com, February 1, 2006.

45. "Q&A: The US and Climate Change," news.bbc.co.uk, February 14, 2002.

46. From http://www.rprogress.org/media/releases/020410_ef.html.

47. From www.newdream.org/newsletter/kickoff.php.

48. From www.computerecycleforeduc.com/ewaste.htm.

49. Ibid.

50. Elizabeth Royte, "E-Waste@Large," *The New York Times*, January 27, 2006.

51. Eric Alterman, "Here's a Plan: Hire the Liar," msnbc.com, February 18, 2005.

52. Jonathan Pinkerton, "Our Guy At 'American Idol'," *Sacramento Bee* (California), February 28, 2006.

53. Hua Hsu, "Vote or Lie," *Village Voice* (New York), November 2, 2004.

54. From usgovinfo.about.com/od/thepoliticalsystem/a/whynotvote.htm.

55. Josh Tyrangiel, "An Eye on the White House, and an Eye on You," *Time*, March 20, 2006.

56. Ibid.

57. "*Washington Post* Poll: Saddam Hussein and the Sept. 11 Attacks," *The Washington Post*, September 6, 2003.

58. From www.whitehouse.gov/news/releases/2002/01/20020129-11.html.

59. Larry Kudlow, "Call It What It Is: Islamophobia," *National Review*, February 24, 2006.

60. From www.pollingreport.com/terror.htm.

61. Pew Global Attitudes Project, "American Character Gets Mixed Reviews," June 23, 2005.

62. "US Experts Resign Over Iraq Looting," news.bbc.co.uk, April 18, 2003.

63. BBC Monitoring Quotes From Middle East Arabic Press, November 5, 2005.

64. Pew Global Attitudes Project, "American Character Gets Mixed Reviews."

65. Associated Press, "FEMA to Stop Giving Out Debit Cards," msnbc.com, September 12, 2005.

66. From www.lvcva.com/press/press-releases-2006.jsp?pressId=440.

67. Howard LaFranchi, "A Turn Inward for US, Europe," *Christian Science Monitor*, September 22, 2005.

6

1. Fritz Klein, *The Bisexual Option: A Concept of One-Hundred Percent Intimacy* (New York: Arbor House, 1978).

2. Stephanie Fairyington, "Bisexuality and the Case Against Dualism," *The Gay & Lesbian Review*, August 31, 2005.

3. "More Women Experimenting with Bisexuality," Associated Press, September 19, 2005.

4. From asexuality.org.

5. "Sexless and Proud," www.abcnews.com, March 23, 2006.

6. Andrew Sullivan, "The End of Gay Culture," *The New Republic*, October 24, 2005.

7. From www.theknot.com/ch_article.html?Object=A50222105815&keywordID=163&keyword Type=2&parentID=527&PARTNER=MSN.

8. From www.census.gov/Press-Release/www/releases/archives/business_ownership/006351. html.

9. "U.S. Secretary of Labor Chao Honors Working Women for Contribution to America's Economic Vitality," U.S. Newswire, March 16, 2006.

10. "Prime Minister's Task Force: Women Entrepreneurs Make Their Mark," *The Toronto Sun*, February 8, 2006.

11. Ibid.

12. From www.naa.gov.au/exhibitions/events/mackay.html.

13. "CDC: Women Waiting Longer to Have First Child," Associated Press (CNN.com), December 18, 2003.

14. Kimberly Hayes Taylor, "Single and Satisfied," *The Detroit News*, October 24, 2005.

15. Anita Gates, "The Week Ahead," *The New York Times*, January 29, 2006.

16. Sarah Womack, "Women Are Powering Ahead in the Race for Riches," *The Daily Telegraph* (London), April 22, 2005.

17. Maria T. Bailey, *Marketing to Moms: Getting Your Share of the Trillion-Dollar Market* (New York: Prima Lifestyles, 2002).

18. Randall Patterson, "Empire of the Alpha Mom," *The New York Times*, June 20, 2005.

19. Patterson, "Empire of the Alpha Mom."

20. From www.thefutoncritic.com/cgi/devwatch.cgi?id=alpha_mom.

21. Tatiana Boncompagni, "Spas' New Message: Bring the Baby, Too," *The New York Times*, January 21, 2005.

22. Laura DeMarco, Newhouse News Service, "Generation X Embraces Family Life," *Times-Picayune* (New Orleans), September 12, 2004.

23. Ibid.

24. Diane E. Lewis, "Number of Dads at Home on the Rise," *The Boston Globe*, June 20, 2004.

25. Jewel Topsfield, "Senator Wants Child Custody Changes," *The Age* (Australia), March 28, 2006.

26. Natalie Hanman, "Logging on to Find Love: Singletons in the UK Are Increasingly Overcoming Their Fears About Online Dating," *Guardian* (London), August 18, 2005.

27. Lynn Welch, "Virtual Matchmaking: Online Dating Goes Mainstream," *The Capital Times & Wisconsin State Journal*, July 28, 2005.

28. Hanman, "Logging on to Find Love."

29. Ibid.

30. Ginia Bellafante, "Indian Nuptials: U.S.-Style," *The New York Times*, August 23, 2005.

31. Barbara Dafoe Whitehead and David Popenoe, "The State of Our Unions," The National Marriage Project, Rutgers, 2005.

32. "Marriage Slump," *Western Daily Press* (U.K.), March 11, 2005.

33. Whitehead and Popenoe, "The State of Our Unions."

34. Ibid.

35. "Unmarried Seniors Living Together Are Increasing: They Face Unique Financial Hurdles," *Times-Picayune* (New Orleans), March 14, 2006.

36. Fay Burstin, "When They Were Young, There Weren't That Many STIs Around: Middle-Age Crisis," *Herald Sun* (Australia), March 16, 2006.

37. From www.unmarried.org/aboutus.php.

38. Peter Ford, "In Europe, Unmarried Parents on Rise, *Christian Science Monitor*, April 17, 2006.

39. Ibid.

40. Alexandra Frean, "Thirtysomethings Choose to Live Together, but Separately," *The Times* (London), December 16, 2005.

41. Pamela Paul, *The Starter Marriage and the Future of Matrimony* (New York: Villard, 2002).

42. Clarence Page, "Trading Races Drama: Can We Ever Get Out of the Skin We Were Born In?" *Chicago Tribune*, March 12, 2006.

43. Sonya Tafoya, "Shades of Belonging," Pew Hispanic Center, December 2004.

44. From www.prcdc.org/summaries/changingnation/changingnation.html.

45. Anthony Crupi, "BET, Infiniti Prep Branded Programming," *Adweek*, January 18, 2006.

46. Steve Maich, "What the Net Taught TV," *Maclean's*, February 21, 2005.

47. Doreen Carvajal, "EU's Proposed Ad Rules Back Product Placement," *International Herald Tribune*, December 13, 2005.

48. From www.mtv.com/onair/dyn/i_want_a_famous_face-2/episode.jhtml?episodeID=81696.

49. Alessandra Stanley, "The Dresses, Low Cut, but the Tones Were Lofty," *The New York Times*, March 6, 2006.

50. "Going Virtual: Flight Training Takes Shape in Cyberspace," Defense Department Documents and Publications, February 16, 2006.

51. *Day to Day*, NPR, August 19, 2005.

52. Ibid.

53. Patrick Klepek, "Online Evolution: Can You Keep a Virtual Economy Afloat?" *Computer Gaming World*, April 1, 2006.

54. *Morning Edition*, NPR, August 25, 2005.

7

1. Marian Salzman and Ira Matathia, *Trends Voor de Toekomst* (*Next: Trends for the Near Future*) (Amsterdam: Anthos, 1997).

2. From www.gailsheehy.com/Game/game.htm.

3. Oprah Winfrey, "Age: This Month's Mission," *O, The Oprah Magazine*, October 2003.

4. Oprah Winfrey, "Transformation: This Month's Mission," *O, The Oprah Magazine*, January 2004.

5. Mintel International Group, "Marketing to Children Aged 7–10," January 2006.

6. From www.teenresearch.com/PRview.cfm?edit_id=280.

7. Lisa Kassenaar and Cotten Timberlake, "For Teens, Wall Street Bonuses Mean Money in the Bag," Bloomberg.com, November 3, 2005.

8. "Nearly 3 in 10 Young Teens 'Sexually Active'," MSNBC.com, January 31, 2005.

9. From www.ja.org/about/about_newsitem.asp?StoryID=183.

10. Larry Elliott, "Mamma May Not Know Best," *Guardian* (London), February 6, 2006.

11. Rick Montgomery, "The Elastic State of Growing Up: More Young Adults Stay Longer in the Nest," *Kansas City Star*, April 24, 2005.

12. Alison Aproberts, "Generation Yo-Yo: Grown, but Not Gone," *The Sacramento Bee*, March 26, 2006.

13. Lev Grossman, "Grow Up? Not So Fast," *Time*, January 24, 2005.

14. Montgomery, "The Elastic State of Growing Up."

15. From http://strategis.ic.gc.ca/epic/internet/inoca-bc.nsf/vwapj/EN_CTR.pdf/$FILE/ EN_CTR. pdf.

16. Lucinda Schmidt, "No Empty Nest, Just a Very Crowded House," *The Sydney Morning Herald*, March 22, 2006.

17. Vanessa Richardson, " 'Generation Debt' Is Going Deep Into the Red," MSNBC.com, February 8, 2006.

18. Adam Sternbergh, "Up With Grups," *New York*, April 3, 2006.

19. Michelle Slatalla, "Online Shopper: The Search for Grown-Up Pants," *The New York Times*, March 23, 2006.

20. Jenn Abelson, "Hot Trend in Fashion: Maturity," *Boston Globe*, March 5, 2006.

21. From www.un.org/esa/population/publications/worldageing19502050/pdf/81chapteriii.pdf.

22. From www.realage.com/reg/regvar/st1.aspx?mod=LONGFORM.

23. From http://www.nclnet.org/news/2004/antiaging.htm.

24. "Body of Work: More Upscale Products Appealing to an Older and Increasingly Diverse Market Make the Body and Bath Categories an Opportunity for Supermarkets," *Supermarket News*, February 6, 2006.

25. "A New Generation of Cosmeceutical Ingredients," *NutraCos*, August 31, 2005.

26. From www.surgery.org/download/2005stats.pdf.

27. Jen Haberkorn, "Forever Young," *The Washington Times*, July 29, 2004.

28. From www.surgery.org/download/2003-stats.pdf.

29. From www.facemd.org/media/stats_polls/AAFPRSMEDIA2005.pdf.

30. Ibid.

31. Arlene Weintraub, "Selling the Promise of Youth," *Business Week*, March 20, 2006.

32. From www.bbc.co.uk/radio4/reith2001/

33. From www.un.org/esa/population/publications/worldageing19502050/pdf/80chapterii.pdf.

34. From www.investor.harley-davidson.com/demographics.cfm?bmLocale=en_US.

35. Bill Pennington, "Boarding without a Nose Ring," *The New York Times*, December 23, 2005.

36. From http://www.pewinternet.org/pdfs/PIP_Seniors_Online_2004.pdf.

37. John Reinan, "Older Gamers Take Up Virtual Pastimes," *Star Tribune* (Minneapolis), March 8, 2006.

38. Rachel Breitman, "Sexual Revolution Finds Seniors Willing Recruits: Medical Enhancement Heats Up Those Golden Years," *Edmonton Journal*, March 2006.

39. From www.gailsheehy.com.

40. Jane Juska, *A Round-heeled Woman: My Late-Life Adventures in Sex and Romance* (New York: Villard, 2003).

41. Breitman, "Sexual Revolution Finds Seniors Willing Recruits."

42. "Older, Wiser and Richer . . . Meet the Sugar Mummy," *Yorkshire Post* (England), August 15, 2005.

43. From http://www.aarp.org/research/press-center/presscurrentnews/a2003-10-13-junecleavers. html.

44. Tom O'Konowitz, "Here's to You, Mrs. Robinson: Older Women Dating Younger Men Find Greater Acceptance. Just Ask TV's Latest Trophy Boyfriend," *Chicago Daily Herald*, April 28, 2005.

45. Ibid.

46. From http://www.cdc.gov/hiv/topics/surveillance/resources/reports/2004report/pdf/2004 SurveillanceReport.pdf.

47. From www.ncbi.nlm.nih.gov/entrez/query.fcgi?cmd=Retrieve&db=PubMed&list_uids= 8267490&dopt=Abstract.

48. Jocelyn Noveck, "It's Not Just Your Kid's Internet: Online Dating Appeals to More Mature Folks, Too," Associated Press, March 15, 2006.

49. Paula Span, "Heaven Can Wait: At 71, Jim Martin Has Put Off the Promised Land of Retirement to Keep Working. You May Be Joining Him," *The Washington Post*, September 11, 2005.

50. Grace Lichtenstein, Elaine Robbins, and Michael Dupuis, "The 15 Best Places to Reinvent Your Life," *AARP the Magazine*, May-June 2003.

51. Span, "Heaven Can Wait."

52. Liz Pulliam Weston, "The Myth of the $1 Million Retirement," MSN Money, February 16, 2006.

53. From uk.virginmoney.com/Images/FreeForAYearPension_tcm19-13457.doc.

54. From www.census.gov/Press-Release/www/releases/archives/aging_population/006544.html.

55. From assets.aarp.org/rgcenter/il/2006_09_caregiver.pdf.

56. Liz Taylor, "Shop for Eldercare Like You Would for a Car," *The Seattle Times*, March 20, 2006.

57. "27th Annual Franchise 500," *Entrepreneur*, January 2006.

8

1. From www.privacyrights.org/ar/idtheftsurveys.htm#BBB06.

2. "Butters Churns Huge Interest in Organic Farming," *Chicago Sun-Times*, June 29, 2005.

3. Thomas Mucha, "New Names for Old Companies," *Business 2.0*, November 1, 2005.

4. Maureen Dowd, *Are Men Necessary?* (New York: Putnam, 2005).

5. Mark Jacob, "Doing a Heckuva Job with Nicknames," *Chicago Tribune*, January 1, 2006.

6. "Queen Rania's Reign," *Psychology Today*, May/June 2003.

7. From www.deeyah.com/News.aspx.

8. From www.deeyah.com/Bio.aspx.

9. Bob Hicks, "She's Cultivating the Urbanites," *The Oregonian*, June 17, 2005.

10. Barbara Mahany, "The Leader of the Farmgirl Pack," *Chicago Tribune*, July 24, 2005.

11. "National Survey Results Show Generational Differences in Political Attitudes Says Frank N. Magid Associates," Business Wire, March 23, 2006.

12. Ibid.

13. Ibid.

14. Mary Meitus, "A New-Year Serving of Trends Past, Present," *Rocky Mountain News*, December 28, 2005.

15. "Cast from the Past," *In Store*, February 14, 2006.

16. Ibid.

17. Michael Hill, "Ages of Rock," *The Baltimore Sun*, January 29, 2006.

18. Walter Humes, "Get on the Net and Find Your True Identity," *The Times Educational Supplement* (London), February 4, 2005.

19. Ibid.

20. "How Americans Use Instant Messaging," Pew Internet & American Life Project, September 1, 2004.
21. "The Road Ahead," *Time*, October 24, 2005.
22. Ibid.
23. Malcolm Gladwell. Ibid., also from "The Road Ahead," Time, October 2005.

9

1. "The Rise of the Superbrands," *The Economist*, February 3, 2005.
2. Archna Shukla and Chaitali Chakravarty, "It's a Crowd of Brands Out There," *India Times*, April 7, 2004.
3. Marian Salzman and Ira Matathia, *Trends Voor de Toekomst* (*Next: Trends for the Near Future*) (Amsterdam: Anthos, 1997).
4. From www.tippingsprung.com.
5. Tom Peters, "The Brand Called You," *Fast Company*, August/September 1997.
6. Tom Doctoroff, *Billions: Selling to the New Chinese Consumer* (New York: Palgrave Macmillan, 2005).
7. Peters, "The Brand Called You."
8. Salzman and Matathia, *Trends Voor de Toekomst*.
9. "Dechert LLP Annual Report on Trends in Trademarks," June 2005.
10. From www.wipo.int/edocs/prdocs/en/2006/wipo_pr_2006_437.html.
11. From www.allaboutbranding.com.
12. From www.internetworldstats.com/stats2.htm#north.
13. From www.netratings.com/pr/pr_060302.pdf.
14. Ibid.
15. Salzman and Matathia, *Trends Voor de Toekomst*.
16. "America's Most Admired Companies 2006," *Fortune*, March 6, 2006.
17. From www.allaboutbranding.com.

10

1. "The Weird and Wonderful World of the Blended Family," *Irish Independent*, September 19, 2005.
2. Irene Shapiro, "New Holiday Rituals for Untraditional Families," secondwivescafe.com.
3. From www.capitalonehealthcarefinance.com/fertility.
4. David Plotz, "The Booming Baby Market: In the Lucrative Fertility Industry, Babies Are the Product and Almost Everything Has Its Price," *Chicago Sun-Times*, March 5, 2006.
5. Jim Hopkins, "Egg-Donor Business Booms on Campuses: Students Offered Up to $35,000 to Sell Eggs," *USA Today*, March 16, 2006.
6. Claudia Dreifus, "An Economist Examines the Business of Fertility: A Conversation With Debora Spar," *The New York Times*, February 28, 2006.
7. From www.cdc.gov.
8. Jennifer Egan, "Wanted: A Few Good Sperm," *The New York Times*, March 19, 2006.
9. From mattes.home.pipeline.com.
10. Egan, "Wanted."

11. Joseph P. Kahn, "Meet the Parent: Single Motherhood Has Changed, and So Has Its Image in Society," *The Boston Globe*, March 13, 2006.
12. Mark Landler, "Quoth the Raven: I Bake Cookies, Too," *The New York Times*, April 23, 2006.
13. Amy Harmon, "Hello, I'm Your Sister. Our Father Is Donor 150," *The New York Times*, November 20, 2005.
14. From www.donorsiblingregistry.com.
15. Blake Morrison, "A Generous Donation," *Guardian* (London), March 11, 2006.
16. Harmon, "Hello."
17. Charlotte Kemp, "Hunt for the Donor Superdads," *Daily Mail* (London), April 3, 2006.
18. From fccncalif.org.
19. Lynette Clemetson, "Adopted in China, Seeking Identity in America," *The New York Times*, March 23, 2006.
20. From www.obets.ua.es/pioneur/difusion/PioneurExecutiveSummary.pdf.
21. Nancy Churnin, "The Cyber Street Corner: Get to Know Networking Sites and Keep Your Kid Safe From Internet Predators," *The Dallas Morning News*, March 16, 2006.
22. Nic Fleming, "One-Night Stands Immoral, Say 9 in 10 Women," *The Daily Telegraph*, March 31, 2006.
23. Ibid.
24. From www.hpa.org.uk/hpa/publications/ann_rep_2004/annual_report.pdf.
25. Lucy Siegle, "Just Say 'No,' " *The Observer*, October 23, 2005.
26. Adam McCulloch, "I Want Your Text," *Sunday Telegraph Magazine* (Australia), November 6, 2005.
27. Debra L. Oswald and Brenda L. Russel, "Perceptions of Sexual Coercion in Heterosexual Dating Relationships: The Role of Aggressor Gender and Tactics," *Journal of Sex Research*, February 1, 2006.
28. David Brooks, "Rethinking Relationships," *The New York Times*, April 17, 2005.
29. From www.cdc.gov/nchs/products/pubs/pubd/ad/361-370/ad362.htm.
30. Sharon Jayson, "Teens Define Sex in New Ways: Shocked Parents Don't Understand Casual Attitude," *USA Today*, October 19, 2005.
31. Jeff Daniel, "Hooking Up: More Than a Kiss But How Much More?" *St. Louis Post Dispatch*, July 24, 2005.
32. From www.unece.org/stats/trend/ch2.htm.
33. Katie Allen, "Number of Households Expected to Jump," Reuters, March 14, 2006.
34. G. D. Gearino, "When Did Fido Become Family?" *The News & Observer* (North Carolina), February 19, 2006.
35. Jenifer Goodwin, "Heads They Win, Tails They Win," *The San Diego Union-Tribune*, March 12, 2006.
36. Guy Friddell, "A Dog's Love Makes the Whole Family a Bit Warmer," *The Virginian-Pilot & The Ledger-Star*, September 8, 2005.
37. From www.americanheart.org/presenter.jhtml?identifier=3035327.
38. From www.churchill.com/pressReleases/010306.htm.
39. Karl A. Van Asselt, "Meow Money, Meow Money, Meow Money," *Desert Morning News* (Salt Lake City), January 14, 2005.
40. From www.thepetprofessor.com/press/press.aspx?id=1843.

41. From www.appma.org/press_industrytrends.asp.

42. L. Phillips Brown, "Pet Supplements Roar!" *Nutraceuticals World*, March 1, 2006.

43. From www.appma.org/press_industrytrends.asp.

44. Stepanie Denton, "It's a Dog's Life," *Post Magazine* (London), March 9, 2006.

45. From www.pinnacle.co.uk/pet/about.php3.

46. Deborah Ball, "Pet Food Goes Gourmet With Condiments and Stew," *The Wall Street Journal*, March 20, 2006.

47. Steve Barnes, "Designer Dogs: From Puggles to Whoodles: Bow Wow Wow!" *Albany Times Union* (New York), March 23, 2006.

48. Raahkee Mirchandani, "Designer Dogs: Meet the Puggle," *New York Post*, November 4, 2005.

49. Ibid.

II

1. Marian Salzman and Ira Matathia, *Trends Voor de Toekomst* (*Next: Trends for the Near Future*) (Amsterdam: Anthos, 1997).

2. From www.hgtv.com/hgtv/about_us/.

3. Elizabeth Large, "Sitting This One Out: The New Decade Has Seen People Turn Their Focus Inward, Making Havens of Their Homes," *Sun-Sentinel* (Fort Lauderdale, Florida), April 1, 2005.

4. "Interior Design Expert Offers Home Decor Tips for 2006," PR Newswire, February 14, 2006.

5. Kermit Baker, "Architects Rate Home Offices Most Popular Special Function Room," *AIArchitect*, September 2005.

6. From www.idc.com.

7. From www.census.gov/prod/2005pubs/p23-208.pdf.

8. Peta Tomlinson, "A Space of Your Own," *South China Morning Post*, February 10, 2006.

9. Yvonne Jeffery, "Small Office, Home Office Is SOHO Smart," *Calgary Herald*, January 7, 2006.

10. From www.ml.com.

11. Jon Weinbach, "Productivity in the Privy: For Workaholics, the Bathroom Has Become the Final Wired Frontier," *The Wall Street Journal*, February 10, 2006.

12. Magnus Wood, "Marketing Society—Marketers, Go Home," brandrepublic.com, August 10, 2005.

13. Marge Colborn, "Super Bowl Parties Spur Last-minute Decor Changes," *Chicago Tribune*, February 4, 2006.

14. John Kenneth Galbraith, *The Affluent Society* (New York: Mentor: 1957).

15. Polly Curtis, "They're Making 'Em Like They Used To," *Guardian* (London), February 9, 2005.

16. Sherri Mandel, "In Our Cleaning Rituals, A Glimpse of the Divine," *Forward*, March 30, 2001.

17. Katrina Burroughs, "Fantasy Kitchens," *The Times* (London), April 2, 2006.

18. From www.marketresearchworld.net.

19. Burroughs, "Fantasy Kitchens."
20. Stephanie Rosenbloom, "The Bachelor Pad Still Lives," *The New York Times*, March 26, 2006.
21. Burroughs, "Fantasy Kitchens."
22. From www.sleepfoundation.org.
23. Simon Mills, "Meet the Luxorexics," *Sunday Times* (London), March 5, 2006.
24. Dawn Fallik, "Just Too Wired: Why Teens Don't Get Enough Sleep," *Philadelphia Inquirer*, March 28, 2006.
25. "Most Children Have TV in Bedroom," news.bbc.co.uk, February 1, 2006.
26. Cathy Booth-Thomas, "Tween Eye for Design," *Time*, September 29, 2003.
27. From www.uli.org.
28. Ibid.
29. From www.ippr.org/centreforcities/articles/?id=2051.
30. Joel Kotkin, "City of the Future: Unless It Keeps Its Citizens Safe, the Modern Metropolis May Go the Way of Ancient Rome," *The Washington Post*, July 24, 2005.
31. From www.defra.gov.uk/rural/pdfs/research/pop_trends_rural_areas.pdf.
32. Sarah Womack, "High Cost of Living Sends 116,000 out of London to Seek Their Rural Idyll," *The Daily Telegraph* (London), September 30, 2005.
33. Rick Lyman, "In Exurbs, Life Framed By Hours Spent in the Car," *The New York Times*, December 18, 2005.
34. Ibid.
35. From www.world-wire.com/news/1115040001.html.
36. From www.energy.gov/taxbreaks.htm.
37. Sean Coughlan, "Power From the People," *BBC News Magazine*, March 9, 2006.
38. From www.dti.gov.uk/energy/consultations/pdfs/microgeneration-est-summary.pdf.
39. Coughlan, "Power From the People."
40. Christopher Solomon, "The Swelling McMansion Backlash," realestate.msn.com.
41. Les Christie, "Die, Die, Monster Home! Die," CNNMoney.com, August 18, 2005.
42. Kevin G. Demarrais, "Fuel-Sipping Hybrids: Is That All There Is?" *The Record* (New Jersey), October 5, 2005.
43. From media.ford.com.
44. From www.jdpower.com.
45. Demarrais, "Fuel-Sipping Hybrids: Is That All There Is?"
46. From www.hybridcars.com/lexus-gs450h.html.
47. "The Globalist Quiz: Home Sweet Home," *The Boston Globe*, February 12, 2006.
48. Ibid.
49. Frank Furedi, "Singleton Society," spiked-online.com, October 11, 2002
50. From www.jrf.org.uk.
51. "Nurses 'Quitting to Buy Houses,' " news.bbc.co.uk, June 19, 2005.
52. Leo Hickman, "Is It OK . . . to Buy a Second Home," *Guardian* (London), February 21, 2006.
53. Ibid.
54. Alan J. Heavens, "Sales of Second Homes Surged in 2005," Knight Ridder, December 18, 2005.

55. Tomoeh Murakami Tse, "2 Legs Up With a 2nd Home," *Washington Post*, Saturday, April 15.

12

1. Marian Salzman and Ira Matathia, *Trends Voor de Toekomst* (*Next: Trends for the Near Future*) (Amsterdam: Anthos, 1997).
2. Michelle Conlin, "The Easiest Commute of All: The Ranks of Remote Workers Are Swelling As Companies See the Sense in Freeing Them," *Business Week*, December 12, 2005.
3. From www.conferzone.com.
4. "Worldwide Wi-Fi Hotspots Hits the 100,000 Mark," Business Wire, January 24, 2006.
5. Ibid.
6. From www.ferris.com.
7. Chris Nuttal, "A Technology Odyssey: Our Man in California Peers Into the Future to See How the Industry Will Look and Finds a World Without Boxes," *Financial Times*, December 14, 2005.
8. Natalie Hanman, "World in Motion," *Guardian* (London), January 30, 2006.
9. Amy Kolz, "Don't Call Them Slackers: Partners May Think This Generation of Associates Is Less Committed to Their Work—They Just Shouldn't Say It Out Loud," *The American Lawyer*, October 2005.
10. Nathan Hurst, "More Will Be Laboring During the Holiday," *The Boston Globe*, September 4, 2005.
11. Ellen Galinsky et al., "Overwork in America: When the Way We Work Becomes Too Much," Families and Work Institute, March 15, 2005.
12. Shirleen Holt and Kristi Heim, "5 Years After the Bust, A Sober New Reality: Dot-Coms and Tech Startups," *Seattle Times*, August 21, 2005.
13. Conlin, "The Easiest Commute of All."
14. Maz Partasides, "It Pays to eBay: 70,000 Brits Quit Work to New Fortune," *Daily Star* (London), February 10, 2006.
15. Francine Pullman, "Sales on the Bay a Lifestyle Decision," *Townsville Bulletin/Townsville Sun* (Australia), November 18, 2005.
16. From www.thefutureofwork.net/assets/Business_Community_Centers.pdf.
17. Ibid.
18. From www.internethomealliance.com.
19. From www.the-hub.net/.
20. Robert Putnam, *Bowling Alone* (New York: Simon & Schuster, 2000).
21. From www.thefutureofwork.net.
22. Conlin, "The Easiest Commute of All."
23. Richard Florida *The Rise of the Creative Class* (New York: Basic Books, 2004).
24. Ibid.
25. "The Wheel Deal," *Wallpaper*, June 2005.
26. Ibid.
27. From www.influxinsights.com/index.php?id=597.
28. From buschowhenley.co.uk/projects/office/004.htm.
29. Pham-Duy Nguyen (Bloomberg News), "Seattle Workers Fight Dark Season with Sunlamps," *The San Diego Union Tribune*, December 31, 2005.

30. "Best New View," *Wallpaper*, January 2005.
31. Robin Pogrebin, "High-Rises That Have Low Impact on Nature," *The New York Times*, February 2, 2006.
32. From www.servicemasterclean.com/cleanoffice/2005ocm.pdf.
33. From www.census.gov/prod/2004pubs/c2kbr-33.pdf.
34. From www.teleworkexchange.com.
35. Barbara Rose, "Employees' Priorities a Mystery to Employers: Pay, Flexibility Rank High for Workers," *San Jose Mercury News*, November 26, 2005.
36. Stephen Overell, "The Sinking of the 'Free Agent' Myth," *Financial Times*, September 19, 2005.
37. Ibid.
38. Ibid.
39. Ibid.
40. Adina Genn, "Women-Owned Businesses without Employees Are Fastest Growing Sector," *Long Island Business News* (New York), February 10, 2006.
41. Laura Koss-Feder, "My Boss, My Wife," *Time*, August 27, 2001.
42. "Randstad Survey Reveals Romance in Workplace Trends," PR Newswire, February 1, 2006.
43. From www.weforum.org/pdf/summitreports/am2006/future.htm.
44. From http://www.ilo.org/dyn/empent/docs/F111PUB105_01/PUB105_01.htm/
45. Richard Freeman, "What Really Ails Europe (and America): The Doubling of the Global Workforce," *The Globalist*, June 3, 2005.
46. Ibid.

13

1. Thorstein Veblen, *The Theory of the Leisure Class* (New York: Penguin Classics, 1994 reprint).
2. Susan Owens, "Why Some Say Yes to Excess, While for Others It's a No-No," *Australian Financial Review*, March 4, 2006.
3. Ibid.
4. Rosie Murray-West, " 'Good Gifts' Enjoy a Bumper Christmas," *Daily Telegraph* (London), Dec 31, 2005.
5. "Inconspicuous Consumption," *The Economist* (U.S. Edition), December 24, 2005.
6. Rana Foroohar and Mac Margolis, "Maximum Luxury," *Newsweek International*, July 25, 2005.
7. Janny Scott and David Leonhardt, "Class in America: Shadowy Lines That Still Divide," *The New York Times*, May 15, 2005.
8. David Smith and John Elliott, "Where Have All the Shoppers Gone?" *Sunday Times* (London), May 15, 2005.
9. Minya Oh, " 'Bling Bling' Added to *Oxford English Dictionary*," MTV.com, April 30, 2003.
10. Michele Ingrassia, "The Shape of Things to Come," *New York Daily News*, April 18, 2004.
11. Heidi Dawley, "Here's a Life Lesson: Greed Is Not Good," *Media Life*, February 13, 2006.
12. From www.unitymarketingonline.com/reports2/luxury/pr1_q4_2005.html.
13. Anjana Ahuja, "Are You Experienced?" *The Times* (London), February 17, 2006.
14. "New Study Anticipates the Travel X-Factor for the 2020 Consumer," PR Newswire, November 8, 2005.

15. From www.sony.net/SonyInfo/QUALIA.
16. Smith and Elliott, "Where Have All the Shoppers Gone?"
17. Foroohar and Margolis, "Maximum Luxury."
18. Sid Cohen, "The New Face of Customer Service," *Business Day* (South Africa), February 27, 2006.
19. Chris Jones, "Stuff the Cupcakes. The Hersheyizer Has a Show to Do," *Chicago Tribune*, June 12, 2005.
20. Bruce Horovitz, "A Whole New Ballgame in Grocery Shopping," *USA Today*, March 8, 2005.
21. Sofie Belle, "The Beauty Doctors: Medically Based Brands Are Changing the Face of Cosmetics," *South China Morning Post*, October 28, 2005.
22. Michael Kahn, "Nike Has a Message for Shoppers Looking for the Hottest Shoe Design: Just Do It—Yourself," Reuters News, June 1, 2005.
23. "Space As Mood," *The Scotsman*, February 25, 2006.
24. Marcus Fairs, "Mallorca," *Icon*, June 2005.
25. From www.cooperativebank.co.uk.
26. From www.fairtrade.org.uk.
27. Tyler Mack, "Shed That Brand: Eugene's Newest Clothing Store Banks on Substance of Its Style," *The Register-Guard* (Eugene, Oregon), January 1, 2006.
28. "Natural and Ethical Consumers 2005," Datamonitor, February 21, 2005.
29. "Ethical Marketing: A Question of Ethics," *Brand Strategy*, June 9, 2005.
30. "Consumer Attitudes: Brands' Behavioral Therapy," *Marketing Week*, November 10, 2005.
31. Marian Salzman and Ira Matathia, *Trends Voor de Toekomst* (*Next: Trends for the Near Future*) (Amsterdam: Anthos, 1997).
32. From www.comscore.com/press/pr.asp.
33. From www.nielsen-netratings.com/pr/pr_051229.pdf.
34. Michael Barbaro, "Internet Sales Show Big Gains Over Holidays," *The New York Times*, December 30, 2005.
35. Kurt Badenhausen and Maya Roney, "Next Generation," *Forbes*, June 2, 2005.
36. From www2.acnielsen.com/news/20051019.shtml.
37. Gary Rivlin, "EBay's Joy Ride: Going Once . . . " *The New York Times*, March 6, 2005.
38. Bob Tedeschi, "Everyone's an Editor as Wiki Fever Spreads to Shopping Sites," *New York Times*, April 24, 2006.
39. From www.statistics.gov.uk.
40. Pia Sarkar, "Disposable Chic: For Retailers, Fashion Turnover Gets Ever Faster, Cheaper," *San Francisco Chronicle*, November 8, 2005.
41. "Inconspicuous Consumption," *The Economist*.
42. "Luxury, for a Fraction," *Wausau Daily Herald* (Wisconsin), March 26, 2006.
43. Lucia Adams, "Go On, Treat Yourself Abroad," *The Times* (London), March 31 2006.
44. Chris Hastings, "Over-27s Need Not Apply to Soho House," *The Sunday Telegraph* (London), February 19, 2006.
45. Mary Jordan, "Russians Spread Money, Cultural Wealth around London," *The Wall Street Journal Europe*, October 31, 2005.
46. Eric Pfanner, "From Show to Know: Why Consumers Buy," *International Herald Tribune*, December 7, 2005.

47. Dexter Roberts and Frederik Balfour, "To Get Rich Is Glorious: More Chinese Are Becoming Millionaires—and Driving a Fast-Growing Market for Luxury Goods," *Business Week*, February 6, 2006.

48. Pfanner, "From Show to Know."

49. Tom Pattinson, "Priceless Artworks Return to China as Mao's Work Undone," *The Sunday Times* (London), May 23, 2005.

50. Susan Moor, "As Transparent As a Bowl of Borscht—It Is Not Clear Precisely Who or What Is Driving a Burgeoning Russian Art Trade," *Financial Times*, March 4, 2006.

51. Catherine McKinley, "Vietnam's Big Spenders Increasingly Look for Luxury," *The Wall Street Journal*, November 23, 2005.

14

1. A. Elizabeth Sloan, "What, When, and Where America Eats," *Food Technology*, January 2006.

2. Emma McLaughlin and Nicola Klaus, *The Nanny Diaries* (New York: St. Martin's Press, 2002).

3. Jane Green, *Babyville* (New York: Broadway Books, 2004).

4. From www.wholefoodsmarket.com/company/pr_10-21-04.html.

5. "Organic Food and Beverages," Mintel, August 2004.

6. From www.organicmonitor.com/700140.htm.

7. From www.npr.org/templates/story/story.php?storyId=5303546.

8. From www.3i.com.

9. "New Directions in Food Marketing," *Food & Pack* (Australia), April 1, 2006.

10. Ibid.

11. Dow Jones Newswire, December 30, 2005.

12. From www.ota.com/pics/documents/2004SurveyOverview.pdf.

13. From www.ota.com/news/press/147.html.

14. John Mooallem, "Twelve Easy Pieces," *The New York Times Magazine*, February 12, 2006.

15. From www.soilassociation.org.

16. From "City Chicks," news.bbc.co.uk, October 20, 2005.

17. Jerry Shriver, "New on the Menu for '06," *USA Today*, January 6, 2006.

18. *All Things Considered*, NPR, March 5, 2005.

19. Pia Catton, "Taste: Remedial Cooking," *The Wall Street Journal*, November 25, 2005.

20. *On the Media*, NPR, October 7, 2005.

21. Ibid.

22. Frederick Kaufman, "Debbies Does Salad," *Harper's*, October 1, 2005.

23. Nigella Lawson, *How to Eat* (New York: Wiley, August 2002).

24. Charles Taylor, "Food Porn," salon.com, April 18, 2003.

25. From www.marketresearch.com.

26. From www.efanet.org/activities/documents/EFALetterFP7.pdf.

27. From www.nutrition.org.uk.

28. From www.marketresearch.com.

29. From www.eufic.org/en/journalist/food_allergy.htm.

30. "School Caterer Demands More Cash," news.bbc.co.uk, March 21, 2005.

31. "Officials, Experts Grapple With School Lunch Problem," CNN.com, December 11, 2003.
32. "School Dinners Around the World," news.bbc.co.uk, March 12, 2005.
33. Palavi Gogoi, "No Feast for Food Marketers," *Business Week*, December 8, 2005.
34. "Ten Trends to Watch in Packaged Goods in 2006," Datamonitor, December 9, 2005.
35. From www.teausa.com/general/teaandhealth/218g.cfm#cardio.
36. From www.hsph.harvard.edu/press/releases/press01052004.html.
37. Mark Duff, "Coffee Is 'Health Drink' Says Italian," news.bbc.co.uk, March 7, 2004.
38. Sloan, "What, When, and Where America Eats."
39. From www.worldethnicmarket.com/exhibit/.
40. A. Elizabeth Sloan, "Top 10 Global Food Trends," *Food Technology*, April 2005.
41. Julie Sahni, "The Indian Spice Kitchen," *Specialty Food*, January 10, 2006.

15

1. Marian Salzman and Ira Matathia, *Trends Voor de Toekomst* (*Next: Trends for the Near Future*) (Amsterdam: Anthos, 1997).
2. "Talking to Yourself," *The Economist*, April 20, 2006.
3. *60 Minutes*, CBS News, November 20, 2005.
4. Ibid.
5. Timothy L. O'Brien, "Is Poker Losing Its First Flush?" *The New York Times*, April 16, 2006.
6. Sarah Kershaw, "Hooked On the Web: Help Is on the Way," *The New York Times*, December 1, 2005.
7. From www.online-publishers.org/?pg=press&dt=032906.
8. Frank Rose, "ESPN Thinks Outside the Box," *Wired*, September, 2005.
9. Paul Hyman, "Video Companies Encourage 'Modders'," *The Hollywood Reporter*, April 9, 2004.
10. Janet Kornblum, "Teens Hang Out at MySpace," *USA Today*, January 8, 2006.
11. Saul Hansell, "For MySpace, Making Friends Was Easy. Big Profit Is Tougher," *New York Times*, April 23, 2006.
12. Dawn C. Chmielewsk, "Studios Not Sure Whether Web Innovator Is Friend or Foe," *Los Angeles Times*, April 10, 2006.
13. Andreas Kluth, "Among the Audience," *The Economist*, April 20, 2006.
14. Ibid.
15. "It's the Links, Stupid," *The Economist*, April 20, 2006.
16. From www.kff.org/entmedia/upload/Executive-Summary-Generation-M-Media-in-the-Lives-of-8-18-Year-olds.pdf.
17. From www.npd.com/dynamic/releases/press_060117.html.
18. From www.dfcint.com/news/prnov92005.html.
19. From www.ce.org.
20. From www.theesa.com.
21. "Men Shell Out More on Games Than Tunes," Reuters (MSNBC.com), April 7, 2005.
22. From www.ce.org.
23. "Dance Dance Revolution Used in U.S. State School Program," www.gamasutra.com, January 25, 2006.

24. Joyzelle Davis, "DVRs to Become Commonplace," *The Rocky Mountain News*, February 1, 2006.
25. From cms.ihrsa.org/IHRSA/viewPage.cfm?pageId=615.

conclusion

1. Tom Nissley, "Where Were You When You Realized the World Is Flat (Or Have You?): Conversation with Thomas L. Friedman," Amazon.com.
2. From www.earth-policy.org/Updates/2005/Update46.htm.

index

Robinson, Mary, 29
Roddick, Anita, 98
Rolling Stones, 120, 121, 133
Roosevelt, Theodore, 26
Rosen, Larry, 194
Rosenberg, Simon, 85
Rothenberg, Ron, 120
Round-heeled Woman, A (Juska), 122
Roy, Olivier, 24
rural living, 183–84
Russia, 33, 63–64, 187, 230–31
Ryan, Kevin P., 226
Ryan, Matthew, 5

Samsung, 151
Sarbanes-Oxley Act, 4, 21
Saturday Night Live, 19, 265
science, as unifying force, 30–31
seasonal affective disorder (SAD), 200
Seepe, Sipho, 28
Seligman, Martin, 5
Sex and the City, 109, 117, 161, 166
sexuality, 96–97
Sheehan, Cindy, 17
Sheehy, Gail, 113, 122
She's the Man, 97
Sifry, David, 34
Single Mothers by Choice, 161
Siwei, Cheng, 40
Skype, 150, 151, 196, 270
Slatalla, Michelle, 117
sleep, as luxury, 180–81
Smith, Paul, 222
social liberalism, 66–67
Solomon, Christopher, 185
Soviet Union, 30, 63, 187, 208
Spain
    Catalonia and, 54, 128
    gourmet foods, 251
    Islam and, 64–65
    Latin America and, 26
    smoking bans, 60
Span, Paula, 124
Spar, Debora L., 160
Spencer, Genia, 206
Stanley, Alessandra, 108
Starbucks, 48, 249
Starter Marriage and the Future of Matrimony
    (Paul), 104
Status Anxiety (de Botton), 80

Stewart, Martha, 95, 98, 152, 173, 178, 213
Stiglitz, Joseph, 29
Stone, Sharon, 72, 117
Sullivan, Andrew, 97
Sullivan, Martin, 88
Summers, Lawrence, 39
Susanka, Sarah, 184

Talk to the Hand (Trusse), 4
Target, 214–15
Taylor, Charles, 244
Taylor, Jim, 114
technology
    biology and, 159, 224
    business and, 175–76, 191–95, 198, 204,
        206–7
    cars and, 187, 276
    communication and, 150–51, 154
    consumers and, 15, 138, 143–45, 213
    entertainment and, 177, 181, 253–56, 258,
        262
    environmental impact, 83
    globalization and, 1, 23, 26, 31–32, 36
    information and, 40, 208, 209
    interactive, 143–45
    nutrition and, 233–34, 247, 250
        @Index:politics and, 85
    reality and, 95, 111
    social impact, 5, 267–69, 271–72
    word of mouth and, 226–27
Technorati, 34
TechnoStress (Rosen and Weil), 194
Teen Research Unlimited, 114
teens
    bedrooms of, 181–82
    dating and sex, 115
    increasing sophistication of, 114
telecommuting, 192–94
"Television without Frontiers Directive," 107
terrorism, 4, 9, 10, 14, 32, 59, 65, 87,
    183, 212
Tobar, Hector, 82
tourism
    disease and, 13
    eco-tourism, 150
    globalization and, 34, 140
    Russia and, 63
    space tourism, 155
    U.S. and, 61
Toyota, 50, 150–51, 186–87